Sierra Leone Krio

Sierra Leone Krio

Language, Culture, and Traditions

Selase W. Williams
Tom Spencer-Walters

HAMILTON BOOKS
AN IMPRINT OF
ROWMAN & LITTLEFIELD
Lanham • Boulder • New York • London

Published by Hamilton Books
An imprint of The Rowman & Littlefield Publishing Group, Inc.
4501 Forbes Boulevard, Suite 200, Lanham, Maryland 20706
www.rowman.com

86-90 Paul Street, London EC2A 4NE, United Kingdom

Copyright © 2024 by The Rowman & Littlefield Publishing Group, Inc.

All rights reserved. No part of this book may be reproduced in any form or by any electronic or mechanical means, including information storage and retrieval systems, without written permission from the publisher, except by a reviewer who may quote passages in a review.

British Library Cataloguing in Publication Information Available

Library of Congress Cataloging-in-Publication Data

Names: Williams, Selase W., author. | Spencer-Walters, Tom, author.
Title: Sierra Leone Krio: language, culture, and traditions / Selase W. Williams, Tom Spencer-Walters.
Description: Lanham: Hamilton Books, 2024. | Includes bibliographical references and index. | Summary: "This book fills the void in the literature about the Sierra Leone Krio people by delineating the connective tissue between their history, language, culture, traditions, and contemporary poetry. While the Krios have often been characterized as fully anglicized, our work demonstrates how deeply rooted Krio is in West African behaviors, practices, communication, tradition, and creativity."— Provided by publisher.
Identifiers: LCCN 2024014722 (print) | LCCN 2024014723 (ebook) | ISBN 9780761874508 (paperback) | ISBN 9780761874515 (epub)
Subjects: LCSH: Krio language. | Krio literature. | Creoles (Sierra Leone) Sierra Leone—Social life and customs.
Classification: LCC PM7875.K73 W55 2024 (print) | LCC PM7875.K73 (ebook) | DDC 427.9664—dc23/eng/20240401
LC record available at https://lccn.loc.gov/2024014722
LC ebook record available at https://lccn.loc.gov/2024014723

∞™ The paper used in this publication meets the minimum requirements of American National Standard for Information Sciences—Permanence of Paper for Printed Library Materials, ANSI/NISO Z39.48-1992.

We dedicate this book to our ancestors who fought for freedom from all forms of oppression and for their rightful place in history, but specifically to those whose sacrifices and tenacity made Krio possible, and to their progeny who follow in their footsteps to advance an agenda that supports a culturally and linguistically diverse world.

Contents

Figures	ix
Tables	xi
Acknowledgments	xiii
Introduction	1
PART I: HISTORY	13
Chapter 1: History of the Krio People and Their Language	15
PART II: KRIO LANGUAGE	39
Chapter 2: Language Basics	41
Chapter 3: Greetings and Simple Sentences	59
Chapter 4: Complex Sentences Structures	83
Chapter 5: African Linguistic Foundations in Krio and the Diaspora	109
PART III: KRIO CULTURE AND TRADITIONS	135
Chapter 6: Elements of Krio Culture	137
Chapter 7: Krio Traditions	167
Chapter 8: Krio Folk Wisdom : Parables and Riddles	183
Chapter 9: Krio Stories and Trickster Narratives	201
Chapter 10: Poetry in Sierra Leone Krio and Jamaican Patois	219
Afterword	259

Appendix	263
Glossary	267
Bibliography	275
Index	281
About the Authors	293

Figures

2.1. Basic Sentence Structure of Krio.   54

2.2. Structure of Krio Noun Phrase.   55

2.3. Structure of Krio Verb Phrases.   56

2.4. Tree Diagram of a Krio Sentence.   57

3.1. Krio Personal Pronouns by Function.   60

3.2. Multiple Realizations of de in Krio.   69

4.1. Serial Verb Constructions with "Mental" Verbs.   84

4.2. Complex Sentences with Infinitive Clause.   101

4.3. Underlying Structures of Relative Clause.   103

6.1. The kaba slɔt (traditional Krio dress), modeled by
Mrs. Milbank Rowe. *Photograph courtesy of Mrs.* Milbank
Rosetta Rowe.   146

6.2. Kapɛt slipas (carpet slippers).   147

6.3. Example 1 of fabric print dress.   148

6.4. Example 2 of fabric print dress, modeled by Dr. Princess
Dougan. *Photograph courtesy of Dr.* Princess Dougan.   149

6.5. Sawa-Sawa (sorrel) leaves.   150

6.6. Sawa-Sawa (sorrel) cooked.   151

6.7. Krenkren (brambly plant) cooked.   152

6.8. Jɔlɔf Rɛs (Jollof Rice).   153

6.9. Bitas (bitter leaves; Vernonia Amygdalina).   154

6.10. Kasada (cassava root).	155
6.11. Fufu (Foofoo).	156
6.12. Kasada bred (Cassava bread).	157
6.13. Kola nɔt (Kola nut).	158
6.14. Kanya (snack of peanuts and sugar).	159
6.15. Jinja kek (Ginger cake).	160
6.16. Kɔngu (snack of peanut butter rolled into rings or balls).	161
6.17. Rayz bred (rice bread).	162
7.1. Example 1 of bod os (wood plank house with mountain view in background).	179
7.2. Example 2 of bod os (wood plank house in an urban setting).	180
7.3. Example of ton os (concrete houses).	181

Tables

1.1. Ethnic Affiliation of Liberated Africans in 1848 Freetown Census. 24

1.2. Settler Speech Reported by Rankin in 1834. 30

2.1. Minimal Pairs Differentiated by Tone (H = High tone, L = Low tone). 47

2.2. Three Levels of Noun Specificity. 51

2.3. Creating Nouns Out of Verbs with di. 52

2.4. Krio Subject Pronouns. 55

4.1. Krio Emphatic Pronouns. 91

5.1. Commonality of "Sweet Mouth" in Three African Languages. 110

5.2. Multiple African Language Sources for Some Krio Words. 113

5.3. Merger of Igbo Nouns with Preposition na. 122

5.4. Second-Person Singular/Plural Pronouns in Five Languages. 131

Acknowledgments

I want to extend a very heartfelt thank you to Dr. Modupe Broderick, who was not only my first Krio teacher, but who also met us at Lumley Field, helped us find housing, and opened doors for recording sessions with many research informants.

Thanks to all of my Sierra Leonean friends, neighbors, and associates, especially the residents of Leicester Village who welcomed me and my family into their community, and who engaged us in all community activities, including many fireside gatherings where my knowledge of the language was deepened and my appreciation for Krio stories began.

Thanks to Eugenia Chinsman, who recognized the importance of this book and began scheduling speaking tours even before this book was in print.

My unending gratitude goes to my wife, Deborah McDuff Williams, who encouraged me to publish this book long ago, for her support and patience throughout the process, and whose love and artistic creativity inspire me every day.

My acknowledgements would not be complete if I did not bestow a wealth of gratitude to my oldest daughter, Beth Williams, for serving as my in-house interpreter and translator as I was learning the Krio language that she picked up so easily in the village at the age of seven.

—*Selase* W. Williams

First, I dedicate this work to the memory of my mentors, Professors Eldred Jones and Clifford Fyle, who saw and nurtured my passion in everything Krio. Your inspiration was palpable.

To my wife, Desiree, thank you so much for your enduring and loving support of this project almost since its inception. I couldn't have done it without your patience and understanding.

xiv   *Acknowledgments*

I am most grateful to family members and close friends from around the world for all your encouragement and help, most notably, the late Judge Linda Spencer-Walters, Mrs. Marvella McEwen, and Mrs. Princess Patnelli, for sharing your outstanding knowledge of Krio culture and traditions. Thank you too, Chelsea Renner, for providing technical support when most needed.

To my sisters and brothers in the Krio Descendant Union, both in California and globally, I say thank you for constantly providing me a platform from which I could examine various strands of our Krio language and culture, and that have now found their way into this book.

—Tom Spencer-Walters

* * *

We both greatly appreciate the comments of reviewers and critics of our earlier scholarship on Krio society and African diasporan phenomena, as well as those who saw the value in publishing our work. A special thanks to the director and technicians in the Instructional Learning Center at California State University, Northridge who shared their expertise and provided us with the technical wherewithal to convert nearly one hundred Krio stories from reel-to-reel tapes to digital files.

Introduction

Sierra Leone Krio: Its Language, Culture, and Traditions is the product of a collaboration between an African American linguist and a scholar of Communications and Comparative Literature. While each brings his own disciplinary expertise and perspective to this project, it is their shared interest in providing a fuller and more comprehensive picture of the Sierra Leone Experiment, what led up to it, and the linguistic and cultural realities produced by that experiment that has given them a common purpose. That purpose is to compile a story of the Krio people of Sierra Leone, their history, their language, their culture, and their traditions, that goes deeper, more systematically, and more holistically than has been done before. In this book, significant new insights are extracted from recent scholarship on the social, political, religious, and economic dynamics that were operative during the founding and subsequent years of the creation of Krio society. Other insights are gathered from little-known, early accounts of various segments of this community, including information on the language spoken by sub-components of this community during the early stages of its development. The text details the history, process, participants, and outcomes of this unique African/European contact experience that was launched in the late eighteenth and early nineteenth centuries in and around the area of Sierra Leone now called Freetown.

RELATIONSHIP TO EXISTING LITERATURE

Over the past few decades, there has been increasing interest in and scholarship on Krio language, culture, and traditions. Three publications in particular have added to the authors' understanding of certain aspects of the social, political, and economic circumstances that existed around the time that the Krio, as a people, were being conceived. One of those publications is Akintola J. G. Wyse's landmark work, *The Krio of Sierra Leone: An*

2   *Introduction*

Interpretive History (1989). Different from earlier books that have discussed Krio people, this book does so with a focus on the common people, rather than on the elite and on the future of the Krios due to the political dynamics operating in Sierra Leone. He identifies the British colonial influence and much larger indigenous groups outside of Freetown as major factors that have impacted the political life of the Krios. Wyse discusses the tensions between Western civilization and traditional African culture. However, its focus was largely historical and political, with anecdotal references to linguistic and cultural phenomena in the Krio community.[1] A second work, *New Perspectives on the Sierra Leone Krio*, is an edited volume by Mac Dixon-Fyle and Gibril Cole (2006) that provides diverse perspectives on topics ranging from history, politics, religion, and language. This book's primary aim was to take the pulse of research on the Krios at that time.[2] Third, Gibril R. Cole's 2013 *The Krio of West Africa: Islam, Culture, Creolization, and Colonialism in the Nineteenth Century* engages in a much needed, and often overlooked, discussion of the Muslim (*Oku*) Krios, their physical space and worship activities, and their relationship with Christian Krios, other indigenous groups in the Western Area, and West Africa at large. This scholarship shed important light on the role of the Oku Krios in asserting their African identity in the evolution of Sierra Leone Krios as a recognized entity.[3]

Only a small number of books have been published on Krio language. The most prominent work is that of Clifford N. Fyle and Eldred D. Jones, *A Krio-English Dictionary*, published in 1980. With over 30,000 entries, it is, by far, the most serious and most authoritative study of the language to date. As a dictionary, its primary purpose was to list Krio words in alphabetical order, with English meanings, etymologies, and infrequently offered sample sentences using the words listed. It includes a very good description of the phonemic system, but only a short description of the grammar.[4] Jones and Fyle were preceded by Jack Berry's 1966 *Dictionary of Sierra Leone Krio*, which appeared as a government report that was a real asset to those beginning to do research on Krio, but it does not contain a description of the grammar or a discussion about the origins of Krio words.[5] Although neither of these important works are still in print, they were invaluable sources for our book.

A more recent 2022 publication is *Next Gen Krios' Krio-English Dictionary*, by Atinuke Scott-Boyle et al. It is both a Krio-English and English-Krio dictionary but does include a brief discussion of the theories on the origin of creole languages and a short section on grammar.[6] In addition to this, Hanne-Ruth Thompson and Momoh Taziff Koroma published in 2014 *Krio Dictionary and Phrasebook*. The number of entries is much fewer than either of the other dictionaries cited but includes a very useful description of the

Introduction 3

basic grammatical elements of the language and practical expressions for everyday use, especially for travelers.[7]

Publications focused on Krio culture and oral traditions are Eyamidé E. Lewis-Coker's 2013 *Motherland Sierra Leone: Anansi Stories*, Daphne Barlatt Pratt's 2017 *Krio Salad: Folktales, Poems, Parables, and Wise Sayings*, and Lewis-Coker's 2018 *Creoles of Sierra Leone: Proverbs, Parables, and Wise Sayings*. Different from our presentation and analysis of Krio culture and traditions, *Motherland* is essentially a collection of folktales written in Krio. They are, therefore, not accessible to non-speakers of Krio or those who can speak Krio at some level but are unable to read Krio. *Krio Salad* caters to audiences who would like to be able to read and write Krio through accessing folktales, parables, and the like.[8] A good addition to this book is a section on original Krio poetry written by Pratt. While Pratt's focus here is on her poetry, our book introduces the reader to a variety of Krio and Jamaican Patois poets whose pieces provide historical, linguistic, and cultural linkages between Sierra Leone and the Krio Diaspora. Lewis-Coker's second book presents a sizeable collection of proverbs, parables, and wise saying, with useful literal English translations and interpretations. Our effort in *Sierra Leone Krio* went farther to examine the function and utility of proverbs, parables, and wise sayings within the much larger social and cultural templates of Krio and Diasporan societies.

CENTRAL QUESTIONS AND CONCEPTS ADDRESSED

The fundamental questions the authors attempt to answer in this book are: (1) What are the components and systems that constitute Sierra Leone Krio Language? (2) What is/are the origins of Krio Language? (3) What constitutes Krio culture and traditions? (4) What lessons does Krio teach us about the social dynamics that give birth to African diasporic societies? and (5) What is unique about the Krio story?

As we sought the answers to these questions, we discovered that there were four pervasive forces that were determinant in bringing Krio language and culture to fruition:

1. Accessibility of linguistic and cultural material,
2. Social Inclusivity,
3. Simplification of complex linguistic and cultural systems, and
4. African Authenticity.

The level of *accessibility* to the linguistic and cultural material that existed in the Sierra Leone Colony at the time Krio language and culture were being

4   *Introduction*

developed was critical. Although we know that there were formerly enslaved and liberated Africans from various parts of Africa and Europeans, primarily from England, did they have ready and equal access to each other's language and culture? On the surface, it might appear that the formerly enslaved African participants depended heavily on the English language for their communication with the British administration and among themselves. Even references in the literature to Krio as an "English-based" creole strongly suggest that the African members of the community depended heavily on English as the foundation for their communication. But, did they really have substantive access to English? Did the British have access to the languages and cultures of the newly freed Africans?

The second operative force was *social inclusivity*. In the multiethnic, multilingual African communities that were situated together in the villages, either by choice or by necessity, there was an impulse to include everyone in a very communal way in what would become their future. This is not to suggest that there were not differences between the various groups that spawned Krio culture. In fact, there was sometimes open hostility between different groups, even physical warfare, but there was an unspoken imperative for inclusivity, for sharing their own language and culture with those from different cultures. The British community, conversely, was not only much smaller, but also more elitist and exclusionary in their interactions with the Africans. The colonizers saw African cultures as inferior to theirs. Consequently, there was little, or no, incentive for the British to learn the languages or cultures of the African groups.

Third, in the process of trying to be inclusive, the African residents who played a major role in establishing the Krio community found it necessary to engage in *simplification* of their linguistic and cultural wealth to facilitate the sharing with those outside of their primary group. While they recognized both the differences and the commonalities in their linguistic and cultural makeup, there was also a profound understanding and appreciation of the fact that they had all arrived there, figuratively speaking, on the same boat, and that their fates were bound together by history. The colonialists, however, viewed their language and culture to be superior to those of the Africans and, therefore saw the sharing unidirectionally. It was expected that the Africans would aspire to speak and to act like the colonialists. Nonetheless, they, too, had to subscribe to the principle of simplification to some extent.

Finally, and, in some senses, the most important of the operative forces, was the imperative for those of African descent to protect their *African authenticity*, the essence of who they were as African people. While the British administration was absolutely in control of the inner-workings of the Colony, it could not control the identity or selfhood of the recently freed Africans. As the text will demonstrate, through a variety of inter-relational dynamics,

Introduction 5

including the unique status and role of the Yoruba ethnic group in the Colony, both the "Liberated Africans" and local indigenes reinforced the principle of retaining their African authenticity throughout the "Kriolization" process.

THE UNIQUE CONTRIBUTIONS OF THIS BOOK

The authors of this book are attempting to fill a void in the literature on Krio language and culture, emphasizing the need for a more holistic analysis of the various component parts, language, history, oral literature, traditions, and ceremonies, within the context of the social, religious, economic, and political dynamics that have existed. Literature on the Krio language has focused largely on words, in particular dictionaries, leaving out how those words are used within a communication system and what worldview is represented through that language. By the same token, the authors try to show the identity of the people and their values through their oral traditions, sacred ceremonies, dress, food, and religion.

To those ends, the authors provide more detailed, extensive, and more systematic descriptions of both the language and the culture of the Sierra Leone Krio people than has previously existed. Wherever possible, they provide concrete evidence and facts to support any claims they make, not relying on assumptions, anecdotes, or speculation. The work debunks earlier claims and assumptions that English is the base language that undergirds Krio language, presenting hard evidence from the African source languages that lay the substratum foundation for the language, while, at the same time elucidating the role that English has played. Both linguistic and cultural evidence are provided that demonstrates that it was not one African ethnic group, but a number of such groups that set the foundation for the Krio community because of the commonalities or similarities that existed therein. Thus, the claim that local indigenous groups played a significant role in the creation of Krio language and culture finds support from specific examples. Just as aspects of Krio grammar find their antecedents in specific African languages that were prominent during the formulation of the society, so too do certain elements of Krio culture find their antecedents in specific African cultures.

This manuscript is also unique in that it draws upon some of the most recent scholarship on various aspects of the Krio community, while, at the same time using well-known, established sources, and introduces the reader to little-known older accounts of Krio people and their history. Each set of source material provides different layers and perspectives of the Krio story. The authors believe that a synthesis of the work produced by other authors, along with their own independent work, present a more comprehensive, and

6 *Introduction*

therefore more complete, and perhaps a more accurate picture or the essence of the Krio people.

Finally, but very importantly, this is the only book on Krio language and culture, to our knowledge, that demonstrates concrete linguistic and cultural connections between the Krio community and other African diasporan communities. For solid historical reasons, the authors have looked most closely at connections between the Krio community and Jamaican Creole, and Gullah. No connections have been claimed that could not be substantiated with concrete evidence and historical facts.

ORGANIZATIONAL STRUCTURE OF THE BOOK

The manuscript is divided into three parts which bring together the most current and insightful analysis of the interrelationship among Krio history, language, and culture to-date. Part I focuses on History and draws its conclusions from both recent scholarship and little-known, early accounts of the Krio people. The chapter details the unique histories and backgrounds of the formerly enslaved Africans and those enroute to enslavement who came to constitute Krio society, while referencing early accounts of the language spoken by the most dominant groups. It is also argued in this chapter that, while Yoruba was perhaps the most significant contributor to Krio Language, it is also argued that the Yoruba contributions were reinforced by similar language features and structures among other Kwa Languages and, very importantly, Temne, a prominent local indigenous language. Arguments are also presented for why these languages rather than others contributed so much.

Part II, Krio Language, presents a linguistically informed description of basic and complex sentences for use by those wishing to learn the language, as well as for those who are interested in studying linguistic systems and patterns. Integrated into the description of the language are folktales, proverbs, and scenarios that exemplify the use of the language in the culture. While these elements provide further examples of various aspects of the language in context, they also prepare the readers for the in-depth discussion of the variety of folktales, proverbs, and parables that follow. Part III, Krio Culture and Traditions, is a collection of Krio oral literature and folk wisdom that is analyzed into types, purposes, and themes which demonstrate how these are tools of socialization for children and reminders of the norms and the expectations for adults. In addition to explicating the cultural treasures of the Krio people, examples of contemporary Krio poetry are offered, along with the poetry of two literary artists from Jamaica, as representative of literature that demonstrates the closeness of Sierra Leone Krio to Creole languages from other parts of the African diaspora.

CHAPTER SUMMARIES

Chapter 1: "History of the Krio People and Their Language" details the unique histories and backgrounds of the "Black Poor," the "Nova Scotians," the "Maroons," and the "Liberated Africans," as they were inserted into the British experiment to create a model African subject. Different from other descriptions of these groups, the authors draw heavily upon some of the most recent scholarship on these groups and their social, political, and economic interactions with each other and the colonial administration. In addition, the authors refer to little-known early accounts of the language spoken by some of the repatriated Africans, early census data, and other documents that uncover the ethnolinguistic identities of these groups. To the degree possible, the principal contributors to the Krio language and culture that emerged in this early nineteenth-century community are identified, with explanations for their ascendancy. The contention that Krio language is fundamentally English is challenged with clear linguistic evidence.

Chapter 2: "Language Basics" introduces the reader to the essential building blocks of Krio language. It begins with the Krio sound system, identifying the vowels, consonants, and diphthongs that exist, and how they resemble or differ from the English sound system. An important part of this chapter is a description of the interplay between tone and intonation, making it similar to other tone languages. After providing examples of the various parts of speech (that is, nouns, verbs, adjectives, adverbs, prepositions), the chapter will demonstrate that the basic structure in simple declarative sentences in Krio is the Noun Phrase followed by the Verb Phrase.

Chapter 3: "Greetings and Simple Sentences" presents the most common greetings used in the Krio community as formulas for social interaction in a society which relies heavily on oral communication and is reflective of an African worldview. It is shown that Krio has a variety of simple sentence types, ranging from straightforward declarative statements to Equational Sentences, Locative Sentences, and different kinds of Questions, expressed in the affirmative or the negative. A fundamental feature of Krio sentences is the use of consistent, unchanging, pre-verbal markers to communicate notions such as Tense and Aspect, along with uninflected verbs.

Chapter 4: "Complex Sentence Structures" describes the mechanisms available in Krio for expressing more complex statements and propositions. It begins with a critical analysis of Serial Verb Constructions, a feature that is not only very different from English, but is also multifunctional. Serial verbs may arise from the need to express directionality, instrumentality, purposiveness, sequentiality, or may be purely idiomatic. Krio is also considered a "thematic language" because of its frequent usage of devices for highlighting

8   Introduction

one element in a sentence in relation to other elements. Emphasis, Focus, and
Contrast are the major vehicles for achieving this. It is in this chapter that the
authors demonstrate how Krio speakers communicate complex tense/aspect
notions by using pre-verbal markers in combination. As in other languages,
Krio has structures for identifying Relative Clauses, Infinitive Clauses,
and Compounds, either alone or in combination. The final section of this
chapter focuses on Duplication as a tool for communicating intensity, changing the class of a word, or mimicking the sound of something or the very
absence of sound.

   Chapter 5: "African Linguistic Foundations in Krio and the Diaspora"
identifies a number of phonological, syntactic, and semantic features commonly found in West African languages that also exist in Sierra Leone
Krio. It will be argued that these features constitute the very essence of the
Krio language and are in no way peripheral. The composition of the sound
system, the rules of pronunciation, syntactic structures, the way in which
concepts like tense and aspect are expressed, the prevalence of serial verb
constructions, the expression of adjectival concepts as verbs, and many other
features make Krio more Kwa-like than Indo-European. Examples from
Kwa languages demonstrate the similarities. However, this chapter also demonstrates that other African languages, including those indigenous to Sierra
Leone, that contain linguistic features that are similar to prominent Kwa
features, buttressed the adoption of such features into Krio. Temne is one of
those languages. It will also be shown that, while the vast majority of Krio
vocabulary are English derivatives, as noted by Fyle and Jones in the 1980 *A
Krio-English Dictionary*, they differ significantly from English in meaning
and in grammar. Finally, a review of languages in the diaspora, in particular
Jamaican Creole and Gullah, reveal the persistence of a number of these
African features far from the African continent.

   Chapter 6: "Elements of Krio Culture" provides answers to the question: What are the key elements of Krio culture that have existed for nearly
two centuries and how do they help to sustain Krio society? The chapter opens with a description of the major religions operating in Krio society,
Christian and Muslim, and their shared relationships within Krio culture. The
chapter then examines a plethora of popular beliefs and practices that give
poignant insights into Krio behavior in everyday life. Finally, it addresses the
uniqueness of Krio traditional dress, food culture, and architectural structures
that have directly impacted the image of Krio society over the years.

   Chapter 7: "Krio Traditions" that are covered in this chapter are: (a) the
celebration of birth (Pul Na Do or Kɔmɔjade), in which the child is introduced
to the world; (b) the Krio wedding engagement ceremony (Put Stɔp) illumi-
nated through a skit adapted from Spencer-Walters' previously unpublished
play (*Put Stɔp*, 1977); (c) a descriptive analysis of various feasts honoring the

Introduction

dead and celebrating life (Awujɔ); and (d) a brief and general description of secret societies, specifically ɔjɛ, ɔntin, and gɛlɛdɛ, and their function in Krio society. The overarching goal of this chapter is to show how these traditions have contributed to defining the foundation of Krio society, how closely connected they are to the daily lives of the people, and how fervently they continue to enrich Krio language and culture in different ways. These cultural customs and ceremonies carry Yoruba names and demonstrate the persistence and continuity of the essence of Yoruba life among the Krio people.

Chapter 8: "Krio Folk Wisdom: Parables and Riddles" introduces the reader to the world of proverbs and riddles in Krio culture. Proverbs, which the Krio regularly refer to as [*parebul*], and riddles [ridulz] are integral components of the communication arsenal of Krio communities everywhere. They enrich the language by transforming ordinary experiences and linguistic expressions into meaningful interpretations in the lives of individuals or the community. *Parebulz* and *ridulz* are therefore best suited to teaching the young about values in Krio culture, while simultaneously exposing them to the richness of the language and the beauty and resourcefulness of their environment. Riddles, especially, are frequently used in Krio communities to test verbal agility and quick wits of participants, and few will shy away from such challenges which are viewed as play.

Chapter 9: "Krio Stories and Trickster Tales." Krio folk tales which are popularly known as *nansi toris*, play a very crucial role in Krio society. In this chapter, we introduce our readers to this West African tradition. They serve to entertain and to educate, but more importantly, they help to develop positive values in young people; positive values such as being responsible, loving, and compassionate to others. One's social obligations are largely dependent upon our understanding and interpretation of these oral traditions. Therefore, this chapter carefully selects tales (many of which were performed by elders in the villages) that deal with various life experiences. While most West African cultures have folktales that feature animal characters, we explore the likelihood that the Krio people named their tradition after *Anansi*, the trickster spider in the Akan tradition of Ghana.

Chapter 10: "Poetry in Sierra Leone Krio and Jamaican Patois." Poetry has been a written art form in Sierra Leone since the late 1800s when educated Krios engaged in what can be referred to as "newspaper poetry." Since then, poetry in Krio has expanded and taken on a character of its own. In this chapter, a selection of original Krio poems written by Krio poets are offered, most with English translations. The chapter also features two distinguished, award-winning Jamaican poets, Lorna Goodison and Andrene Bonner whose selections were translated into Krio to show the close historical, cultural, and linguistic ties to Sierra Leone and Jamaica.

PROSPECTIVE AUDIENCES

The very nature of this book makes it appealing to a wide and diverse audience.

Academics

In the academy, there is tremendous interest in cross-cultural, multi-disciplinary scholarship. This makes the text of special interest to those in Anthropology, African and African Diaspora Studies, Linguistics, Comparative Literature, History, Creole Studies, and International Studies.

New Urban Populations in Sierra Leone

A 2022 census reports that 43.8% of the total population of Sierra Leone is now living in the urban centers of the country, placing additional motivation for speakers of indigenous Sierra Leonean languages to learn Krio as their daily mode of communication. Thus, Krio has become the de-facto official language of the country. More advanced learners of the language will appreciate learning about the structure of Krio Language, its African origins, and the interrelationship between language and culture. Those who are native speakers of indigenous Sierra Leone languages (for example, Temne, Mende, and Sherbro) should have a special interest in learning about the contributions of their ethnic groups to the development of Krio language and culture as a nineteenth-century invention.

Krio Descendants Internationally

Thousands of individuals of Krio descent now live in North America and Europe. Many of those individuals have never lived in Sierra Leone, but are hungry for more information about the language and culture of their parents, grandparents, and ancestors.

Students Pursuing International Careers

Students of all backgrounds are pursuing careers in the foreign service, international business, world health, or human rights. They will find this book enlightening about the history of Africa and the complex interrelationships between African peoples and peoples from Europe.

Introduction 11

Military and Professionals Needing
Language Certification

In addition, there are university students, military personnel, and professional workers who need language certification in their various levels of professional endeavor. It is important to note here that Krio is one of over a hundred languages selected by the American Council for the Teaching of Foreign Languages (ACTFL) to help meet language certification requirements primarily for university students and branches of the military.

NOTES

1. Akintola J. G. Wyse, *The Krio of Sierra Leone: An Interpretive History* (London: C. Hurst, 1989).

2. *New Perspectives on the Sierra Leone Krio*, ed. Mac Dixon-Fyle and Gibril Cole (New York: Peter Lang, 2006).

3 . Gibril R. Cole, *The Krio of West Africa: Islam, Culture, Creolization, and Colonialism in the Nineteenth Century* (Athens: Ohio University Press, 2013).

4. *A Krio-English Dictionary*, ed. Clifford N. Fyle and Eldred D. Jones (Oxford: Oxford University Press, in collaboration with the Sierra Leone University Press, 1980).

5 . Jack Berry, *A Dictionary of Sierra Leone Krio*, U.S. Department of Health, Education, and Welfare, Contract Number OE-5-15-028 (Evanston, IL: Northwestern University Press, 1966).

6. Atinuke Scott-Boyle, Dennisia Lightfoot-Boston, Francois Baudouin, Juliet Sho-Cole, Malvia Coomber, Rhian Milton-Cole, Sharon Sho-Cole, and Yamide Rogers, *Next Gen Krios': Krio-English Dikshɔnɛri (Dictionary)* (Sierra Leone: NGK Oganisation, 2022).

7. Hanne-Ruth Thompson and Momoh Taziff Koroma, *Krio Dictionary and Phrasebook, Krio-English/English-Krio: A Language of Sierra Leone* (New York: Hippocrene Books, 2014).

8. Eyamidé E. Lewis-Coker's *Motherland Sierra Leone: Anansi Stories* (Bloomington, IN: AuthorHouse, 2013); Lewis-Coker's *Creoles of Sierra Leone: Proverbs, Parables, and Wise Sayings*, 2nd ed. (Bloomington, IN: AuthorHouse, 2018); and Daphne Pratt's *Krio Salad: Folktales, Poems, Parables, and Wise Sayings* (Freetown: Sierra Leonean Writers Series, 2017).

PART I

History

Chapter 1

History of the Krio People and Their Language

A close Krio translation of this chapter title would be *Usay Krio Pipul Dɛm Kɔmɔt?* [What is the origin of the Krio people?] A history of the Krio people could begin with the late eighteenth century. In fact, most, if not all, previous histories of this unique group of people have begun their chronologies there. We believe such an abbreviated history does not provide enough context to fully understand the circumstances that gave rise to Krio language and culture. Thus, we have chosen to provide a broader and longer picture of the world which made Krio language and culture possible. Had it not been for the centuries of interaction between European powers and the African political entities of the day, Krio language and culture would not have come into existence. This longer view of history has led us to new and significant insights into the Krio people we know today and the languages and cultures that contributed most significantly to the systems and character of Krio.

THE TRANS-ATLANTIC SLAVE TRADE: PLAYERS AND NUMBERS

The story really begins in the mid-1400s. This marks the beginning of a world-altering series of interactions between a number of European powers and West Africa. Philip D. Curtin has chronicled this history very effectively by compiling an extensive set of quantitative data related to the Atlantic slave trade. Given the nature of the slave trade in various periods and at different stages of development in particular geographic areas, the data is more or less available and seldom exactly comparable to earlier or later periods. In spite of these shortcomings, the data is very informative. Curtin summarizes this long history, from the mid-fifteenth century to the late nineteenth century, as follows:

16   *Chapter 1*

In the fifteenth and sixteenth centuries, the Spanish and Portuguese carried the rudimentary institutions of the South Atlantic System from the Mediterranean to the Atlantic Islands, then to Santo Domingo and Brazil. In the seventeenth and eighteenth centuries, the Dutch, English, and French dominated the slave trade, but in the nineteenth century, Brazil and Cuba accounted for the vast majority of slaves imported, and by that time the northern powers had made their own slave trade effectively illegal.[1]

Curtin's book is invaluable as a tool for understanding not only the magnitude of the Atlantic slave trade, but also for understanding why the linguistic features and cultural remnants from various African ethnolinguistic groups show up in particular parts of the world. His work also provides answers to questions like these:

- Which European powers were dominant during certain periods of time?
- Why was their focus on particular regions of West Africa at one time, but not later?
- What role did African political dynamics play?
- Which African ethnic groups were preferred by the recipients of enslaved Africans?

In the next few pages, we will highlight some of the trends and actions that appear to have had the greatest impact on what would eventually result in the evolution of the Sierra Leone Krio.

The data collected by Curtin reveals that the largest number of enslaved Africans during the sixteenth century came from two geographical regions of Africa. One was the area referred to as "The Guinea of Cape Verde," which was principally what we know of as the Senegambia and Sierra Leone. It was called "the Guinea of Cape Verde" because it broadly defines the area east of the Cape Verde Islands. The other was the region south of the mouth of the Congo River, the Congo/Angola area. While there had been conventional trading with the Portuguese in the Senegambia region before the mid-1500s, the break-up of the Jolof Empire in the middle decades resulted in warfare between the members of the confederation. This warfare produced prisoners that could be sold as slaves. These enslaved Africans could be found in significant numbers in sixteenth-century America. However, Curtin claims that, after this period, the Wolof, people from Senegal and Gambia, "never again provided significant numbers for the slave trade."[2]

A study done in Las Charcas (modern day Bolivia) shows that although the Wolof were dominant in the middle decades of the sixteenth century, a shift took place during the second half of that century to the Bight of Biafra (southern Nigeria/western Cameroon). This was followed by another shift to Angola (central Africa) around 1594, with Angola becoming the most important source of enslaved Africans by 1600. This strongly suggests that the Wolof had little or no significant influence on the language and culture of enslaved African communities after the end of the sixteenth century.

According to Curtin, "the large flow [of enslaved Africans] from Congo is again partly the result of African political history, but with more direct European participation. This quarter century in history of the Kingdom of Kongo was a period when the early good relations with the Portuguese began to deteriorate, when the central authority of the kingdom declined, and when the Portuguese began their exploration and penetration of the Kingdom of Ndongo."[3] From 1614 until 1640, the Portuguese actually launched military operations in the interior of Angola, taking slaves directly, catapulting the slave trade to a different level. It is not a coincidence that the Portuguese began enslaving Africans directly just as their colony on the islands of Sao Thome and Principe, off the coast of Angola, had begun to experience an increased demand for free labor to work the expanding sugar plantations. In fact, considerations of both supply and demand were ongoing motivating forces in the trade of enslaved Africans.

Approaching the end of the sixteenth century, in 1580, the Spanish and Portuguese crowns were unified, placing them in almost complete control of the Atlantic slave trade for nearly a century. So much in control of the slave trade was the Spanish Empire in supplying the Spanish colonies that most slaving ships from other countries, thereafter, had to become parties to *asientos*, contracts between the crown and either private entities or other sovereign powers, granting them permission to ship a specific number of enslaved Africans from particular regions to particular destinations. Asientos were granted to the Dutch in 1675, the Portuguese in 1694, the French in 1701, and the English in 1713. Although there were multiple players in the Atlantic slave trade at this point, it should be recognized that "about 60 per cent of the slave trade in the seventeenth century still went to the Hispanic colonies, and about 40 per cent to Brazil alone."[4]

Based on the meticulous research conducted by K. G. Davies on the financial aspects of the Royal African Company, which appeared in his 1957 publication, *The Royal African Company*, Curtin calculated the estimated number and origin of enslaved Africans traded by this company, as well as the areas to which they were shipped, between 1673 and 1689. Curtin's estimates of the exports may reflect a prevalent pattern of the British slave trade during the seventeenth century:

27.3% (24,400) were exported from the Windward Coast (Liberia/Ivory Coast),
20.9% (18,600) from the Gold Coast (Ghana),

18   *Chapter 1*

15.7% (14,000) from Ardra & Whydah,
12% (10,700) from the Senegambia and Sierra Leone region,
12.0% (10,700) from Angola,
6.7% (6,000) from Benin & Calabar, and
5.4% (4,800) from other areas.[5]

A couple of observations are instructive here. First, it should be noted that the largest percentages of the Africans enslaved by the British during the latter quarter of the seventeenth century were from the Windward Coast and Gold Coast. Consequently, it is safe to assume that a large percentage of the Africans enslaved by the British from those regions were members of the Kwa Language Family, most notably speakers of Akan. Second, even though the shift in the overall slave trade was from the Senegambia/Sierra Leone region to the Congo/Angola area, only 12% of all of the exported captives taken by the Royal African Company were from Congo/Angola during this period. Not reflected in the numbers above were the locations where these Africans were shipped. During this period of the British slave trade, 38.4% were shipped to Barbados, 33.6% were shipped to Jamaica, 10.1% were shipped to Nevis, and 17.9% were sold elsewhere. These latter figures are indicative of the degree to which the slave trade was geared toward supplying free labor to work the expanding sugar plantations in the Caribbean. The fact that Jamaica was one of the largest producers of sugar cane was a major factor in the British decision to seize control of Jamaica from the Spanish in 1655.

In spite of the fact that the English had gained dominance over the other European traders in the eighteenth century, the Royal African Company had become weakened by its wars with the Dutch (1665–1667) and the French (1689–1697). Because the British Crown refused to provide needed financial support to the Royal African Company, the British slave trade was taken over, almost totally, by private trading companies and pirates. Thus, the British slave trade was much less regulated, much less consistent from one colony to another, and much more dependent on the specific needs of the individual colonies. However, in 1661 through 1667, the British government of the Island of Barbados established the *Barbados Code*, a set of laws, restrictions, and practices for administering the slave trade in Barbados. While other countries had laws and policies that tended to provide certain protections for enslaved Africans, the *Barbados Code* stripped the enslaved Africans of their humanity by legally establishing them as property and giving the plantation owners free rein in the management of their slaves, including brutal punishments for minor infractions. Unfortunately, the other British colonies began to establish their own Slave Codes, based on the basic premises laid down in Barbados.

History of the Krio People and Their Language 19

According to Curtin, "the great majority of slaves imported into British colonies were imported between 1690 and 1870."[6] Although the ethnolinguistic background of the enslaved Africans imported into the various colonies may have differed from one another, based on their availability, the colonies typically made it known what their preferences were, based on what Curtin refers to as "a set of stereotyped 'national characters' highlighting traits that seemed important to slave owners—industry, proneness to rebellion, faithfulness, honesty, or physical suitability for fieldwork."[7] Large markets, like Jamaica, needed to keep a steady flow of enslaved Africans, regardless of their ethnic origin, to meet the demands of the plantations, but the Jamaican planters still had their preferences. While Jamaica preferred Akan peoples between 1751 and 1790, and bought nearly 80% of those from the Gold Coast, they had a change of heart after the revolt in Saint Domingue in 1791. This revolt was sparked by the refusal of the government of the French colony to grant citizenship and freedom to free people of color, which was one of the provisions of the French revolutionary government. The Jamaican government could not afford to assume an increased threat of all out revolt from its enslaved population, many of whom were Akan.

Elizabeth Donnan's research, published in 1928, identifies the clear preferences among the South Carolina planters between 1732 and 1765:

> That these purchasers had decided preferences as to the source of their labor supply is patent from the fact that the advertisements usually mentioned and frequently emphasized the place of origin of the cargo. The favorite negroes were those from Gambia and the Gold Coast. Between 1732 and 1765, at least fifty-three Gambia and twenty-nine Gold Coast cargoes were sold in Charleston. To describe arrivals as "Gambia Men and Women" or "Gold Coast negroes," was a guaranty of high quality.[8]

Donnan goes on to indicate that "the Calabar slaves, were the least desired of all, and the captains were frequently urged not to bring them to this market. The difference in price between a Calabar and a Gambia negro was from 3 to 4 pounds."[9] Interestingly, Georgia and North Carolina had distributions similar to South Carolina, because they were fed by the interstate trade from South Carolina.

This history is particularly important to understanding the establishment and growth of the Krio community in Sierra Leone because significant groups of the Africans who were enslaved in the British colonies became some of the first to populate the British Colony in Sierra Leone. One group, referred to in the literature as the "Black Poor," was promised their freedom from slavery in America and resettlement in London, if they would leave their masters, thereby strengthening British odds of winning the war against

20   *Chapter 1*

the colonies. Once resettled in London, they discovered that their liberators had made no provisions for them to make a decent living, forcing many of them to roam the streets, destitute. As the anti-slavery sentiment began to grow in England, a representative of the group appealed to Granville Sharp, an abolitionist, philanthropist, and influential leader, to transport them back to Africa. Along with another sympathetic Englishman, Henry Smeathman, Sharp was able to secure approval and a grant from the government for this group to start a new life in Africa. In May of 1787, 377 of the original party of 510 Black Poor landed at St. George's Bay in the western region of Sierra Leone. This resettlement was made possible by the leasing of land from the Thaimne-speaking people (that is, the group currently referred to as Temne people). This initial association with the Temne would turn out to be only the first of a significant relationship between the newcomers and the indigenous peoples of Sierra Leone.

A second group of formerly enslaved Africans are referred to as the "Nova Scotians." Their circumstances, very similar to those of the "Black Poor'" resulted from their agreement to defect from service in the colonial army. For their loyalty to the British Crown, they were freed from slavery and promised farmland in Nova Scotia. However, the thickly forested land they were granted as well as the blistering cold weather prevented them from being able to eke out a livable existence there. In a land with few employment opportunities, they found themselves in competition with the white residents. Resentment from the white settlers created a hostile environment, in addition to the already difficult natural environment. After six years of struggling against the odds, one of their leaders, Thomas Peters, born in Yorubaland, protested their conditions to the British government, eventually travelling to London and meeting with Sharp. As perhaps the most prominent abolitionist in London and someone who had developed a plan for repatriating Africans back to their homeland, Sharp was the most logical and likely person to assist the Nova Scotians. In fact, prior to the establishment of the Sierra Leone Company in 1791, Sharp had founded the St. George's Bay Company, a trading company. Thus, Sharp contracted with fifteen ships to carry 1,200 Nova Scotians to Sierra Leone in 1792.

When the Nova Scotians arrived, only five years after the founding of Granville Town by the Black Poor, they found the settlement almost completely destroyed by the Temnes, who had set the town on fire, according to Christopher Fyfe,[10] in retribution for siding with the captain of a British naval ship responsible for burning down one of King Jimmy's towns. Having built their own community once before in Nova Scotia, the new arrivals were up to the task of rebuilding the settlement, renaming it Freetown, the Province of Freedom. Given the larger size of their group, the Nova Scotians came with more skills and experience in managing under adverse conditions.

At the turn of the century, in 1800, eight years after the arrival of the Nova Scotians, a third group of formerly enslaved Africans were transported to Freetown, a group called the "Maroons." The name, "Maroons," is fitting for this group because, for nearly a century, they had been successful in escaping from enslavement in Jamaica, initially under Spanish rule, and later under British rule. The British had been victorious in defeating the Spanish for the lucrative plantations and for their quest to monopolize the slave trade. These runaways took shelter in the rugged mountains around the island and formed an anti-slavery resistance movement. After the Maroon War which began in 1795, the British decided to neutralize this rebellious group by shipping them off the island. After a short residence in Nova Scotia, they, too, were shipped to the place that had become the British resettlement station, Freetown, Sierra Leone. At the time of their relocation, they numbered between 500 and 600 men, women, and children.

By this time, the Colony was under the control of the Sierra Leone Company. According to Joko Sengova, the Sierra Leone Company "held off the Temne while the settlers supported themselves by farming."[11] The presence of the colonial administration and the Christian evangelical missionaries, especially the Church Missionary Society (CMS), as well as the influence of the British benefactors of the recently settled Africans, clearly projected an image of Freetown as being a community steeped in Western European culture and Christian values. It was clearly the goal of the Crown that Freetown would become a model Western-educated, Christian-converted, hard-working, African society for the rest of the African world to emulate.

Anti-slavery sentiments were growing in England in the early nineteenth century, thanks to the abolitionist and humanitarian efforts of individuals like Sharp. The clearest indication of this was the *Act for the Abolition of the Slave Trade*, which was enacted by the Parliament of the United Kingdom on March 25, 1807.[12] In essence, the *Act* (1) prohibited the sale of slaves within British territories going forward, (2) imposed a penalty on those caught engaging in slave trading in the amount of 100 pounds per slave, and (3) identified those empowered to seize the belongings of slave trading operations, including slaving ships and "natives of Africa" on those vessels, most importantly the Royal Navy. As a practical matter, any enslaved Africans seized on slaving ships in the Atlantic Ocean by the navy were to be set free on the west coast of Africa. Between 1808 and 1860, 1,600 slaving ships were seized and 150,000 Africans were freed. These returnees were initially referred to as the "Recaptured Slaves," but were later called the "Liberated Africans." Sengova estimates that approximately 50,000 of them "were resettled in Freetown between 1808 and 1868."[13] The Liberated Africans constituted the largest group to settle in the Colony.

It is undisputed that the largest linguistic group among the Liberated Africans were the Yoruba. However, it is estimated by some that there may have been as many as 200 other African ethnic groups present at one time or another in the colony. What has been amplified in more recent scholarship[14] is the significant number and impact of local, indigenous groups such as the Temne, Mende, Bullom, Koranko, Mandinka, Susu, and Limba on the formation of what became Krio society. C. Magbaily Fyle reminds us that the "original inhabitants [of the peninsula] never went away when the newcomers arrived."[15] Many Krios have not readily accepted their familial affiliation with local indigenous groups because they were stigmatized as being inferior. Thus, this part of the history of Krio society has been under-represented and underappreciated.

Identifying the ethnic and linguistic background of the various groups who settled in the colony provides significant insights into the development of Krio language and culture. It is important to note that none of the groups involved would have identified themselves as "Krio" prior to the middle of the nineteenth century or later. The ethnic makeup of the Black Poor is very sketchy at best, for a host of reasons. At the top of the list is the fact that they had existed in slavery for a multi-generational period of time before they were given a path to freedom by the British during the American Revolution. As a means of containing and controlling the enslaved Africans, the American plantation owners and the local governments used every method possible, including torture, to eradicate African names, languages, and cultures from the enslaved Africans. While the history of the slave trade routes and planter ethnic preferences provide us with some hint as to the ethnic background of enslaved Africans from North American British colonies, assigning ethnic origin to individuals is very difficult, because the British colonists did not keep systematic records of the origin of the enslaved Africans who landed on these shores.

Some of the Nova Scotians, whose histories were very similar to those of the Black Poor, were able to trace their origins to the inland areas of Sierra Leone. Gibril R. Cole, in his "Re-Thinking the Demographic Make-Up of Krio Society," states that "John Gordon and John Kizzell were among those who are said to have hailed from the Yalunka, Koranko, and Sherbro areas."[16] Cole goes on to say that "Christopher Fyle mentions the presence, among the Nova Scotians, of several Koranko who had been sold into slavery through Bunce Island, one of them being Frank Peters, who had been enslaved in South Carolina before returning to Sierra Leone as a Nova Scotian."[17]

According to Cole, "The Maroons who returned to West Africa from Jamaica via Nova Scotia can trace their provenience to the area of modern Ghana."[18] A much earlier source that supports Cole's claim is the statement from R. C. Dallas, in his 1803 book, *History of the Maroons*:

History of the Krio People and Their Language

Some of the old people remember that their parents spoke, in their own families, a language entirely different from that spoken by the rest of the negroes with whom they had incorporated. They recollected many of the words for things in common use and declared that in their early years they spoke their mother tongue. The Coromantee language, however, superseded the others, and became in time the general one in use.[19]

The fact that the Akan (the ethnic group typically referred to by the term "Coromantee") were known to be fierce warriors, helps to explain how the Maroons had the wherewithal and temperament to successfully resist captivity in Jamaica for nearly a century under both Spanish and British rule.

Fortunately, we have much better information on the ethnic backgrounds of the Liberated Africans. They were retrieved from slaving ships in the Atlantic Ocean by the British Navy while enroute to unknown locations in the Caribbean Islands or the Americas. Thus, they had not gone through the trauma of being forced to work on plantations yet, sold, and perhaps sold again, and stripped of their home language and culture. As they landed in the Sierra Leone colony, their identities were documented for the purpose of being placed in one of the rural villages surrounding Freetown along with others from their ethnic group or from an area close to their point of origin.

In reference to the settlement of recaptured Africans from naval ships, Fyfe points out that, "one ship might be filled with people from Congo over two thousand miles to the south; the next might be from Senegal, about five hundred miles to the north."[20] Since the recaptives had come from such distant lands, it would have been impossible for the British to resettle them all in their original homelands. Placing them on the peninsula in nearby villages, under the parish system established by Governor Charles McCarthy was the most practical solution. "Leicester Village, in the mountains behind Freetown, was the first, started by recaptives from the Jolof and Bambara countries. A group of Congo recaptives was sent to a deserted Temne village in the hills west of Freetown, but they preferred the waterside and moved down and built their own Congo Town by the shore. Another group settled east of Freetown at Kissy; they are supposed to have come from the Kise-Kise River north of Sierra Leone."[21] Portuguese Town was founded by a group, all of whom spoke Portuguese. That village was situated on the outskirts of Freetown in a former Temne village headed by a chief called Pa Demba. Cole states that "Hogbrook Village (later named Regent Village) was originally inhabited by people from Vai Country. Mende recaptives were among the earliest inhabitants of PaSanday (Renamed Lumley)."[22] Cole's research reveals that not all of the recaptives were from distant lands. In fact, there is good reason to believe that those from regions only a short distance from Freetown probably returned to their homeland.

24   *Chapter 1*

Tom Spencer-Walters provides us with additional details about the makeup of these villages: "In the small village of Hastings (about 13 miles from Freetown) alone, several of these [ethnic] communities were established: Oku Town for the Yoruba contingent; Egba Town (the home of the Oje and Hunting secret societies) for another Nigerian group; Congo Town, for the Congolese and Angolan groups; and Kossoh Town was the home of the Kossoh from the provinces of Sierra Leone."[23]

From the research done by Cole and others, we have learned that these villages did not all start with only one ethnic group, nor did they remain that way, even if they began that way. It would appear that the longer the villages existed, the more ethnically diverse they became. As early as the 1820s, Regent Village included ethnolinguistic groups from Sierra Leone, like the Kono, Soso, Bulom, Bassa, and Gola, living alongside groups from the coast and inland of Nigeria, namely Igbos, Efiks, Kalabaris, Yorubas, and Hausa. This level of diversity is underscored by Spencer-Walters when he points out that "In Kossoh Town . . . there was a strong presence of the Oku people living side by side with the Kossoh. In Egba Town where the Yoruba were pre-eminent, the Temne, Loko, and Limba populations were quite visible as well."[24] From early on, diversity was the very essence of what would become the Krio society.

According to Fyfe, "In 1808 the whole population of the Colony was under two thousand. Most were 'Settlers' (that is Nova Scotians and Maroons). Each lived in their own part of Freetown, the Nova Scotians from Little East Street to Charlotte Street, the Maroons west of Charlotte Street."[25] With only a few exceptions, the "Black Poor" had disappeared, due to disease, old age, poor health, or the harsh conditions under which they had been forced to live over the years. By 1815, over 6,000 recaptives had been settled in the colony. As the recaptives continued being taken off of slaving ships, thousands of them were being landed in Sierra Leone every year during the 1820s and 1830s. New villages had to be established to accommodate them; Murray Town and Aberdeen west of Freetown; Campbell Town and Benguema near Waterloo.

Curtin reports on the results of the 1848 Census conducted in Freetown. Comprised of 13,273 participants, the census identifies the five largest ethnic groups to be Yoruba, Igbo, Fon, Gun, Hausa, and Mende.[26] In table 1.1, which

Table 1.1. Ethnic Affiliation of Liberated Africans in 1848 Freetown Census

Yoruba	*7,114 (Western Nigeria)*
Ibo	1,231 (Southeastern Nigeria)
Fon, Gun	1,075 (Dahomey, now Benin)
Hausa	657 (Northern Nigeria)
Mende	609 (Sierra Leone)
Sub-Total	10,686

History of the Krio People and Their Language 25

has been extracted from the numbers reported by Curtin, it is obvious that the Yoruba group was, by far, the largest group.

These numbers reflected in table 1.1 and the reports from other chroniclers are very significant to our understanding of the birth of Krio Society and Krio Language. A more detailed presentation of all of the participants in the 1848 census appears in the table constructed by Curtin.[27]

THE ROLE OF THE COLONIAL ADMINISTRATION IN SIERRA LEONE

With such a diverse group of African peoples and such varying experiences coming together in one colony, it is important to describe the European contingent that was present. At the first landing of the Settler populations, there were members of the St. George's Bay Company. Not long afterward, in 1791, St. George's Bay Company was replaced by the Sierra Leone Company. Eventually it was replaced by the British government, as a Crown Colony, in 1808. It appears that at no time were there more than a few hundred Englishmen. The Europeans were always a small, but dominant, group because of the role they performed from the very beginning of the colony.

Spencer-Walters makes it clear what the vision of the British benefactors and colonial power was. As he states it, the "Sierra Leone Experiment" was both "a civilizing project" and

> an opportunity for the British to actualize and expand their empirical and territorial ambitions. It was an opportunity for them to gain strategic influence in a part of the world with which they were already familiar and out of which the expansion of legitimate trade, missionary activities and, consequently, the widespread propagation of British culture can be quickly realized through dedicated converts like freed Africans; free men who have been imbued in the ways of the English and, who are culturally and linguistically adaptable.[28]

The colonists hoped to achieve their goals through two strategic initiatives: (1) converting the African populations to Christianity, and (2) through Western education. Initially, both of these goals were pursued by missionary societies. The CMS, founded in 1808, was the first to engage in this organized activity. Other missionary groups followed, like the Methodist Mission, then the Nova Scotian Methodist Church, and the Huntingdonians. Where there was no missionary organization, there was usually a village pastor to preach the gospel. In 1844, a group of recaptive preachers started their own church, the West African Methodist Church. The face of the Christianizing mission, although predominantly white, was also black.

26   *Chapter 1*

It was the missionary societies that established English schools, first in Freetown proper, and later in the villages. The schools established in Freetown were better funded and of higher quality than those in the villages. The expectation of the colonial authorities was that those in the villages would concentrate on farming. Those who had the means, whether in Freetown or in the villages, sent their children to be educated in England, many returning as doctors, lawyers, administrators, and business owners. The task of educating the "Settlers" was considerably easier because of their previous histories in America, England, or the Caribbean. As Cole describes it, "Christianity was not simply an external imposition but part of an identity that had been forged in the crucible of Atlantic enslavement, resistance, and freedom."[29] Much of the education program was grounded in learning how to read the scriptures, and reinforcing Christian values and Western civilization among the formerly enslaved population.

While village schools were few and far between in the early nineteenth century, a mission school was established in Regent Village in 1820. Two of the most prominent schools established in Freetown were the CMS Grammar School in 1845 and the Annie Walsh Memorial School in 1849. When the missionary schools could no longer afford to provide for the broader, more diverse educational needs, the British Government took over.

ISLAM IN THE DEVELOPING KRIO COMMUNITY

Not everyone in the evolving colony was Christian. A large segment of the village populations followed the teachings of Islam. The most significant number of Muslims were the members of the Yoruba communities, the Oku. "The European missionaries, especially those in the CMS, were adamantly opposed to the presence of Muslims within the colony population and made enormous efforts to rid the Liberated African community of what they perceived as the Islamic menace."[30] It was not only the CMS missionaries who ostracized the Muslims. So too did the more affluent, more highly educated stratum of Freetown society. However, "by the late 1830's onward, colonial administrators began to realize that the economic viability of the colony depended on the growth of the colony-interior trade."[31] The Muslims, most of whom had brought their exceptional mercantile experience and success with them, especially outside of the colony, now found themselves an invaluable asset to the colony administration. By the mid-1800s, Muslim communities thrived in places like Fourah Bay, Fula Town, and Aberdeen. Without their contributions to the colony's economy, it would have suffered a devastating economic decline.

THE AFRICAN MAJORITY

What has not been emphasized enough thus far is the fact that, except for the colonial administrators and the majority of the missionary personnel, the rest of those who inhabited the Colony, that being the remaining "Settlers," the "Liberated Africans," and those indigenous to the surrounding area, were all Africans. This is a critical point for understanding the evolution of Krio Society and the nature of it. "The more educated upper stratum of emergent Krio society was certainly predominantly Christian and may very well have aspired to European cultural values . . . nonetheless, the overwhelming majority of the people continued to adhere to African cultural values and engaged in fluid interactions without regard to differences in religion."[32] Furthermore, the vast majority of those who were African in the colony were working class people. As such, they were less interested in being admitted into the elite social spaces, like the Freemason Lodge, than they were in being initiated into "equally esoteric Yoruba-derived cultural organizations like the Ojeh, Egunuko, Akpansa, Gelede, and Odeh."[33]

Given the extraordinary diversity of the groups that constituted the colony, it is difficult to understand how this community coalesced into a high-functioning society and accepted one language, Krio, as their language of choice, if not their first language. Afterall, there were representatives from nearly 200 different African languages. There were significant differences (and sometimes conflict) between the Settlers and the Liberated Africans. In addition to this, there existed a power differential between the African population, on the one hand, and the European colonialists and missionaries, on the other hand, that was essentially unbreakable. However, there are critical factors, events, relationships, motives, and ambitions that help us make sense out of this complex story. Unravelling these interwoven social and cultural dynamics will also lead us to a better understanding of the origin(s) and construction of the Krio language.

HOW DID KRIO LANGUAGE EVOLVE IN THIS VERY COMPLEX SOCIAL SETTING?

The authors of this book believe that there are fundamental principles, and/ or conditions, that are required to stimulate a creolization process, of which Kriolization is an example. One of those conditions is the existence of a linguistic environment in which at least one indigenous language exists in proximity to, and in interaction with, a language of a socially and politically dominant language. Contrary to the tenets of some theorists, we maintain

28   *Chapter 1*

that the primary agents of change in such situations are the speakers of the indigenous, less prestigious language(s), while the speakers of the politically dominant language are the primary donors of vocabulary. The grammatical structures and systems underlying the indigenous language(s) constitute the framework or template into which the dominant language material is inserted. In the specific case of Sierra Leone Krio, the African language speakers spoke one or more languages and had only those linguistic structures and systems to build upon. They did not have ready access to the grammatical, semantic, or phonological systems of the English language. At best, they only had infrequent, superficial access to English in a classroom setting in which the principal text was the Bible.

As the agents of change, the speakers of the African languages, who were highly motivated to be able to communicate with the various segments of their community, they naturally reduced the complexity of their linguistic systems in order to make them more accessible to others and to accommodate foreign linguistic data they were importing. Linguistic elements that did not fit into their systems, even with some modification to the base structures, were simply rejected. Consistent with this theory and consistent with what we know about natural child language development, we believe that, the children between the ages of two and twelve years old (the critical language-learning period) were the critical agents in synthesizing the various language inputs in their linguistic environment. In other words, the children living in these very diverse linguistic communities were the innovators/creators of the novel creolized language. The phonological, syntactic, and semantic rules formulated by these children, evolved into a coherent and consistent linguistic system.

The various groups which constituted the Krio Society of the early- and mid-nineteenth century played different roles in this linguistic and cultural transformation. An understanding of their roles leads us to a more accurate picture of how Krio Language came into existence and why Yoruba language and culture have had such a dramatic impact on what resulted.

THE DIFFERENTIAL ROLES OF THE PARTICIPANTS

The Settlers (that is, the Black Poor, the Nova Scotians, and Maroons, as a group) played a couple of critical roles. First of all, they were the catalysts for British philanthropists and abolitionists envisioning a society of free, self-governing, independent Africans. The Black Poor and the Nova Scotians drew international attention to the strife of enslaved Africans, yearning to be free and searching for a home where their humanity would be fully recognized. Had it not been for the appeals of the Settlers in the latter part of the eighteenth century, neither the Settlers nor the Liberated Africans would have been thrust together into a community with British colonial administrators, missionaries, and educators.

Second, the Settlers had all spent a substantial amount of time in England, America, or Jamaica where they were forced to incorporate some English elements into their linguistic repertoire, thereby creating a model for the Liberated Africans to try to replicate. It was critical for the Black Poor and Nova Scotians to have some facility in English, since the ability to speak English was thought to be synonymous with intelligence. As Fyfe describes it, "They spoke their own style of English, different from that spoken in England . . . though their dances and some of their customs were African in origin, they had been changed by their residence in America. They were Christians and attended their own churches regularly."[34] Although homeless and destitute in England, they were, in some sense, still viewed as exceptions to other Africans.

The literature does not provide many examples of what might be referred to as "Settler Talk," but Dallas provides us with the following description of the language spoken by the Maroons: "The Maroons, in general, speak, like most of the other Negroes in the island, a peculiar dialect of English, corrupted with African words; and certainly understand our language sufficiently well to have received instruction in it."[35]

Though it is highly unlikely that the Maroons had had much, if any, formal instruction in English, we can be pretty certain that, after nearly a century of contact with the British, the Maroons had developed enough facility in the language to at least understand most of the English spoken to them, even if they may not have been proficient speakers of English themselves.

F. Harrison Rankin, writing in 1836 in a book titled *The White Man's Grave*, provides some interesting, although anecdotal, insights into the subtleties in the language of the different African groups residing in the colony at that period of time. As he reported:

> Shortly after arriving, when Settlers and Maroons were to me as equally black and undistinguishable as Soosoos and Ibboos, I innocently inflicted deep injury on the sensitive mind of the laundress by inquiring why she had omitted to bring home some particular article of dress. . . . The exact idiom which wounded the pride of the Settler has already been forgotten: it was either "What *matter* for you no done bring him?" instead of "What *fashion* for you no done bring him?" or some nicety equally important, and similarly difficult discrimination. It had the effect, however, of changing the mild maiden into a fury; "What! White man come for insult me! Leff me, leff me! Bad man, dis man, for true, 'peak a me so! Me no Maroon, me think; me Settler-girl and you sabby."[36]

30   *Chapter 1*

After attempting to apologize for insulting the young woman, she responded as follows: "Why for, den, you no can 'speak a me like Settler-girl? Why for you done curse me wid Maroon word? Pish, phoo, for true; me sabby de English good; no talk bad-palaver like Maroon girl."[37]

Although we cannot be confident of Rankin's precision in rendering the actual conversation, two things are evident: (1) within the broader Settler community, there was apparently a fairly clear distinction, at least among the African population, between the speech of the Maroons and the speech of those who had been enslaved in America; and (2) regardless of the level of accuracy of Rankin's depiction of the actual conversation, there are a number of lexical, grammatical, and phonological features in his description that find almost exact replicas in present-day Krio.

The example in table 1.2 suggests that although there may have been a considerable amount of variability among the speakers of the incipient Krio language, many elements of modern-day Krio were already baked in.

Finally, another role played by the Settlers was that of the social model the British were aspiring to achieve by educating and Christianizing them. Success to the British would have been transforming the Liberated Africans into the same mold. In fact, those who were interested in upward mobility into Freetown society needed to emulate the exemplars of Krio society.

By contrast to the Settlers, the Liberated Africans had been rescued from slaving ships in the Atlantic Ocean and not subjected to the long-term dehumanizing behavior of the planters nor were they exposed to English speakers over a significant period of time. In other words, the Liberated Africans had not been forced to give up their home languages and cultures. The period of their captivity was unlikely to have been long enough to have been forced to learn English. At most, they may have been exposed to Pidgin English, if they had been held in one of the slaving ports before being thrown on to a ship heading for a life of servitude. Even if that had been the case, the captured

Table 1.2. Settler Speech Reported by Rankin in 1834

1834 Settler Speech	Contemporary Krio	English Translation
leff me	lɛf mi	'leave me alone/get away'
for true	fɔ tru	'honestly/correctly'
curse	kɔs	'defame/disrespect'
sabby	sabi	'know/understand'
dis, den	dis, dɛn	'this/then'
de	di	'the'
done	dɔn	'completive aspect marker'
palaver	plaba	'dispute/argument'

Africans would have become familiar with only a limited number of English words in a very narrow set of interactions with English speakers.

Once situated in the various villages around Freetown, the Liberated Africans were, for all intents and purposes, segregated from the more dynamic interactions between the colonial administrators and the Settlers. Although the missionaries in the colony worked hard at converting the Liberated Africans to Christianity and taught the scripture in English, the Liberated Africans continued practicing their home religious beliefs and retaining their native values, traditions, and languages. In fact, given the ethnic diversity that existed in the villages, the Liberated Africans may have been as challenged to communicate across the linguistic boundaries between some of their African neighbors as they were to communicate with the missionaries, colonial administrators, and other English-speaking members of the larger community.

Even in the early 1800s, the Liberated Africans outnumbered the Settlers and the Europeans in the Colony. The Yoruba were demonstrably the most influential among the Liberated Africans not only because of their numerical superiority, but also because they had linguistic kinship with a number of other groups in the colony who belonged to the Kwa Language Family (for instance the Ibo, Ewe, Akan, Ga, and Bini). The resilience of their religious practices, traditions, ceremonies, and secret societies made them the flag-bearers of *Africanness* and positioned them as the most prominent resistance to the British model they were expected to embrace.

The business activities of the Yoruba required frequent travel into the hinterland, as well as within the colony, leading to deep, abiding relationships across linguistic groups. In the process, they developed social relationships, in addition to their business relations, evolving in many cases to inter-ethnic marriage. Crosscultural marriages like these created a rich environment for cultural exchange and linguistic integration. This kind of cultural sharing is what leads to creolization. This is especially true when partners from different linguistic groups bear children.

The normal process of child language development involves the formulation of linguistic rules based on the linguistic inputs in their environment. Children born in a community in which they are hearing Yoruba at home, other African languages in their village, and English of various kinds at school and in the markets, expanded their vocabulary and are allowed to formulate new rules of grammar, rules of pronunciation, and semantic rules that weaved elements of the contributing languages into a full-blown, novel language. Thus, it was the villages surrounding Freetown, not Freetown proper, that was the *epicenter* of Kriolization.

32   *Chapter 1*

DEBUNKING THE BELIEF THAT ENGLISH
IS THE FOUNDATION OF KRIO

Clifford N. Fyle and Eldred D. Jones, in their monumental work, *A Krio-English Dictionary* (1980), have advanced the claim that the vocabulary of Krio, "at a conservative estimate, is at least eighty percent derived from a single language, English."[38] What most people would conclude from this estimate is that English was the primary source of the Krio Language. However, the operative word in their claim is "derived." Although eighty percent of the vocabulary may be derived from English, the vast majority of those words of English origin frequently, if not typically, carry a meaning or range of meanings different from those words in any British or American variety of English. It is also true that those words most often function grammatically different from their English counterpart and are pronounced differently as well. Fyle and Jones do not claim that Krio is an English-based language or that the foundation of Krio is English. Let us remember that their task was that of documenting the extensive vocabulary of Krio and identifying the etymologies of those words, but not to describe the grammatical usage of those words, other than word class. In other words, their work does not demonstrate how differently these words function, in comparison to their identified etymological sources. It is the semantic characteristics of words, their grammatical functioning, and the phonological aspects of the word that reveal the essence of those words.

The examples that follow demonstrate the asymmetrical relationship between English words and their meaning and usage within the Krio context. Let's start with a very common English word, *take*. It appears in sentences like the following:

Take this food to your father.
Take my book home.
Take me to school.

Yet, when the word was adopted into Krio, its meaning and uses were modified to fit into language patterns more familiar to the new adopters. Look at two examples of *tek* in Krio:

Go tek mi pikin na skul. [Pick up my child from school.]
   (literal: Go tek-hold-of my child Location school)
Di man tek di nɛf kɔt di bif. [The man cut the meat *with* a knife.]
   (literal: The man take-hold-of the knife cut the meat)

History of the Krio People and Their Language   33

Notice that, although the English word *take* has found its way into Krio with the same pronunciation, its meaning in Krio is much narrower, something like "to take hold of something" or "possess something." The Krio word, *tek,* does not possess two critical features found in the English word "take," *movement* and *direction*, which are inherent semantic features of that English word.

Eliciting the exact equivalent of the English sentence, "Take this food to your father," requires a much more complex sentence structure in Krio. In this case what is required is the combination of three verbs, [kɛr + go + gi]:

Kɛr dis it ya go gi yu papa. [Take this food to your father.]
(Literal: Carry this food here go give your father.)

It is safe to say that the Krio word, *tek*, resembles the English word "take" in only a very superficial way, its pronunciation. It does not mean the same thing as "take" in English and attempts at translating the English word "take" into Krio requires a very different grammatical structure and a specific set of verbs. The particular construction needed in this case is referred to in the literature as a *serial verb construction*, which, while widely used in Krio, is, for all intents and purposes, non-existent in English.

Another Krio word that is derived from English is the word *kam*. In this case we can find sentences in which both the Krio and English uses of the word and its English counterpart have the same meaning and the same grammatical structure. Observe the following example:

English Example:
The boy will come. [kəm]

Adopted Krio Meaning:
Di bɔbɔ go kam. [The boy will come.] (literal: The boy FUTURE come)

Notice, however, that these words differ in pronunciation, [kəm] in English versus [kam] in Krio. Having seen the example with "take" above, it is perhaps not surprising that the Krio word, *kam,* can carry meanings very different from its English counterpart when found in other contexts. Look at the following examples:

A de kam go. [I am getting ready to go.] (literal: I Pres. Progr. come go)
A de kam. [I'm leaving (but will return shortly).] (literal: I Pres. Progr. come)
Go kam-o. [Go in peace until we meet again.] (literal: Go come exclamation)

34   *Chapter 1*

It would clearly be inaccurate to say that *tek* and *kam* in Krio are English words when they behave so differently from their English counterparts. At best, they were appropriated from English and inserted into a different set of language structures.

With such a high percentage of the Krio vocabulary derived from English, it is reasonable for someone who is not familiar with the Krio language system to assume that the grammatical, phonological, and semantic systems were adopted along with the words. The evidence presented so far suggests that that is not the case. In fact, it is in the grammatical structures of Krio that we find some of the greatest differences between Krio and English. This will become even more evident in the following chapters that describe the whole system.

Another area in which Krio grammar differs from English is with respect to the ways in which they communicate concepts like *Tense* and *Aspect*. Krio employs *pre-verbal tense/aspect markers* that have fixed meaning and appear in *unmodified* phonological form in front of the main verb of a sentence. Many languages, including English, have grammars in which systematic changes are made within the verb phrase to reflect different tenses, aspects, or moods. Those changes may involve adding a prefix or a suffix to the base form of the verb, or actually changing the phonological shape of the verb itself. A few examples of simple sentences in Krio, along with their English translations, demonstrate the fundamentally different grammatical structures used in these two languages:

1. *Mi mama de go na di makit.* [My mother is going to the market.]
   (Literal: My mother Present Progressive go Loc the market.])
2. *Mi mama bin go na di makit.* [My mother went to the market.]
   (Literal: My mother Past go Location the market.)
3. *Mi mama kin go na di makit.* [My mother usually goes to the market.]
   (Literal: My mother Habitual go Location the market.]

Notice how the Krio verb, *go*, remains constant, regardless of the tense or aspect marker that precedes it, while in the English sentences, the verb, *go*, changes from *going (in Present Progressive)* to *went* (in Past) to *goes* (*in the Simple Present*) to express the different tense/aspect concepts. These few examples demonstrate the consistent usage of Pre-Verbal Markers in Krio. The following three chapters of the book will reveal not only the regularity of meaning expressed by the full set of tense/aspect markers, but also how combinations of these markers, in prescribed sequences work together to communicate a wide range of complex meanings.

This chapter has described in significant detail the long history of the Trans-Atlantic slave trade which provided a picture of the various contours of that trade. We witnessed how different European nations dominated the flow of enslaved Africans from different parts of West and Central Africa, selling them as free labor to various plantations, first in the Spanish colonies, then the Portuguese and others, finally being dominated by the British in the eighteenth and nineteenth centuries. We discovered that the European powers took advantage of conflicts within Africa, which increased the availability of enslaved Africans in certain regions at certain times, but how, when the demand called for it, the slave traders raided villages directly to meet their business needs.

What is of direct import of this history for our purposes is discovering from which African groups slave traders purchased human beings and to which colonies they were sold. Gathering information on the four primary groups that came to constitute Kriodom will be shown to help us understand the grammatical, phonological, and semantic systems that undergird the Krio language. We will also see how closely the linguistic evidence and the cultural evidence are aligned. While most other writers have made broad sweeping claims about the origin(s) or source(s) of Krio language or culture, we will present specific linguistic and cultural evidence to prove, to a high degree of certainty, the source(s) of specific features or characteristics found in Krio. We will show that it is in exactly those areas of language and culture where Krio language and culture differ from English that the African sources provide an explanation.

Although in this chapter, we have provided a limited number of examples of components of Krio Language that are substantively different from English, we have shown that even the words in Krio that appear to be English turned out to be *derived* from English, but *function* very differently than known English dialects. We will explain, to the best of our abilities, why these differences exist.

Chapters 2, 3, and 4 describe Sierra Leone Krio Language in systematic detail. With that foundation, the reader will be ready to compare the grammatical structures, phonology, and semantics of Krio to the parallel language systems that we know were spoken by the various African groups who comprised the Krio community at its founding.

NOTES

1. Philip D. Curtin, *The Atlantic Slave Trade: A Census* (Madison: University of Wisconsin Press, 1969), 15.

2. Curtin, *Atlantic Slave Trade*, 102.

3. Curtin, *Atlantic Slave Trade*, 102.

4. Curtin, *Atlantic Slave Trade*, 126.

36 *Chapter 1*

5. Curtin, *Atlantic Slave Trade*, 122. Our numbers extracted from calculations done by Curtin on commercial trade records analyzed by K. G. Davies, *The Royal Africa Company* (London: Longmans, Green, 1957; repr. New York: Atheneum, 1970).

6. Curtin, *Atlantic Slave Trade*, 154.

7. Curtin, *Atlantic Slave Trade*, 155.

8. Elizabeth Donnan, "The Slave Trade into South Carolina Before the Revolution," *American Historical Review*33, no. 4 (1928): 816, https://doi.org/10.2307/1838372.

9. Donnan, "Slave Trade into South Carolina," 817.

10. Christopher Fyfe, *A Short History of Sierra Leone* (London: Longmans, Green, 1962; 1964), 28.

11. Joko Sengova, "Aborigines and Returnees: In Search of Linguistic and Historical Meaning in Delineations of Sierra Leone's Ethnicity and Heritage," in *New Perspectives on the Sierra Leone Krio*, ed. Mac Dixon-Fyle and Gibril Cole (New York: Peter Lang, 2006), 170.

12. *An Act for the Abolition of the Slave Trade*, 47th George III, Session 1, CAP. 36 [XXXVI], March 25, 1807, Electronic Scholarly Publishing-Foundations of Freedom, http://www.esp.org/foundations/freedom/holdings/slave-trade-act-1807.pdf (accessed February 2, 2024).

13. Sengova, "Aborigines and Returnees," 170.

14. Gibril R. Cole, "Re-Thinking the Demographic Make-Up of Krio Society," in *New Perspectives on the Sierra Leone Krio*, ed. Mac Dixon-Fyle and Gibril Cole (New York: Peter Lang, 2006); Cole, *The Krio of West Africa: Islam, Culture, Creolization, and Colonialism in the Nineteenth Century* (Athens: Ohio University Press, 2013); C[ecil] Magbaily Fyle. "Nationalism should Trump Ethnicity: The Krio Saga in Sierra Leone," *Research in Sierra Leone Studies* (*RISLS*, eJournal) 1, no. 2 (December 2013); and Tom Spencer-Walters, "Creolization and Kriodom: (Re) Visioning the 'Sierra Leone Experiment,'" in *New Perspectives on the Sierra Leone Krio*, ed. Mac Dixon-Fyle and Gibril Cole (New York: Peter Lang, 2006), 223–54; have all provided recent insights into the involvement and integration of Africans indigenous to Sierra Leone who played significant roles in the formation of Krio culture.

15. C. M. Fyle, "Nationalism Should Trump Ethnicity," 9.

16. Cole, "Re-Thinking," 40.

17. Cole, "Re-Thinking," 40.

18. Cole, *Krio of West Africa*, 32.

19. R. [Robert] C. Dallas, *History of the Maroons: From Their Origins to the Establishment of Their Chief Tribe at Sierra Leone* (London: Routledge, 1803; Longman and O. Rees, Paternoster-row, 1803), 32–33, https://repository.library.northeastern.edu/files/neu:m044rf60h (accessed February 2, 2024).

20. Fyfe, *Short History*, 50.

21. Fyfe, *Short History*, 50–51.

22. Cole, "Re-Thinking," 42.

23. Spencer-Walters, "Creolization and Kriodom," 234.

24. Spencer-Walters, "Creolization and Kriodom," 235.

25. Fyfe, *Short History*, 44.

26. Curtin, *Atlantic Slave Trade*, 102.

History of the Krio People and Their Language 37

27. Curtin, *Atlantic Slave Trade*, 245.

28. Spencer-Walters, "Creolization and Kriodom," 231.

29. Cole, *Krio of West Africa*, 4.

30. Cole, "Re-Thinking," 44.

31. Cole, *Krio of West Africa*, 11.

32. Cole, "Re-Thinking," 45.

33. Cole, *Krio of West Africa*, 30.

34. Fyfe, *Short History*, 45–46.

35. Dallas, *History of the Maroons*, 92.

36. F. Harrison Rankin, *The White Man's Grave: A Visit to Sierra Leone in 1834* (London: Richard Bentley, 1836), 105–7.

37. Rankin, *White Man's Grave*, 107.

38. *A Krio-English Dictionary*, ed. Clifford N. Fyle and Eldred D. Jones (Oxford: Oxford University Press; in collaboration with the Sierra Leone University Press, 1980), x.

PART II

Krio Language

Chapter 2

Language Basics

As pointed out in chapter 1, Krio is a creolized language which developed from a predominantly Kwa language family underlying structure with heavy word-borrowing from English. The Krio sound system is demonstrably closer to its West African contributors than to the English sound system. This is observable not only in the inventory of meaningful sounds, but also in the permissible sequence of sounds, and in the suprasegmental area of distinctive tone. Though many of the words found in the Krio lexicon (that is dictionary) are of English origin, the majority of them differ from the English source in pronunciation, meaning, and grammatical functioning. One might say that these English words came into the Krio Language only after being filtered through a West African phonemic and semantic grid, as described in Wayne R. Williams' 1976 dissertation.[1] This information alone strongly suggests that it was the speakers of West African languages who were the *actors* in creating the Krio Language, not passive *recipients*.

KRIO SOUND SYSTEM

Vowels

Krio has seven phonemic vowels (written Krio uses the phonetic symbols i, e, ɛ, a, ɔ, o, and u). That is to say that seven vowels are used to distinguish one word from another, assuming that all other elements in the word are the same (for example, *fɛt* [fight], *fit* [worthy], *fut* [foot]). Their close equivalent sounds in English are presented below to provide a point of reference.

i is pronounced as ea in *beat* (for example, *tik* [tree], *pikin* [child], *titi* [girl], and *tif* [steal]).

e is pronounced as a in *take* (for example, *tek* [take], *mek* [make], *de* [exist/ be], and *pre* [pray]).

42   *Chapter 2*

ε is pronounced as e in bet (for example, *fɛt* [fight], *pɛpɛ* [pepper], *nɛm* [name], and *ustɛm* [when]).

a is pronounced as o in dot in SAE (for example, *tap* [live], *at* [hurt], *fam* [farm], and *makit* [market]).

u is pronounced as oo in boot (for example, *fut* [foot], *butu* [stoop down], and *fufu* [cassava dough]).

o is prounced as oa in boat (for example, *wok* [work], *tot* [carry], *rod* [street], and *sok* [get wet/soak]).

ɔ is pronounced as a in tall (for example, *kɔpɔ* [money], *pɔt* [pot], *ɔl* [all], and *pɔtɔ-pɔtɔ* [mud]).

The readers will notice that the written word in Krio is essentially a phonetic transcription of the actual sounds as pronounced by Krio speakers. In other words, a given sound is consistently represented by the same letter. Written English letters, by contrast, may be pronounced differently depending upon the word it appears in. For instance, the letter *Aa* in written English may represent three different sounds in the following words: fat, father, fate. Phonetically, the vowel sounds in these three words are [ae], [a], and [e], respectively. (Note that in these examples the [] markers indicate the phonetic spelling.)

Diphthongs

Three diphthongs exist in Krio that function the same as the vowels identified above. Two symbols combine to represent one sound. It appears that these diphthongs occur primarily in words of English origin that contain the same diphthong. The following examples demonstrate this:

ay is pronounced as *i* in hide (for example, *usay* [where?], *ayd* [hide], *blay* [basket], and *bay* [buy]).

ɔy is pronounced as *oy* in boy (for example, *bɔy* [servant], *ɔyl* [oil], and *lɔya* [lawyer]).

aw is pronounced as *ou* in out (for example, *aw* [how?], *awa* [hour], *kaw* [cow], and *sawa-sawa* [a leafy plant used to make a particular stew]).

Consonants

The consonant sounds in Krio are also broadly phonetic, meaning that the letter, or written symbol, consistently represents only one sound and each sound is represented by only one symbol (or letter). In other languages, like English, a given sound may be represented by different letters or combination

Language Basics

43

of letters. For instance, the phonetic sound represented by the symbol [f] appears in written English in multiple ways (for example, fat, tough, phone). Because of the one-to-one relationship between Krio sounds and the writing system, learning how to write Krio should be relatively easier than learning to write other languages.

The Krio consonants listed below consistently represent the same sound:

t sound as in Eng. top (for example, *Tunde* [man's name], *titi* [young girl], and *tumbu* [type of fly]).

d sound as in Eng. dad (for example, *dans* [dance], *domɔt* [doorway], and *du* [be enough]).

n sound as in Eng. no (for example, *nɛt* [night], *nɔbɔdi* [nobody], and *nɛm* [name], and *nɛf* [knife]).

m sound as in Eng. mom (for example, *man* [man/person], *makit* [market], and *mɔna* [overwhelm]).

p sound as in Eng. pie (for example, *pikin* [child], *popo* [carry baby on one's back], and *pɔpɔ* [papaya]).

b sound as in Eng. baby (for example, *bit* [beat/whip/pound], *bonga* [type of fish], and *bɛlɛ* [stomach]).

f sound as in Eng. fall (for example, *fala* [follow/accompany], *fɔl* [chicken], and *fiba* [resemble]).

v sound as in Eng. voice (for example, *vɛks* [be angry], and *vup* [loud hit/ sound]).

l sound as in Eng. love (for example, *lili* [little], *Lɔmli* [Lumley Beach], and *lɛk* [like]).

r (See description of this sound and examples of Krio in paragraph below)

g sound as in Eng. go (for example, *Gɔd* [God], *gadin* [garden], and *agidi* [cassava flour]).

k sound as in Eng. cat (for example, *koknat* [coconut], *kalbas* [gord bowl], and *kam* [come]).

s sound as in Eng. sit (for example, *saful-saful* [softly/carefully], *sɛf* [even], and *san-san* sand]).

z sound as in Eng. zip (for example, *baz* [bump/kick], *ziro* [zero], and *zot* [nothing (Ideophone)]).

j sound as in Eng. jog (for example, *jɛge* [cowrie shell], *jamani* [Germany], and *jus* [albino]).

w sound as in Eng. wait (for example, *wata* [water], *awujɔ* [feast], and *wɔwɔ* [ugly]).

y sound as in Eng. you (for example, *yuba* [vulture], *yet* [yet], and *yawo* [bride/bargain]).

ch sound as in Eng. choice (for example, *chɔch* [church], *chɛr* [tear], and *cham* [chew]).

44 *Chapter 2*

sh sound as in Eng. shoe (for example, *shεb* [share/divide], *shub* [push], and *mεnshɔ* [measure food]).

zh sound as in Eng. pleasure (for example, *plεzhɔ* [pleasure], and *mεzhɔ* [clothes fitting]).

gb (See description of this sound and examples of Krio below.)

kp (See description of this sound and examples of Krio below.)

A few of the sounds in Krio are unusual and deserve additional comment here. The symbol [r] in Krio is a uvular/velar fricative, different from the retroflex *r* sound found in English. The English *r* sound is formed by flexing the tongue toward the middle of the roof of the mouth, while the Krio *r* is produced by pushing the uvula toward the velum (the back area of the roof of the mouth), causing a faint, hissing sound at the point of articulation. It occurs in numerous Krio words and is one of the sounds that gives Krio its own unique identity. It occurs frequently in everyday speech (for example, *rayt* [write], *rod* [road], *oroko* [oak tree], *rεd* [red], *rεdi* [ready], *rεs* [rice], *rɔbish* [trash], *rop* [rope], *arata* [rat], *Rijεnt* [a village north of Freetown]).

Also not commonly found in the world's languages are the co-articulated sounds, <u>*gb*</u> and <u>*kp*</u>. These sounds are difficult to pronounce for people from most other languages because they require the speaker to articulate the velar stops (k or g) in the back of the roof of the mouth while simultaneously articulating the labial stops (p or b, respectively) produced by stopping the airflow by pressing the lips together. All of the words in Krio that contain these sounds have their origin in one or more African languages, most often Yoruba. In addition to Yoruba, these co-articulated sounds are found in other Kwa languages, like Ashanti/Twi, as well as in two indigenous language in Sierra Leone, Mende, and Temne. Again, these are sounds that mark Krio as "African." Examples of Krio words that contain these sounds are the following:

gb as in *igbakɔ* [flat wooden spoon], *gbangba-ode* [open area], and *gbag-bati* [over-officiousness].

kp as in *ɔkpɔlɔ* [frog], *kpεkpεkpε* [snacks/odds and ends], and *kpakɔ* [back of the head].

Krio does not possess the two <u>*th*</u> sounds found in English words, phonetically referred to as [*theta*] and [thorn]. Theta is the *th* sound found in words like *think* and *bath*. Thorn is the *th* sound found in words like *this* and *bathe*. Since Krio does not possess either of these two sounds, it must substitute some other sound in their place if the words are adopted into Krio. The theta sound is replaced by *t*, while the thorn sound is replaced by *d*. Without going

Language Basics 45

into too much physiological detail, suffice it to say that all of these sounds involve the tongue touching the teeth. Theta and *t* are articulated with the vocal chords in open position, while thorn and *d* are articulated with the vocal chords in a closed position. When theta and thorn are produced, the tongue only partially obstructs the airflow from the mouth, causing a light hissing sound, but when *t* and *d* are produced, the tongue completely stops the airflow for a brief moment.

To summarize, all four of these sounds, theta, thorn, *t*, and *d*, have a number of similarities, even though they have distinctive differences. In linguistic terms, they are described as follows:

Theta: voiceless, interdental, fricative.
Thorn: Voiced, interdental, fricative.
t: voiceless, alveo-dental, stop.
d: voiced, alveo-dental, stop.

Below are examples of the conversion of English words containing theta or thorn to Krio words with *t* or *d*, respectively:

think becomes reproduced as *tink* in Krio.
Arthur becomes reproduced as *atɔ* in Krio.
thing becomes reproduced as *ting* in Krio.
thank you becomes reproduced as *tɛnki ya* in Krio.
thief becomes reproduced as *tifman* in Krio.
this becomes reproduced as *dis* in Krio.
them becomes reproduced as *dɛm* in Krio.
there becomes reproduced as *de* in Krio.
that becomes reproduced as *dat* (or *da wan de*) in Krio.
other becomes reproduced as *ɔda* in Krio.

Limited Occurrence of Consonant Clusters

Consonant clusters are limited in Krio. Most consonant clusters are found at the beginning of words in Krio, with the second consonant being *r* or *l*. See the following examples:

Examples of Krio words beginning with *Cr*:

tri [three]
pre [pray]
granat [peanut]
krɔ-krɔ [blistering skin]
bra [pal, friend like a brother]

46   *Chapter 2*

drayv [drive]
fray-sup [fry-soup]
Examples of Krio words beginning with *Cl*:
plasas [green leaf stew w/palm oil, beef]
plaba [words, argument]
ple [play]
ples [place]
plit [split]
plɔt [piece of land, plot]
plɛnti [many, much, plenty]

Words of English origin which end in the consonant clusters, *_st* and *_nd* are reduced to a single consonant, *_s* and *_n*, respectively. View examples of this phenomenon:

[first] becomes realized as *fɔs*.
[fast] becomes realized as *fas*.
[lost] becomes realized as *lɔs*.
[land] becomes realized as *lan*.
[ground] becomes realized as grɔn.

Other words of English origin found in Krio that contain clusters beginning with *st_* or *str_* are reduced to *t_* and *tr_*, respectively. A few examples demonstrate this:

[street] becomes realized as *trit*.
[strength] becomes realized as *trɛnk*.
[stick] becomes realized as *tik*.
[stone] becomes realized as *ton*.
[stop] becomes realized as *tap*.

Tone

Krio, like many other West African Languages, is a *tone* language. The tonal nature of Krio is a fascinating topic that deserves much more attention than can be devoted to it in this book. However, here are some of the essential facts. Krio functions with two tones, High (H) and Low (L). As a tone language, Krio words can have different meanings simply by having different tonal assignments, in the same way that Krio words can be differentiated in meaning by having different vowels or different consonants. A very simple example demonstrates this concept. The Krio word that means "to be/exist"

Language Basics   47

is *de* (with High tone), but *de* (with Low tone) is the tense/aspect marker which means "present continuous action." We refer to pairs of words which differ from each other by only one sound as *minimal pairs*. Examples of minimal pairs in Krio with respect to tone are presented in table 2.1 after minimal pairs.

Every word in the Krio lexicon has a characteristic tone when the word is spoken in isolation. We can refer to this as its basic (or citation) tone. For instance, the Krio noun which means "water" (the liquid substance) has a Low-High tone pattern, *wata*, while its verbal counterpart (to water) has a High-Low tone pattern, *wata*. Observe the following sentence:

Mi mama bin kɛr di wata (LH) *go na gadin fɔ wata* (HL) *di plant dɛm.*
[My mother took the water to the garden to water the plants.]

Now look at the following sentences which demonstrate that two words that are identical in every way except for their tonal assignment can significantly change the meaning of a sentence:

A go (H) *bay fish.*
[I went (and) bought (some) fish.] (go, with H tone, is the verb in the sentence.)

A go (L) bay fish.
[I will buy (some) fish.] (go, with L tone, is the Future Tense marker.)

Minimal Pairs Differentiated by Vowels

A few examples of minimal pairs based on different vowels are presented below:

kɔl [call] versus *kol* [cold/coal]
gɔt [innards] versus *got* [goat]
shɔ [sure] versus *sho* [show]

Table 2.1 Minimal Pairs Differentiated by Tone (H = High tone, L = Low tone)

Word A	Tone	Meaning	Word B	Tone	Meaning
Aja	HL	Female returned from Mecca	*Aja*	LL	Attic
Afbak	LH	Slipper	*Afbak*	HL	Soccer half-back
Dɛm	H	Those	*Dɛm*	L	Plural/more than one
De	L	There	*De*	H	Exist/be
Kɔntri	HL	Country	*Kɔntri*	LH	Countryman
Buli	LH	Gourd bottle	*Buli*	HL	bully

48 *Chapter 2*

pɔta [porter] versus *pata* [wash clothes by beating them in water]
ɔla [woman's name] versus *ala* [shout]
mɔta [mortar] versus *mata* [mat]
fayn [pretty] versus *fɛn* [find]
taym [outsmart] versus *tɛm* [time]
os [house] versus *ɔs* [horse] versus as [ass]

Minimal Pairs Differentiated by Consonants

The following examples demonstrate words that are differentiated from other based on different consonants, just as the words above were differentiated by either tone or vowels:

kot [coat] versus *got* [goat]
kro [crow] versus *gro* [grow]
kɔt [cut] versus *gɔt* [gut/innards]
pɔt [pot] versus *bɔt* [but]
pata [plank for beating clothes] versus *bata* [smash, drum]
pak [park] versus *bak* [back or again]
lɛs [reduce (as in price)] versus *rɛs* [rice]
lɛk [like] versus *rɛk* [wreck]

Intonation Patterns

While every Krio word has a basic tone assigned to it, different sentence types have intonation patterns which influence the absolute pitch of the syllables. A comprehensive study of all of the intonation patterns in Krio has not been conducted. However, at least two major intonation patterns will demonstrate this phenomenon, the Simple Declarative Sentence Pattern and the Yes-No Question Pattern. In a *Simple Declarative Sentence*, there is a characteristic falling tone at the end of the sentence. In anticipation of that falling tone, the absolute pitch of every syllable in that sentence is progressively lowered as the end of the sentence is approached. This phenomenon is referred to as *Downdrift* because the pitch drifts in a downward fashion. The relative basic tone in each word is maintained as the overall pitch is in a downward direction. This phenomenon is graphically displayed in the following example:

Simple Declarative Sentence:

A de go na mi os. (Basic Tone sequence is L L H L L H)
  [I am going to my house. / I am going home.]

Language Basics 49

Since the intonation on this sentence type requires falling tone as one approached the end of the sentence, the High tone on *os* is actually lower than the High tone on *go*. For the same reason, the actual pitch on *na* and *mi* is higher than the pitch on *a* and *de*, even though both are assigned a basic Low tone. This demonstrates that the tone on a given word is relative to its surrounding linguistic environment. Language is fluid. As individuals speak, they reach for the target tone, but make sure that a word with a Low tone is always lower in pitch than an adjacent word with a High tone.

In *Yes-No Questions* there is a characteristic rising of pitch toward the end of the sentence. The following Yes-No question attempts to demonstrate this gradual rising pitch while maintaining the High-Low relationship between words with different basic tones:

Yes/No Questions:

Yu de go na yu os? (Basic Tone sequence is L L H L L H.)
  [Are you going home?]

Since the intonation pattern for this sentence-type is Rising, all of the basic tones will get progressively higher than their basic tone as one approaches the end of the sentence.

Nasal Assimilation

Nasal consonants (*m, n, ng, ny*) can be very sensitive to consonants that follow them with respect to the point of articulation of the following consonant. The *m* is articulated using both lips (bi-labial); *n* is articulated by the tongue touching the alveolar ridge behind the front teeth; and the *ng* is articulated by moving the tongue toward the roof of the mouth. Different consonants are also articulated at those points or in those areas of the mouth. The m-sound, in particular, will assimilate to the consonant that follows it.

For instance, the third-person, singular pronoun in Krio is *im* [his/her/its]. If the word following *im* begins with a consonant pronounced with the lips, the *m* in "im" remains in its basic form, as in *im pɔkit* [his/her pocket], *im pikin* [his/her child], *im mama* [his/her/its mother], and *im blay* [his/her basket].

If the word that follows *im* begins with a consonant that is articulated in the alveolar area (behind the teeth), then the *m* is pronounced like its alveolar counterpart, *n*. This can be readily seen in examples like the following:

im trɔsis [his/her pants] is pronounced *in trɔsis*.
im domɔt [his/her entrance/doorway] is pronounced *in domɔt*.
im chɔp [his/her food] is pronounced *in chɔp*.
im sista [his/her sister] is pronounced *in sista*.

50 *Chapter 2*

By the same token, if the word that follows *im* begins with a consonant that is articulated in the velar area, the *m* in *im* becomes pronounced as *ng*, the velar nasal. A few examples demonstrate this:

im gɔt [his/her intestines] is pronounced *ing gɔt.*
im kata [his cloth head ring] is pronounced *ing kata.*
im krɔkrɔ [his/her rash/scab] is pronounced *ing krɔkrɔ.*
im grani [his/her grandma] is pronounced *ing grani.*

If, on the other hand, the word following *im* begins with a vowel, the *i* in *im* tends to be realized as simply a nasalized vowel with no distinctive consonant being articulated. See the examples below, as in *im ɔrinch* [his/her orange] and *im ɛnkincha* [her head scarf].

Although *ny* exists within the Krio sound inventory, it does not appear as the product of a nasal assimilation process. This sound appears in a very small group of words, all of which appear to have simply been borrowed wholesale from an African language or as the British pronunciation of the word [new], *nyu*. Here are some of those words that contain ny:

Bunya [a little over; little gift for regular customer], most likely origin is Temne.
Nyam [eat heartily/voraciously], most likely origin is Fulani, *nyama* [eat] or Jamaican *nyamanyama* [eaten away or chewed].
Nyanga [showiness or coquetry], most likely origin is Temne, *nyanga* [beautiful] or Mende, *nyanga* [ostentation]. This word occurs frequently in Krio in the form *kɔt yanga* [flirt insincerely or play hard to get].
Nyuz [news], of obvious English origin.
Nyu rɛs [freshly harvested rice].

STRUCTURAL ELEMENTS

Nouns

Nouns are very important elements in every language. Nouns are usually defined as "people, places, and things." However, that class of words is a little broader than that. Actions and abstractions can also be nouns, for example "cooking" and "pregnancy." Languages differ in the way(s) they convert actions and abstractions into nouns. In this chapter, among other things, you will learn how speakers of Krio routinely create noun-like entities out of words usually considered members of other word classes, like verbs and adjectives.

Language Basics 51

Generalized Nouns

In Krio, a noun standing alone usually refers to the whole class of people, places, or things with the same characteristics, like the following examples:

Man [men], as in "men are typically stronger than women."
Uman [women], as in "women prepare the food for the celebration."
Gyal [girls], as in "girls must wear dresses to school."
Bɔbɔ [boys], as in "boys enjoy going fishing."
ɔkɔ [grooms], as in "grooms have to attend their bachelor's party."
Yawo [brides], as in "brides are usually very nervous before the wedding."

Particular Nouns

Krio speakers distinguish between the general category of nouns and more specific nouns. Nouns are made more specific by the addition of the definite article, *di* "the," or the indefinite article, *wan* "one," in front of the noun. Look at the examples of generic and more specific nouns in Krio in table 2.2.

In addition to meaning "a/an," the word, *wan*, can also retain its meaning as the number, "one." Consequently, *wan bɔbɔ* can ambiguously mean [one boy] or [a boy]. Only the context of the sentence will clarify which meaning is being used at any given point in time.

Concept of Plural

In Krio, the concept of plural is realized by adding the third-person plural pronoun, *dɛm,* after the noun. This is the consistent and only mechanism for expressing plurality in Krio. Many languages use a variety of devices for expressing plurality. In English the concept of plural is achieved by changing the singular form of a noun by (1) adding the suffix -s/es, (2) changing the vowel, (3) adding -en, or (4) using some other unique device. Observe the regularity with which dɛm is added to a singular Krio noun and how the English singular forms change to indicate more than one:

Table 2.2. Three Levels of Noun Specificity

Mass Nouns	Indefinite Nouns	Definite Nouns
man [men]	wan man [a man]	di man [the man]
uman [women]	wan uman [a woman]	di uman [the woman]
gyal [girls]	wan gyal [a girl]	di gyal [the girl]
bɔbɔ [boys]	wan bɔbɔ [a boy]	di bɔbɔ [the boy]
os [houses]	wan os [a house]	di os [the house]
chɔch [churches]	wan chɔch [a church]	di chɔch [the church]
trɔki [turtles]	wan trɔki [a turtle]	di trɔki [the turtle]

52   *Chapter 2*

wan man [a/one man] in the singular becomes *di man dɛm* [the men].
wan uman [a/one woman] in the singular becomes *tri uman dɛm* [three
women].
wan pikin [a/one child] in the singular becomes *di pikin dɛm* [the children].
wan fɔl [a/one chicken] in the singular becomes *fo fɔl dɛm* [four chickens].
wan bɔbɔ [a/one boy] in the singular becomes *di bɔbɔ dɛm* [the boys].
wan chɔch [a/one church] in the singular becomes *di chɔch dɛm* [the
churches].
wan fut [a/one foot] in the singular becomes *tu fut dɛm* [two feet].

Nominalized Verbs and Adjectives

As stated above, not all nouns are concrete, like a person, a place, or a thing.
An action (verb) or a descriptive feature (adjective) can be transformed into
a noun simply by placing the Definite Article, *di* [the], in front of a verb or
an adjective. Look at the following examples of this phenomena in table 2.3.

Examples of adjectives being transformed to nouns will be described in
chapter 4 in the discussion of relative clauses, where nominalized adjectives
are more frequently found.

Verbs

There are essentially two kinds of verbs in Krio, Action Verbs and Stative
Verbs. Like the category suggests, action verbs involve some kind of action,
while stative verbs relate to a state of being. Later chapters will show how
action verbs and stative verbs differ grammatically in their functioning.
Examples of these two kinds of verbs are identified below:

Action Verbs
kuk [cook], *bit* [beat/pound], *lan* [teach], *sing* [sing], *waka* [walk], *sɛl*
[sell], *so* [sew], *tot* [carry]

Table 2.3 Creating Nouns Out of Verbs with *di*

Verbs	Verbs Converted to Nouns
waka [walk]	*di waka* [the walk or the trip]
kuk [cook]	*di kuk* [the food preparation]
it [eat]	*di it* [the food/meal]
bit [beat]	*di bit* [the beating/spanking]
drayv [drive]	*di drayv* [the driving/the drive]
vɛks [to be angry]	*di vɛks* [the anger]

Language Basics   53

Stative Verbs
tinap [stand], *slip* [sleep], *de* [exist/be located], *sidɔm* [sit], *at* [hurt], *biliv* [believe], *fɔdɔm* [fall]

Adjectives

Adjectives describe or clarify the nouns that follow them. Although adjectives in Krio can be converted to verbs or nouns when placed in the appropriate grammatical structure, adjectives customarily are positioned in front of nouns. Examples of Krio adjectives are listed below:

> *Big* [big/large], *fat* [fat], *langa* [long/tall], *fayn* [pretty/beautiful], *dia* [expensive], *wɔwɔ* [ugly], *koto-koto* [rocky, damaged (road)], *bod* [wooden], *ɔt* [hot], *wam* [warm].

Adverbs

Adverbs indicate concepts such as time, manner, intensity and are usually found directly after verbs in Krio sentences and usually qualify the verbal action. The Krio adverbs identified below demonstrate the variety found:

> *Tide* [today], *tumara* [tomorrow], *jisnɔ* [very soon], *kwik* [quickly], *saful* [slowly/carefully], *ɔredi* [already], *paopa* [at all costs], *nɛks tumara* [day after tomorrow].

BASIC SENTENCE STRUCTURE

Sentences are essential units of communication in every human language. But the structure of sentences varies from one language to another. The most basic sentences in Krio and in English are comprised of a Noun Phrase followed by a Verb Phrase. A structural chart reveals both the linear sequence of components and the hierarchical relationships between the components to each other. Figure 2.1 visually presents the structure of basic sentences in Krio.

The central word in a Noun Phrase (NP) is a Noun (sometimes substituted by a Pronoun), just as the central word in a Verb Phrase (VP) is a Verb. As the terms Noun Phrase and Verb Phrase imply, these phrases may include words in addition to nouns/pronouns and verbs, respectively. The words that comprise the Noun Phrase and Verb Phrase must occur in a prescribed sequence. Thus, children growing up in a Krio speaking community must learn not only what words make up these phrases but also the correct order in which these words must appear in the phrase.

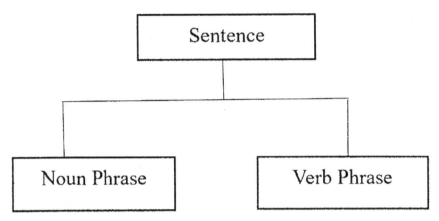

Figure 2.1. Basic Sentence Structure of Krio.

Structure of the Krio Noun Phrase

There is a variety of possible combinations of words that can make up a Noun Phrase in Krio. Figure 2.2 is a representation of those various combinations. To orient the reader, parentheses () indicate optional categories, words that may exist in a Noun Phrase or not. The curly brackets {} identify the alternative possibilities in a given position. Finally, the order of categories in the linear string indicates the required sequence of words in the Noun Phrase.

The outside curly brackets indicate that an NP in Krio must contain either a Noun or a Pronoun. These are the only two categories of words that are not surrounded by parentheses, in other words are not optional. If the Pronoun is selected, none of the other categories are relevant. However, if the NP contains a Noun, it may be preceded, first, by a Definite Article, *di* [the]; an Indefinite Article, *wan* [a], or a Possessive Pronoun. Second, the Noun may be preceded by an Adjective. Finally, the Noun may be followed by the Plural Marker, *dɛm*.

Below are examples of the various combinations of words that can exist in the Krio Noun Phrase:

Noun: *polisman* [policeman], *drayva* [chauffer/taxi driver], *ɔkpɔlɔ* [frog]
Noun + Plural Marker: *ticha dɛm* [teachers], *edmasta dɛm* [principals]
Possessive Pronoun + Noun: *mi pikin* [my child], *yu mama* [your mother], *im papa* [her father]
Definite Article + Noun: *di bɔbɔ* [the boy], *di man* [the man], *di titi* [the girl]

Language Basics

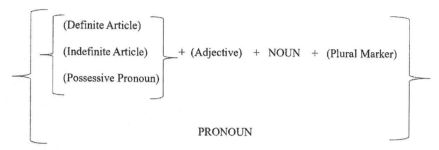

Figure 2.2. Structure of Krio Noun Phrase.

Definite Article + Noun + Plural Marker: *di bɔbɔ dɛm* [the boys], *di titi dɛm* [the girls]

Indefinite Article + Noun: *wan bɔbɔ* [a boy], *wan uman* [a woman], *wan os* [a house]

Definite Article+Adjective+Plural: *di wɔwɔ dɔg* [the ugly dog], *di blɛnyay man* [the blind man]

Possessive Pronoun+Adjective+Noun+Plural: *mi gud-gud padi dɛm* [my old friends].

The Subject Pronouns are presented in table 2.4 as one-word Noun Phrases that can stand-alone as subjects in Krio sentences.

Demonstrative Pronouns

There is a set of Demonstrative Pronouns that can function like the Subject Pronouns in a Noun Phrase. In Krio the indefinite article, *wan*, is part of the demonstrative pronouns. The set of demonstrative pronouns are list below:

dis wan ya [this], (literally "this one here")
da wan de [that], (literally "that one there")
dɛm wan ya [these], (literally "them ones here")
dɛm wan de [those], (literally "them ones there")

Table 2.4. Krio Subject Pronouns

	Singular	*Plural*
1st Person	*a* [I]	*wi* [we]
2nd Person	*yu* [you]	*una* [you (all)]
3rd Person	*i* [he, she, it]	*dɛm* [they]

56   *Chapter 2*

Structure of the Verb Phrase in Simple Declarative Sentences in Krio

Now, let's look at the second major part of Krio sentences that was presented in figure 2.2. Using the same conventional notations used above to represent the structure of the NP, figure 2.3 is a representation of the structure of Krio Verb Phrases. Curly brackets indicate alternative possible components, while the parentheses indicate components that are optional, meaning that they may be included in the structure or not. For the purposes of demonstration, we will focus on the structure of Simple Declarative sentences, those that simply make a straightforward statement. Observe figure 2.3:

Notice that the first possible element(s) in the Verb Phrase in that of Tense or Aspect Marker. As the labels indicate, this element expresses the tense or aspect of the verbal action. Next is the Verb itself. If the sentence is intended to express "direction," but that meaning is not a semantic feature of the Verb, a Directional Verb may follow the central verb to supply that meaning. An Object Noun Phrase may follow the Verb to indicate the thing, person, or place being acted upon. Finally, a Locative Phrase may be included in the sentence to indicate where the action is taking place.

To demonstrate this, we have selected the Present Continuous Marker, *de*, that indicates that the action is going on in the Present.

Figure 2.4 represents the integration of the two structures, NP and VP that comprise one particular sentence.

The sentence generated by the sentence structure and its meaning are presented below:

Mi pikin de go na di makit. [My child is going to the market.]

Examples of other sentences that could be generated by the integration of the Noun Phrase structure in figure 2.2 and the Verb Phrase Structure in figure 2.3 are presented here.

1. *Tunde de go na skul.* [Tunde is going to school.]
2. *Di titi de sɛl kasada na di trit.* [The young girl is selling cassava in the street.]
3. *Di uman dɛm de drink di wata.* [The women are drinking the water.]

$$\left\{ \begin{array}{l} \text{(Tense Marker)} \\ \text{(Aspect Marker)} \end{array} \right\} + \text{VERB} + \text{(Directional Verb)} + \text{(NP)} + \text{(Locative Phrase)}$$

Figure 2.3.   Structure of Krio Verb Phrases.

Language Basics

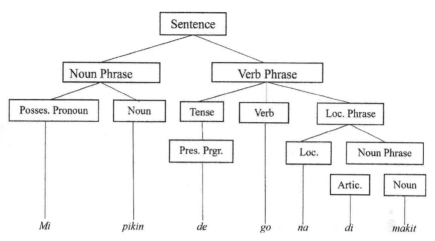

Figure 2.4. Tree Diagram of a Krio Sentence.

4. *Di pipul dɛm de kam na ya.* [The people are coming here.]
5. *Im papa de drayv di motoka na bush.* [Her dad is driving the car in the forest.]

In this chapter, we have introduced the readers to many of the basic elements that constitute Sierra Leone Krio Language. That included a survey of the sound system, the basic operation of Krio sentence structure, and a small sample of the Krio lexical universe. In chapter 3 we will expand the readers knowledge of the various components that make up Krio sentences as well as introducing them to those features that make Krio a unique, systematic, cohesive, and independent language.

NOTE

1. Wayne R. Williams, "Linguistic Change in the Syntax and Semantics of Sierra Leone Krio," PhD diss., Bloomington, Indiana University, 1976.

Chapter 3

Greetings and Simple Sentences

Throughout the African world greetings carry a very important social function in society. It is not merely a nod to a neighbor, friend, or merchant, it is a way of connecting with another person on a very human level. Consequently, "hello" or "hi" is not sufficient. One must engage in a question-and-answer conversation that shows one's concern for the other person's well-being, that of his/her family members, and any other relevant matters, such as the ease of travel or one's work situation. Greetings are also an opportunity to show respect for a person based on their age, station in life, or level of friendship.

Krio Greetings: Afrocentric Social Events

An informal greeting exchange between individuals of relatively equal age and stature might go something like this:

A. *Kushe-o.* [Hello, my friend!] (familiar)
B. *O, Kushe ya*! [Greetings to you too!]

A. *Bo, aw yu du*? [How are you doing, my friend?]
B. *A tɛl Gɔd tɛnki.* [I give thanks to God.] *Aw di go de go*? [How are things going with you?]

A. *a de fɔdɔm grap.* [Everything is okay.] *We yu mama*? [How is your mother?]
B. *I de.* [She is alive and well.]

A. *We yu brɔda*? [How about your brother?]
B. *I wɛl.* [He's doing well too.] *Aw yu fambul dɛm*? [How is *your* family doing?]

60   *Chapter 3*

A. *Dɛm ɔl wɛl.* [They're all fine.] Mɔs kam fɛn mi, ya! [Come over sometime!]

B. *ɔlrayt, wi go si.* [Alright, see you soon.]

A. *Yɛs-o, wi go si.* [Okay, see you soon.]

Obviously, there can be many variations on this exchange, but the main point is that the exchange is meaningful, caring, and sincere, not perfunctory. As you will see later in this chapter, greetings can be shaped by factors of age, gender, and stature of those engaged in the exchange. Because greetings make extensive use of personal pronouns, the next section of this chapter will delineate the various personal pronouns in Krio.

Personal Pronouns Used in Krio Greetings

In many languages, there are completely different sets of pronouns that correspond to their grammatical functions in a sentence, for instance, subject, object, or possessive. While there are some differences between these functional sets in Krio, the differences are very minimal. Note that the set of plural pronouns are constant regardless of their function, as is the case with second person plural. Notice that Krio has a singular and plural form for "you" (*yu* and *una*). The language has only one form for masculine, feminine, and neutral in third-person, singular (*i* covers [he, she, and it]). It is also important to point out that all of the Krio pronouns in these sets carry Low Tone, with the exception of *una*, which has High-Low Tone. Table 3.1 shows the full set of Krio personal pronouns:

Table 3.1 Krio Personal Pronouns by Function

Function	Person	Singular	Plural
Subject			
	1st	*a* [I]	*wi* [we]
	2nd	*yu* [you]	*una* [you]
	3rd	*i* [he, she, it]	*dɛm* [they]
Object			
	1st	*mi* [me]	*wi* [us]
	2nd	*yu* [you]	*una* [you]
	3rd	*am* [him, her, it]	*dɛm* [them]
Possessive			
	1st	*mi* [my]	*wi* [our]
	2nd	*yu* [your]	*una* [your]
	3rd	*im* [his, her, its]	*dɛm* [their]

Greetings and Simple Sentences 61

Familiar Greetings

As stated above, greetings are social events, making them sensitive to social factors such as age, status, and gender of the participants. Familiar Greetings are those which can be used anytime of the day among contemporaries of all ages and both sexes.

A. *Kushɛ-o!* [Greetings to you.]
B. *O kushɛ ya.* [Greetings to you too.]

A. *Bo, aw yu du?* [Hey, Man, how are you doing?]
B. *A wɛl.* [I'm fine.]

A. A(w) du o! [Hi there.]
B. *O, aw di bɔdi?* [Hi, how are you doing?] (Literally: "How is the body?"])

A. Aw di go de go? [How are things going?] (Literally: "How is the going goin?")
B. *A de fɔdɔm grap.* [I'm hanging in there.] (Literally: "I am falling down and getting up.")
   Or: *A de manej.* [I'm doing ok.]

Greeting Between Younger Person and Older Woman

A. *Ma, kushɛ, ma.* [Hello, Mam.]
B. *Kushɛ, mi pikin.* [Hello, my child.] *Aw yu du?* [How are you?]

A. A wɛl ma. [I'm fine.] Aw di bɔdi, ma? [How are you feeling, Mam?]
B. *A tɛl Gɔd tɛnki.* [I'm fine, thanks.] *Tɛl yu mama adu fɔ mi, ya?* [Give your mother my regards, ok?]

A. Yɛs, ma. [Yes, Mam.]

Greeting Between Younger Person and Older Man

A. *Pa, kushɛ, sa.* [Hello, Sir.]
B. *Kushɛ, mi pikin.* [Hello, my child.]

A. Aw di de, sa. [How is your day going?]
B. *Di de fayn.* [It's a beautiful day.] *Usay yu de go naw?* [Where are you going?]

62   *Chapter 3*

    A. A de go skul, sa. [I am going to school.]
    B. *Mekes ya.* [Hurry back.]

    A. Yɛs, sa. [Yes, Sir.]

Greetings Different Times of the Day

Morning

    A. *Bo, mɔnin o.* [Good morning.]
    B. *O, mɔnin o.* [Good morning to you too.] *Aw di mɔnin?* [How is everything this morning?]

    A. Di mɔnin fayn. [Everything's fine.]

Afternoon

    A. *Aftanun o.* [Good afternoon.]
    B. *O, aftanun o.* [Good afternoon to you too.] *Aw di aftanun?* [How is everything this afternoon?]

    A. I nɔ bad. [Pretty good.]

Evening

    A. *Gudivin, Pa Dɛka.* [Good evening, Mr. Decker.]
    B. *O, gudivin, mi pikin.* [Good evening, my child.] *Aw di ivin?* [How are you this evening?]

    A. Di ivin fayn, Sa. [Fine, Sir.]
    B. *Usay yu kɔmɔt so?* [Where are you coming from?]

    A. A kɔmɔt tɔn, Sa. [I'm coming from town.]
    B. *Tɛl yu dadi adu fɔ mi, ya.* [Tell your dad "Hi" for me.]

    A. A go tɛl am, Sa. [I'll tell him, Sir.]

FORMULAIC FAREWELLS

Greeting can go on for some period of time, depending upon how well the individuals know each other and depending upon the circumstances of their interaction. Some greetings may last a few minutes while others may last until

Greetings and Simple Sentences 63

the parties are far from each other. Two individuals walking in the opposite direction may only exchange a few comments, while those who might meet in the marketplace may have occasion for a more lengthy conversation. In either case, the exchange has to come to an end at some point. There are somewhat formulaic expressions that signal the end of the exchange. Some of these are listed below:

1. *Wi go si (ya, sa, or ma)*. [See you later (friend, Sir, or Mam).]
2. *Na go dat (ya, sa, or ma)*. [I have to being going now.]
3. *Na in dat (ya, sa, or ma)*. [Goodbye for now.]
4. *Mekes o*. [Hurry back.]
5. *Waka saful saful*. [Travel safely.]
6. *Gɔd go wit yu*. [Godspeed.]

Tense and Aspect in Simple Sentences

When we talk about Tense, we are making reference to the time in which something happens. When we talk about Aspect, we are referring to a manner or mode of action. Was the action one that happens frequently? Is it ongoing? Is the most important feature of the sentence to inform the reader/listener that the action being referred to is over? In some cases, the verbal marker, or markers, reflect both Tense and Aspect in the sentence.

Let's begin with a sentence in which the pre-verbal Marker communicates both Tense and Aspect:

Di man de sɛl di fish. [The man is selling the fish.]

We see that the pre-verbal Marker, *de* (Low Tone), when used alone, indicates that the action is taking place at the present time, but is ongoing. For this reason, we refer to this marker as the Present Progressive Marker.

If a Krio speaker wants to communicate that the action took place in the Past, the verbal marker, *bin* (Low Tone) would be present in front of the verb, like the following sentence:

Di man bin sɛl di fish. [The man sold the fish.]

If the man is going to sell the fish in the future, the speaker would use the Future Tense Marker, *go* (Low Tone) as in the following sentence:

Di man go sɛl di fish. [The man will/is going to sell the fish.]

These three verbal markers express *Present*, *Past*, and *Future* in Krio.

64 *Chapter 3*

Two more aspect markers that will be discussed in this chapter are those that communicate *Habitual* or *Frequent* action and *Completed* action. *Kin* (Low Tone) is the verbal Marker that indicates Habitual or Frequent Action. To indicate that the man frequently or usually sells fish, one would use this marker. Notice that the direct object noun now has to be expressed in the generic sense *fish*, not the specific sense, *di fish*, because the man cannot sell the same fish on multiple occasions. Observe the use of kin in this sentence:

Di man kin sɛl fish. [The man sells fish or the man frequently sells fish.]

The second Aspect Marker to be discussed here is the Completed Aspect, indicated by the marker, *dɔn* (High Tone). Different from the Past Tense Marker, *bin*, the Completed Aspect Marker, *dɔn*, is used to indicate that whatever action is being referenced, it has been completed at the time the statement is made. Notice that this is the only marker with High Tone.

Di man dɔn sɛl di fish. [The man has sold that particular fish.]

If the generic form of the noun phrase, *fish*, without the Definite Article, *di*, the sentence takes on different meaning, as the following sentence demonstrates:

Di man dɔn sɛl fish. [The man used to sell fish.] Or [The man no longer sells fish.]

The list presented below summarizes the five Tense/Aspect Markers covered in this chapter:

de (Low Tone) = Present Progressive Marker
bin (Low Tone) = Simple Past Tense Marker
go (Low Tone) = Future Tense Marker
kin (Low Tone) = Habitual/Frequent Action Marker
dɔn (High Tone) = Completed Action Marker

Examples of these various Tense/Aspect markers will help the reader better understand the use of these markers in Krio sentences, reinforce the patterns, and see them in context. The first set of examples will sort the sentences by Tense/Aspect marker. Then, the examples will appear randomly:

Present Progressive

1. *Dɛm de it granat sup.* [They are eating chicken in peanut sauce.]
2. *Wi de wok na di rod.* [We are working on the road.]
3. *Di pikin de rid mi buk.* [The child is reading my book.]
4. *Im mama de so im trɔsis.* [His mother is sewing his pants.]
5. *Wetin im mama de du?* [What is his mother doing?]

Simple Past Tense

1. *Dɛm bin kuk rɛs.* [They cooked rice.]
2. *I bin sidɔm na chia.* [He sat on the chair.]
3. *Di ɔkpɔlɔ bin jomp na di tebul.* [The frog jumped up on the table.]
4. *Tunde bin fɔdɔm na grɔn.* [Tunde fell down on the ground.]
5. *Wetin di uman bin se?* [What did the woman say?]

Future Tense

1. *Wi go go na King Jimi Makit.* [We are going to go to King Jimmy Market.]
2. *Dɛm go bil di skul na di il.* [They will build the school on the hill.]
3. *Dɛm go bay kaw-bif na makit.* [They're going to buy beef at the market.]
4. *Di edman go mit di tifman.* [The village chief will meet with the thief.]
5. *Di ol uman dɛm go bit am.* [The elder women will beat him.]

Habitual Action

1. *Mi anti kin sɛl ɔkrɔ na makit.* [My aunt usually sells ocra in the market.]
2. *Dɛm ɔnkul kin vɛks.* [Their uncle gets angry frequently.]
3. *Joko kin ambɔg im sista.* [Joko often teases his sister.]
4. *Di kɛkɛ kin kam siks oklɔk.* [The local public transport comes at 6:00.]
5. *Di ol man dɛm kin drink Ginis.* [The old men like to drink Guiness.]

Completed Action

1. *Di titi dɔn it.* [The little girl has finished eating.]
2. *Di polisman dɔn kam.* [The policeman has arrived.]
3. *Di ren dɔn kam.* [It has already started raining.]
4. *Ayo dɔn kuk di plasas.* [Ayo has cooked the leafy vegetable soup.]
5. Mi wɛf dɔn bɔn gyal-pikin. [My wife has given birth to our daughter.]

66   *Chapter 3*

Vocabulary—Action Verbs

1. *shɛb* [share]
2. *tot* [carry]
3. *bit* [beat, spank, pound]
4. *ayd* [hide]
5. *kɔt* [cut,slice]
6. *fɛn* [find]
7. *ambɔg* [tease, pester]
8. *was* [wash]
9. *tif* [steal]
10. *fray* [fry]
11. *drɛb* [drive away, chase away]
12. *shub* [push]

EQUATIONAL SENTENCES WITH *NA*

Equational sentences utilize the copula verb, *na*, to reveal an equal relation-ship between the noun phrases that appear on either side of the verb. The copula in Krio, different from English and many other languages, does not change in form based on the subject of the sentence. It remains constant. One common use of this sentence type is in identifying an object or person, using Demonstrative Pronouns as the Subject of the sentence. The sentence pattern for this kind of sentence is as follows:

Demonstrative Pronoun + na + Noun Phrase Object

See how they are used in equational sentences:

1. *Dis wan ya na buk.* [This is a book.]
2. *Da wan de na kɛkɛ.* [That is a local public taxi.]
3. *Dɛm wan ya na got dɛm.* [These are goats.]
4. *Dɛm wan de na fɔl dɛm.* [Those are chickens.]
5. *Da wan de na mi buk.* [That is my book.]
6. *Dɛm wan ya na Bayo im got dɛm.* [These are Bayo's goats.]
7. *Dis wan ya na mi mama im mata-odo.* [This is my mother's mortar.]

In addition to using the demonstrative pronouns as the subject of equa-tional sentences, one can also use Demonstrative Adjectives, along with a specific noun, to provide more detailed information about the specific noun. The demonstrative phrases, all of which have two parts, *dis-ya, da-de, dɛm-ya*, and *dɛm-de*, actually wrap around the noun they are modifying. Look at the sentence pattern for such sentences below.

Examples:

1. *Dis man ya na polisman.* [This man is a policeman.]
2. *Da bɔbɔ de na mi brɔda.* [That boy is my brother.]
3. *Dɛm titi de na im pikin dɛm.* [Those girls are her children.]
4. *Dɛm os ya na bod os dɛm.* [Those houses are wooden houses.]

Equational sentences are also generalizable to any sentence in which one is claiming that the NP on one side of the copula verb, *na*, is the same thing or same person as the NP that appears on the other side of *na*. A classic case is when a person is equated with the profession they are in. The examples below clearly demonstrate this:

1. *Jɔn na polisman.* [John is a policeman.]
2. *Tunji na ticha.* [Tunji is a teacher.]
3. *Di man na fishaman.* [The man is a fisherman.]
4. *Mi brɔda na klak.* [My brother is a clerk.]
5. *Im papa na dɔkta.* [Her father is a doctor.]
6. *Wi ɔnkul na injinia.* [Our uncle is an engineer.]
7. *Dɛm mama na makit uman.* [Their mother is a market woman.]

LOCATIVE SENTENCES WITH *DE* (H)

Essential to stating the location of anything in Krio Language is the verb, *de* (Hi Tone), which can be translated into English as "to exist" or "to be at a place." That verb is usually followed by a prepositional phrase. The generic preposition in Krio is *na* (Low Tone) which can variably mean "in, at, on," depending upon the context and semantic features of the location identified. An example of a sentence that contains the verb, *de*, and the preposition, *na*, is the following:

Modupɛ de na im os. [Modupe is in his house/at home.]

The reader will note that the verb, de, with no Tense/Aspect marker in front of it indicates the Present Tense. This is because *de* is a Stative Verb. A fuller discussion of the functioning of Stative Verbs will be covered in Chapter 4. A few more sentences demonstrate the use of *de* to identify location in the Present Tense:

68   *Chapter 3*

1. *Di bɔd de ɔp na di tik.* [The bird is in the tree.]
2. *Im mama de na di makit.* [His/her mother is at the market.]
3. *Wi kɔpɔ de na di bank.* [Our money is in the bank.]
4. *Di pikin dɛm de na skul.* [The children are in school.]
5. *A de na mi motoka.* [I am in my car.]
6. *Di ol pa de na im chia.* [The old man is in his chair.]

Notice that, in English, the form of the verb that expresses location/ existence, "to be," has to follow Subject/Verb agreement rules of English, depending upon whether the Subject NP is singular or plural and first, second, or third person. Consequently, we see "is, am, or are" in the translation of the verb, *de*, in the Present tense.

With the exception of the "Present" tense, the verb, *de,* functions just like other verbs in Krio, in the sense that it can be preceded by other Tense/Aspect Markers to modify the temporal or aspectual intent of the sentence. Look at the following locative sentences in which *de* is expressed in different tenses and aspects:

1. *Modupɛ bin de na im os.* [Modupe was in his house/at home.]
2. *Modupɛ kin de na im os.* [Modupe is usually at home.]
3. *Modupɛ go de na im os.* [Modupe will be/is going to be at home.]
4. *Modupɛ dɔn de na im os.* [Modupe used to be at his house.]

Although *na* is perhaps the most frequently used preposition in Krio, there is a number of other prepositions that provide greater specificity of the location. Look at the following prepositions and a sample of sentences utilizing them:

biɛn [behind], *ɔnda* [under], *pantap* [on top of], *nia* [near]
insay [inside of], *oba* [over], *pan* [on/at], *tru* [through]

Examples:

1. *I de biɛn di chɔch.* [It/He is behind the church.]
2. *Di rɛs de nia di mata-odo.* [The rice is near the mortar.]
3. *Di pɔt de pantap di kuka.* [The pot is on top of the stove.]
4. *Im dɔg de ɔnda di tebul.* [Her dog is under the table.]

Greetings and Simple Sentences   69

UNRAVELING THE MULTIPLE
REALIZATIONS OF *DE* IN KRIO

In order to avoid confusion, it is important to point out that there are a number of words in Krio that are spelled *de*. The word meaning "to exist" carries the High Tone. With a Low Tone, the word can mean either, "there," sometimes in combination with a demonstrative pronoun (that is, *dis* "this" or *dat* "that"), as will be demonstrated later in the chapter. It can also communicate Present Progressive (the tense/aspect marker) where the word carries a Low Tone. Finally, *de*, with a High-Falling tone means "day." Figure 3.2 reveals in a schematic way of viewing the way these four morphemes operate in the language.

SUBSTANTIVE QUESTIONS

What are referred to as "substantive questions" here are those questions that solicit specific information from the person, to whom they are directed. Yes/No questions, which will be discussed in another chapter, are questions that simply try to determine the veracity or falsity of a proposition. Substantive questions are often referred to as "WH-questions" in English, because they virtually all involve words that begin with "Wh." Substantive questions in Krio all begin with one of the words listed on the next page.

de (high tone) "to be/exist/live"

Examples:	Usay mi buk de?	"Where is my book?"
	Mi buk de na tebul.	"My book is on the table."

de (low tone) "there"

Examples:	A bin go de.	"I went there."
	Da bɔbɔ de.	"That boy (there)."

de (low tone) "Present Continuous Action"

Examples:	Di bɔbɔ de go na skul.	"The boy is going to school."
	Mi mama de kuk rɛs.	"My mother is cooking rice."

de (high-falling) "day"

Examples:	Aw di de?	"How is everything today?"
	Di de fayn.	"Everything is fine."

Figure 3.2.   Multiple Realizations of de in Krio.

70   *Chapter 3*

Wetin? [What?]
Usay? [Where?]
Udat? [Who?]
Ustɛm? [When?]
Wetin du? [Why?]
Us? [Which?]
Uskayn? [What kind of?]
Aw? [How?]

Substantive questions demonstrate a prominent feature of Krio Language, the predisposition to maintain consistent word-order over a wide range of different kinds of sentences. The question word, which appears at the beginning of the sentence, replaces the component of the sentence about which specific information is being solicited. That component may be the Subject of the sentence, the Direct Object of the Verb, an Adverb, or a Prepositional Phrase (like location). The remaining components of the sentence continue in the same order they would have been in if the sentence was a declarative sentence rather than a question. This differs from English in that, in questions, the auxiliary verb that indicates tense is inverted with the subject of the sentence. Krio questions do not undergo such a conversion.

For example, look at the declarative sentence like the one below:

Di bɔbɔ bin rid im buk na di skul yɛstade. [The boy read his book at school yesterday.]

If the subject of the sentence is in question (Q-Subject), the following would be the result:

Udat bin rid im buk na di skul yɛstade? [Who read his book at school yesterday?]

In the same way, if the direct object (Q-Direct Object) is in question, the question would be the following:

Wetin di bɔbɔ bin rid na di skul yɛstade? [What did the boy read at school yesterday?]

Q-Prep Phrase would result in the sentence below:

Usay di bɔbɔ bin rid im book yɛstade? [Where did the boy read his book yesterday?]

Greetings and Simple Sentences 71

And, one final example, (Q-Time), would result in the sentence that follows:

Ustɛm di bɔbɔ bin rid im buk na di skul? [When did the boy read his book at school?]

An additional set of substantive questions will further demonstrate the use of WH-question words and the consistent word order of the remaining components of the sentence:

1. *Udat bin tif mi kɔpɔ?* [Who stole my money?]
2. *Wetin di uman dɛm go sɛl na di makit?* [What will the women sell in the market?]
3. *Usay di pikin dɛm kin go skul?* [Where do the children go to school?]
4. *Wetin du di titi de kray so?* [Why is the little girl crying like that?]
5. *Us sing di kwaya go sing?* [Which song will the choir sing?]
6. *Uskayn drink dɛm dɔn gi wi?* [What kind of drink have they given us?]
7. *Aw di ɛnjinia go tret di rod?* [How will the engineer straighten the road?]
8. *Udat di ticha bin tich na di skul?* [Who did the teacher teach at the school?]
9. *ɔmɔs yu de sɛl di pɔpɔ?* [How much does the papaya cost?]
10. *Wetin du yu dɔn bit yu pikin so?* [Why did you spank your child like that?]

Responding to Substantive Questions

Sentences that respond to substantive questions reinforce the predisposition for maintaining a consistent word order in various Krio sentence types. Below are substantive questions and plausible responses to them:

Examples with *ustɛm*

Ustɛm yu mama bin go na makit? [When did your mother go to the market?]
I bin go na makit na mɔnin. [She went this morning.]

Ustɛm yu papa go kam na os? [When is your father going to come home?]
I go kam na os ivintɛm. [He will come home this evening.]

Ustɛm Fumikɛ go fray di fish? [When is Fumike going to fry the fish?]
I go fray di fish afpas wan. [She is going to fry the fish at 1:30.]

Ustɛm yu yɛri dat? [When did you hear that?]
Yɛstade na di awujɔ. [Yesterday at the ceremonial feast.]

Examples with *udat*

Udat bin it di plasas? [Who ate the green stew.]
ɔsɛ im pikin bin it di plasas. [Ose's kid ate the green stew.]

Udat go so di lapa? [Who is going to sew the lapa skirt?]
Di titi im mama go so am. [The little girl's mother is going to sew it.]

Udat kin tich ridin na di skul? [Who teaches reading at the school?]
Mista Margay kin tich am. [Mr. Margay teaches it.]

Udat de dans na di trit? [Who is dancing in the street?]
Di dɛbul de dans na di trit. [The masquerader is dancing in the street.]

Udat dɔn rid im buk? [Who has finished reading his book?]
Gres ɛn Joko dɔn rid dɛm buk. [Grace and Joko have finished reading their books.]

Examples with *uskayn*

Uskayn fish yu de sɛl? [What kind of fish are you selling?]
A de sɛl snapa ɛn kuta. [I am selling snapper and barracuda.]

Uskayn bif una bin si na di makit? [What kind of meat did you see in the market?]
Wi bin si ɔg bif ɛn got. [We saw pork and goat.]

Uskayn os dɛm kin bil na Fritɔn? [What kind of houses are built in Freetown?]
Dɛm kin bil bɔd os ɛn blɔk os. [They build board houses and cement block houses.]

Uskayn plasas yu mama go kuk? [What kind of plasas is your mom going to cook?]
I go kuk pɛtɛtɛ lif dis ivin. [She is going to cook potato leaf this evening.]

Uskayn ɛnkincha Anti tay na im ed? [What kind of head tie is Auntee wearing?]
Anti bin tay wan fayn fayn ɛnkincha na im ed. [Auntee wore a beautiful scarf.]

Greetings and Simple Sentences

Examples with ɔmɔs

ɔmɔs kɔpɔ yu gɛt? [How much money do you have?]
A gɛt twɛnti lion nɔmɔ. [I only have 20 leones.]

ɔmɔs yia yu ol? [How old are you?]
A ol twɛnti-wan yia. [I am 21 years old.]

ɔmɔs pipul dɛm tap na da os de? [How many people live in that house?]
Et pipul dɛm tap na da os de. [Eight people live in that house.]

ɔmɔs di uman de sɛl im plantin? [How much do the woman's plantains cost?]
I de sɛl dɛm tri fɔ fayv lion. [She sells them 3 for five leones.]

Typical Conversation in the Market

A. *Sista, mɔnin-o.* [Sister, good morning.]
B. *O, mɔnin-o.* [Oh, good morning to you.] *Aw yu du?* [How are you?]

A. A tɛl Gɔd tɛnki. [I give thanks to God.] Aw di fambul dɛm? [How is your family?]
B. *Dɛm ɔl de.* [They are all alive and well.] *We yu pikin dɛm?* [How about your children?]

A. Dɛm wɛl. [They're fine.] Uskayn fish yu gɛt tide? [What kind of fish do you have today?]
B. *A gɛt kuta, mina, ɛn bonga, fresh wan dɛm.* [I have fresh barracuda, minnows, bonga.] *ɔmɔs yu want?* [How many do you want?]

A. ɔmɔs fɔ di kuta? [What's the price of the barracuda?]
B. *A kin sɛl dɛm, wan fɔ twɛnti-fayv lion.* [I usually sell them for 25 leones each.]

A. Eee! Mi mami, I dia-o! [Wow! Girlfriend, that's expensive!]
B. *ɛnti yu no aw wisɛf de bay frɔm di fishɔman dɛm?* [Don't you know how we have to buy from the fishermen?] *Grɔn dray fɔ ɔlman.* [Everyone is struggling.]

A. Yu nɔ go lɛs mi lilibit? [Aren't you going to reduce the price a little for me?]
B. *Yu na mi gud kɔstamɛnt.* [You are one of my good customers.] *So, fɔ yu a go sɛl di kuta wan fɔ twɛnti lion.* [So, for you, I will sell the barracuda for 20 leones each.]

74   *Chapter 3*

A. ɔrayt, mek a gɛt tu kuta. [Ok, give me 2 barracuda.] ɔmɔs fɔ yu plantin?
   [How much are the plantains?]
B. *Tri fɔ fayv lion.* [Three for five leones.]

A. Luk di kɔpɔ. [Ok, here's the money.] Wi go si nɛks wik. [I'll see you
   (again) next week.]
B. *ɔrayt. Gɔd go wit yu.* [Alright, God travel with you.]

A. Tɛl dɛm ɔl adu fɔ mi, ya. [Give your family my regards.]
B. *ɔrayt. wi go si.* [Ok, see you.]

NEGATION

Negation in Action Sentences

Krio possesses a Negative Marker, *nɔ*, to transform an action sentence from
the affirmative to its negative counterpart. The marker is placed at the beginning of the Verb Phrase. The sentence pattern looks like this:

Subject NP + *nɔ* + Tense/Aspect + Verb + Object NP + (Prep P)

The following sentences demonstrate this pattern:

A de rid mi buk. [I am reading my book.]
A nɔ de rid mi buk. [I am *not* reading my book.]

A bin rid di pepa. [I read the paper.]
A nɔ bin rid di pepa. [I *didn't* read the paper.]

I go was im klos. [She's going to wash her clothes.]
I nɔ go was im klos. [She's *not* going to wash her clothes.]

I go was di plet dɛm. [She's going to wash the dishes.]
I nɔ go was di plet dɛm. [She is *not* going to wash the dishes.]

Bayo kin ple na trit. [Bayo often plays in the street.]
Bayo nɔ kin ple na trit. [Bayo *doesn't* usually play in the street.]

Greetings and Simple Sentences 75

Negation in Locative Sentences

The functioning and location of the Negative Marker in Locative Sentences is the same as in Action Sentences. The negative marker is placed at the beginning of the Verb Phrase, followed by a possible Tense/Aspect Marker, in front of the Verb, *de*, "to be/exist," then, a Prepositional Phrase or location noun (for instance *Fritɔng* [Freetown] or *makit* [market]). The sentence pattern is represented by the following string of components:

Subject NP + *nɔ* + Tense/Aspect + *de* + Prep P or Location

Observe examples of Locative Sentences in their negative forms:

1. *Di man nɔ de na di os.* [The man is not in the house.]
2. *Dɛm nɔ bin de na di makit.* [They weren't at the market.]
3. *Modupɛ nɔ kin de na chɔch.* [Modupe isn't usually at church.]
4. *Wi nɔ go de na os tumara.* [We're not going to be at home tomorrow.]
5. *Mi brɔda nɔ bin de na wok ples Sɔnde.* [My brother wasn't at work on Sunday.]

Negation in Equational Sentences

The signaling of negation in Equational Sentences differs from that of the other two sentence types discussed above. Equational Sentences are those which "equate" the Subject NP with the NP that follows the Equational Verb, *na* [is equivalent to]. The negative form of *na* in Equational Sentences is *nɔto*. As we indicated earlier in this chapter, the regular pattern for an affirmative Equational Sentence is as follows:

NP + *na* + NP

A few examples show affirmative Equational Sentences:

1. *Mi na pikin.* [I am a child.]
2. *Di man na polisman.* [The man is a policeman.]
3. *Da uman de na sɛktri.* [That woman is a secretary.]
4. *Dis langa bɔbɔ na Tunde.* [This tall boy is Tunde.]
5. *In na di edman.* [He is the headman/chief.]

The pattern for its negative counterpart is cited below:+

NP + *nɔto* + NP

76   *Chapter 3*

Examples of Equational Sentences in the negative form are offered here:

1. *Mi noto pikin.* [I am not a child.]
2. *Di man noto polisman.* [The man isn't a policeman.
3. *Da uman de noto sɛktri.* [That woman isn't a secretary.]
4. *Dis langa bɔbɔ ya noto Tunde.* [This tall boy isn't Tunde.]
5. *In noto di edman.* [He isn't the headman/chief.]

The sentence patterns shown above and examples demonstrate that negation in Krio is systematic, or governed by grammatical rules. Which Negative
marker is to be used and its position in a sentence is dependent on the sentence type.

Negative Harmony Rule

Krio contains a group of words referred to as Indefinite Quantifiers. Within
this group there are two sub-sets, one positive, the other negative. Below are
the two sub-sets:

The Positive Sub-set consists of words like *ɛni* [any], *ɛnibɔdi* [anybody], *ɛniting*
[anything], and *ɛniwe* [anywhere]. The Negative sub-set contains words like *nɔ*
[no], *nobɔdi* [nobody/no one], *natin* [nothing], and *nɔwe* [nowhere].

Accompanying this group of words is what we refer to as the Negative
Harmony Rule, of which there are two parts:

Negative Harmony Rule—Part One:

*If a Krio sentence contains a verb that is marked as negative, all instances
of Indefinite Quantifiers in that sentence must appear in their negative form.*
Examples of this rule application in Krio sentences are presented below:

1. *A nɔ de go nɔwe.* [I'm not going anywhere.]
2. *Yu sista nɔ bin sɛl natin na di makit.* [Your sister didn't sell anything in
   the market.]
3. *Dɛm nɔ go gi natin to nobɔdi.* [They're not going to give anybody
   anything.]
4. *Mi mama nɔ kin kɔs nobɔdi.* [My mother would never swear at anyone.]
5. *Da edman de nɔ go chenj natin.* [The village chief won't change
   anything.]

Greetings and Simple Sentences 77

Notice that all of the English translations require the indefinite quantifiers in such sentences to be in the positive forms. For the negative form of indefinite quantifiers to appear in a sentence in which the verb is negative would be considered ungrammatical.

Negative Harmony Rule—Part Two:

If the subject of a Krio sentence is a member of the sub-set of negative indefinite quantifiers, then the accompanying verb must be marked as negative.
Examples of Part Two of the Negative Harmony Rule appear in the sentences below:

1. Natin nɔ de na di pala. [Nothing is in the living room.]
2. Nɔbɔdi nɔ go go na im os. [Nobody will go to his house.]
3. Nɔbɔdi nɔ lɛk am. [Nobody likes him/her.]
4. Natin nɔ de na di frij. [Nothing is in the refrigerator.]
5. Nɔ kuta nɔ bin de na di makit tide. [There wasn't any barracuda in the market today.]

YES/NO QUESTIONS

In Chapter 2, in the discussion of tone as distinctive in Krio, it was indicated that sentence intonation can influence the absolute tone of words in a sentence. Yes/No Questions presents an occasion in which intonation plays a major role. In Krio, the only difference between a Declarative Sentence and a Yes/No Question is, in fact, intonation. While the intonation in declarative sentences *falls* downward toward the end of the sentence, the intonation on a Yes/No Question *rises* toward the end of the sentence. The effect of this on the absolute tone of words in the sentence changes, but the relative tone between High and Low is maintained. The word order in a Yes/No Question in Krio remains the same as in its corresponding declarative sentence.

Declarative Sentence: *Olu de go na di makit.* [Olu is going to the market.]
Yes/No Question: *Olu de go na di makit?* [Is Olu going to the market?]

Notice that English Yes/No Questions are signaled not only by rising intonation, but also, and perhaps more importantly, by grammatical inversion of the Subject Noun Phrase (*Olu* in this case) and the Auxiliary Verb (*is* in this case). In the examples below, the word order in the Krio questions on the left remains the same as in a declarative sentence. The English translations

78 *Chapter 3*

demonstrate the inversion of the auxiliary verb (did, is, will, or are) and the subject NP:

1. *Di man bin tif yu kɔpɔ?* [*Did* the man steal your money?]
2. *Yu mama go kuk fufu tide?* [*Is* your mother going to cook fufu today?]
3. *Ola na yu fɛjɛ?* [*Is* Ola your girlfriend?]
4. *I go bay da mɔtoka de?* [*Will* she buy that car?]
5. *Dɛm de bil os na bush?* [*Are* they building a house in the woods?]

There is a word in Krio that can be used to announce a Yes/No Question. The word is *ɛnti* with Low-High tone. Its meaning can generally be interpreted as "Is it the case that" or "isn't it the case that." The intonation pattern described above for Yes/No Questions still applies and the dominant word order persists. A few examples demonstrate this Krio signaling device:

ɛnti yu brɔda go kam? [Isn't your brother going to come?]
ɛnti yu mama go de na os? [Won't your mother be home?]
ɛnti una bin no? [Didn't you all know?]
ɛnti di man bin gɛt fɔ go ɔspitul? [Didn't the man have to go to the hospital?]
ɛnti ɔl man lɛk fɔ si yu dawnfɔl. [Isn't it true that everyone likes to see you humbled?]

These Yes/No Questions in Krio can be answered in either the affirmative or the negative. If the response is in the affirmative, the respondent will usually begin with the word, *yɛs* (with Low-Rising tone). If the response is negative, one will typically begin with the word, *nɔɔ* (with Low-Rising tone). And, of course, the verb in the response in the negative will carry the Negative Marker in the VP. A few examples demonstrate responses to Yes/No Questions:

1. *Joko bin tif mi kɔpɔ?* [Did Joko steal my money?]
   Nɔɔ, I nɔ bin tif yu kɔpɔ. [No, he didn't steal your money.]
2. *Yu mama go* kuk fufu tide? [Is your going to cook fufu today?]
   Yɛs, I go kuk fufu tide. [Yes, she is going to cook fufu today.]
3. *Ola na yu fɛjɛ?* [Is Ola your girlfriend?]
   Nɔɔ, Ola nɔto mi fɛjɛ. Na mi padi. [No, she's not my girlfriend. She is my friend.]
4. *I go bay dis* motoka ya? [Is he going to buy this car?]
   Nɔɔ, i nɔ go bay da wan de. [No, he's not going to buy that one.]
5. *Yu* fambul dɛm de bil nyu os? [Are your relatives building a new house?]
   Yɛs, dɛm de bil os na bush. [Yes, they're building a house in the woods.]

Greetings and Simple Sentences 79

STATIVE AND ADJECTIVAL VERBS

This section of the chapter focuses on verbs that express a "static condition" or a "state of being." One such verb has already been introduced, the verb *de*, meaning "to exist" or "to be at a place." Remember, this verb carries high tone and appears in Location sentences like the one below:

Di man *de* na im os. [The man is in his house.]

When there is no Tense/Aspect Marker in front of a Stative Verb, it indicates the Simple Present Tense. So, the man is in his house right now. This sentence pattern can be represented in the following way:

NP + 0 Tense/Aspect + Stative Verb = "Simple Present"

However, as we saw in the section on Locative Sentences, stative verbs are compatible with many Tense/Aspect markers, with the expected interpretation. Look at the following examples:

Di man go de na im os. [The man will be in his house.] [Future]
Di man bin de na im os. [The man was in his house.] [Past]
Di man kin de na im os. [The man is often/usually in his house.] [Habitual]

Other stative verbs behave the same way in Krio. Observe this behavior with a sample of other stative verbs:

1. Olu sidɔm na di chia. [Olu is sitting in the chair.]
2. Dɛm pikin de tap na di bod os. [Those children live in the wooden house.]
3. Di ol man gri. [The old man agreed.]
4. Di ɔda man nɔ gri. [The other man didn't agree.]
5. Wi sabi da pɔsin de. [We know that person.]
6. I bin mɛmba mi. [She remembered me.]
7. A nɔ mɛmba dɛm nɛm. [I don't remember their name.]
8. Di pipul dɛm kin gladi na mared. [People are usually happy at a wedding.]
9. Di dɔg bin kɔmɔt na di bed. [The dog got off of the bed.]
10. ɔgɔsta im mama lɛk di man. [Augusta's mother likes the man.]

80   *Chapter 3*

Stative Verbs Behavior with the Present Progressive Marker

When the Present Progressive Marker, *de* (Low Tone), is used in front of most Stative Verbs it communicates a different meaning than when it is placed before action verbs. That special meaning is "to be in the process of" or "preparing to." However, *de*, the Present Progressive marker is semantically incompatible with some stative verbs, including *de*, meaning "to exist" or "be at a place." Observe examples of sentences containing stative verbs which are semantically compatible with *de*:

1. *Di bɔbɔ de kɔmɔt skul.* [The boy is on his way out of school.]
2. *Suleman de rɛdi fɔ ledɔm.* [Suleman is getting ready to lie down.]
3. *A de mɛmba naw wɛtin i bin se.* [I am starting to remember what she said.]
4. *Ola de wɛr im sus.* [Ola is putting her shoes on.]

Listed below is a list of sentences demonstrating the variety of stative verbs in different grammatical contexts:

1. *Di tri bɔbɔ dɛm sidɔm na di grɔn.* [The three boys are sitting on the ground.]
2. *Modupɛ gɛt bɔku kɔpɔ.* [Modupe has a lot of money.]
3. *Di man dɛm nɔ gri.* [The men do not agree.]
4. *ɔltɛm a kin yɛri im dɔg.* [I always hear his dog.]
5. *i lɛk da gyal de.* [He likes that girl.]
6. *i lɛk da gyal de bad.* [He loves that girl.]
7. *Usay yu tap?* [Where do you live?]
8. *Mi sista tinap bɛn di mangro tik.* [My sister is standing behind the mango tree.]
9. *Tunde de wɛr im trɔsis.* [Tunde is putting on his pants.] (in the process)
10. *Usay Joko kɔmɔt?* [Where is Joko from?]

Adjectival Verbs

One of the interesting features of Krio Language is that a number of words belonging to one word class can also function in one or more other word classes. Such is the case with *Adjectives*. One of their functions is to describe the features of a noun, but they also can function as verbs. In fact, Krio Adjectives can function as Stative Verbs. To achieve this, the Adjective is placed in the *Verb* position in the sentence. Below are Adjectives shown functioning as an adjective in one sentence, followed by a sentence in which the same word functions as a verb:

Adjective: *Yu pikin na big gyal.* [Your child is a big girl.]
Verb: *Yu gyal pikin big-o.* [Your daughter is really big.]

Adjective: *Da pɔsin de na wɔwɔ man.* [That person is an ugly man.]
Verb: *Da man de wɔwɔ.* [That man is ugly.]

Adjective: *Yu na trangayes bɔbɔ.* [You are a stubborn/hard-headed boy.]
Verb: *Yu tu trangayes.* [You are very stubborn/hard-headed.]

Adjective: *Yu nɔ gɛt bɔku kɔpɔ.* [You don't have a lot of money.]
Verb: *Yu kɔpɔ nɔ bɔku.* [Your money isn't a lot.]

Adjective: *Yu bin gɛt fayn os.* [You had a beautiful home.]
Verb: *Yu os bin fayn.* [Your home was beautiful.]

ADVERBS

Adverbs are words that qualify the verb in a sentence, whether the verb is active or stative. Krio possesses numerous adverbs or adverbial phrases that indicate the time the verbal statement is taking place. Some adverbs have more liberal placement in the sentence. Although typically placed at the end of the Verb Phrase, depending upon the semantics of the sentence or the emphasis being placed on the adverb, it can be found at the beginning of the sentence or immediately after the verb. A few sentences demonstrate the use of temporal adverbs in Krio:

1. *Yɛstade nɔbɔdi nɔ bin kam na mi shɔp.* [Nobody came to my store yesterday.]
2. *Dɛm go bigin wok jisnɔ.* [They will begin working shortly.]
3. *Bayo nɔba drayv go Bo.* [Bayo never drove to Bo.]
4. *Wi go mit Olamide na mi os afpas siks.* [We'll meet Olamide at my house at 6:30.]
5. *ɔgɔsta go go na makit nɛks tumara.* [Augusta will go to the market the day after tomorrow.]

In addition to a wide range of temporal adverbs, including the days of the week, times of the day, and months of the year, Krio has a group of General Adverbs which describe the conditions or nature of the verbal action in the

82   Chapter 3

sentence. A few examples of sentences containing general adverbs demonstrate the use of them in Krio sentences:

1. *Kwaku bin se i lɛk Pamɛla bad.* [Kwaku said that he was in love with Pamela.]
2. *Di pikin dɛm kam kwik.* [The children came quickly.]
3. *Duya, una waka saful nia di wata.* [You all, please be careful near the wata.]
4. *Olu kin it bɔku-bɔku.* [Olu eats a lot.]
5. *Di bɔbɔ dɛm awangɔt pas mak.* [The boys are excessively greedy.]

SUMMARY

All human languages are comprised of basic lexical, grammatical, and phonological building blocks, upon which more complex and nuanced sentences are based. This chapter has described the basic building blocks for Sierra Leone Krio. The more sophisticated features of Krio that are presented in chapter 4 will be easier to comprehend because of the foundational components presented in this chapter.

Chapter 4

Complex Sentences Structures

Every human language employs words in different ways to communicate the range of human thoughts, actions, and emotions. In one language a particular concept might be expressed by a single word, but in another language that same concept might require a full sentence.

SERIAL VERB CONSTRUCTIONS

In fact, in Krio, two or more verbs must work in combination in the same sentence to communicate concepts that are communicated by a single verb in many other languages. This phenomenon is referred to as serial verb constructions. In the following pages, we describe the conditions under which these serial verbs occur in Krio.

Mental Verbs

There is a sub-set of Stative Verbs that we refer to as "Mental Verbs," because they involve concepts like "hoping," "thinking," "believing," "remembering," and "understanding." One might say that the speaker is mentally processing a second proposition. That proposition is stated in an embedded sentence that is introduced by the verb, *se* [say]. Look at the sentence below:

Tunde bin biliv se im pikin go kam na os kwik.
[Tunde believed his child was going to come home quickly.]

Figure 4.1 represents the structural tree that shows the relationship between the components of the sentence above:

Notice that this particular sentence structure results in a sequence of two verbs (Mental Verb + *se*) and demonstrates the characteristic structure involved in Serial Verb Constructions. In such serial verb constructions, the

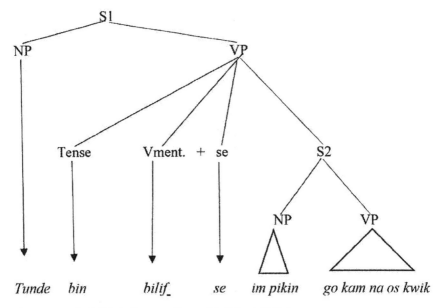

Figure 4.1. Serial Verb Constructions with "Mental" Verbs.

Tense/Aspect marker (*bin* in this case) appears only once, in front of the first verb. The second verb carries no separate Tense/Aspect marker, instead it assumes the tense or aspect of the main verb in the sentence. Since mental verbs are, by their very nature, also stative verbs, if this sentence was in the Present Tense, the first verb would be marked with Zero Tense Marker and the sentence would read as follows:

Tunde bin biliv se im pikin go kam na os kwik.
[Tunde believes his child was going to come home quickly.]

Additional examples of Mental Verbs in sentences that result in serial verb constructions are identified below:

1. *A bin mɛmba se i nɔ go kam.* [I remembered that she is not going to come.]
2. *Di edman op se ɔlman go de de.* [The chief hopes everyone will be there.]
3. *Wi ɔl no se di ticha gɛt sɛns.* [We all know that the teacher is smart.]
4. *i tink se di pati nɔ go fayn.* [He thinks the party is not going to be very good.]
5. *Modupɛ biliv se im pikin nɔ tif natin.* [Modupe believes his son didn't steal anything.]

Complex Sentences Structures 85

Serial verbs in Krio can be used to communicate "directionality," "instrumentality," "Indirect Object," "Sequentiality," or "Initiation." In addition to these, serial verbs can also be very idiomatic, meaning that they are unique to one verb or one situation, but do not generalize across a sizeable subset of verbs. Each of these types of serial verbs deserve our attention.

Serial Verbs with Directional Function

The directional function of serial verbs in Krio is used almost exclusively with motion verbs or verbs that have motion implied in their meaning. The verbs that satisfy this function (*go* [go], *kam* [come], and *kɔmɔt* [come out of/from]) are selected based on their relationship to the speaker. Observe the serial verb usage with the verb, *waka* [walk].

1. *Di pikin dɛm de waka go na skul.* [The children are walking to school.] (away from speaker)]
2. *Di pikin dɛm de waka kam na skul.* [The children are walking to school.] (toward speaker)]
3. *Di pikin dɛm de waka kɔmɔt na skul.* [The children are walking out of the school.]

Notice that the second verb in the series in the third sentence, *kɔmɔt*, is conveying directionality in relation to the school and the speaker.

Other verbs that require a serial verb to communicate directionality:

rɔn [run], as in *rɔn* go [run to (away from speaker)]
rɔn kam [run to (toward speaker)]
drayv [drive] as in *drayv* X go [drive X to (away from speaker)]
drayv X *kam* [drive X to (toward speaker)]
sɛn [send/throw] as in *sɛn* X *go* [send X to (away from speaker)]
sɛn X *kam* [send X to (toward speaker)]
kɛr [carry/take] as in *kɛr* X *go* [Take X to (away from speaker)]
bring [bring] as in *bring* X *kam* [bring X to (toward speaker)]
tek [take possession of] as in *tek* X *go* [take X to (away from speaker)]
tek X *kam* [bring X to (toward speaker)]
fes [no meaning without serial verb] as in *fes* X *kam* [go get X bring (toward speaker)]
drɛb [no meaning without serial verb] as in *drɛb* X *go* [chase away from speaker]
drɛb X *kam* [chase X toward (direction of speaker)]
tif [steal] as in *tif* X *kɔmɔt* [steal from]

86 *Chapter 4*

It should be noted that the "X" in the expressions above is a place holder for a Noun Phrase Direct Object of the primary verb. The following sentences show how these noun phrases add critical meaning to the sentences:

1. *Di uman bin bring ɔl im pikin dɛm kam na di skul tide.* [The woman brought all of her children to the school today.]
2. *Di ɔntingman bin drɛb di tifman go na do.* [The hunter chased the thief out the door.]
3. *ɔse ɛn im fambul dɛm go waka kam na wi os dis ivin.* [Ose and his family will walk to our house this evening.]
4. *Kɛr dis chia go gi yu ɔnkul.* [Take this chair to your uncle.]
5. *Di man bin drayv im anti go na di ɔspitul.* [The man drove his aunt to the hospital.]

Serial Verbs with Instrumental Function

Krio uses the verb, *tek*, to identify the instrument to be used in performing a particular act or to identify the materials or ingredients needed to make or prepare something. Different from the directional serial verbs (*go*, *kam*, and *kɔmɔt*), which appear as the second verb in the series, the verb, *tek*, assumes the first position in the verb phrase by identifying the *instrument to be used*, the *second verb describes how the instrument will be used.* The sentences below are clear examples of how serial verb constructions are used to express "instrumentality."

1. *I tek im an bit di bɔbɔ.* [He spanked the boy.] (literal: He take his hand hit the boy.)
2. *Dɛm go tek di kasada mek fufu.* [They will make foofoo out of cassava.] (literal: They FUTURE take the cassava make foofoo.)

Additional sentences demonstrate the breadth of usage of the Instrumental Function of serial verbs in Krio. Note that not all of the *instruments* are physical objects that are controlled by one's hands. Some sentences reveal instrumental serial verbs being used metaphorically. See the examples below:

1. *Tela dɛm kin tek gara so fayn dɔkɛt ɛn lapa.* [Tailors can make beautiful skirts and blouses out of tie-dyed cloth.]
2. *Wetin yu kin tek mek rayzbred?* [What do you make rice bread out of?]
3. *A tek mi yay si am.* [I saw it with my very eyes.]
4. *Di uman tek nɛf kɔt di bif.* [The woman cut the meat with a knife.]
5. *Bami tek sɛns kech am.* [Bami used his wits to catch him.]

Complex Sentences Structures 87

Indirect Object Function

In English, action verbs are typically followed by a Noun Phrase, which is the Direct Object. If an Indirect Object is present in the sentence, it appears after the Direct Object in the form of a Prepositional Phrase that begins with "to" or "for." Examples of this are presented below:

A. Mr. Smith carved the wooden horse for his son.
B. She dispatched the letter to her friend.

In Krio, the Indirect Object function is frequently produced by a serial verb construction that begins with the verb, *gi*, meaning "to give." Look at the following sentences to see how Indirect Objects are presented in Krio:

1. *Kɛr da blay de go gi yu mama.* [Take that basket *to* your mother.]
2. *Udat bin sɛn di buk kam gi mi?* [Who sent the book *to* me?]
3. *A go sɛl di kuta gi yu, wan fɔ twɛnti lion.* [I will sell the barracuda *to* you, one for twenty leones.]
4. *Fes di plasas kam gi yu ɔnkul.* [Get the plasas *for* your uncle.]
5. *A bin bay di bia gi Pa Jɔnsin.* [I bought the beer *for* Mr. Johnson.]

This is a specialized use of the verb, *gi*, indicating that an object is being acted upon to someone or for the benefit of someone. So, one cannot simply substitute *gi* for the English words "to" or "for" wherever they may occur.

Serial Verbs with Purposive and/or Sequential Action Function

One of the most productive, or frequently used, functions of serial verbs in Krio is in the expression of a *sequence of actions* or *to show the purpose of an action*. In either case, the directional verbs, *go* and *kam*, are pivotal elements. The most accurate translations of sentences containing this kind of serial verb construction are [go or come *to do* X] or [go or come *and do* X,] with X being almost any verb. Look at the following sentences which demonstrate the wide use of serial verb constructions in this way:

1. *Nain, i go tɛl di edman.* [Then, she went and told the headman.]
2. *Wi ɔl go go makit go bay kpɛkpɛkpɛ.* [We will all go to the market to buy odds and ends.]
3. *Tunde bin go tek mi sista na skul.* [Tunde went to pick up my sister from school.]

88   *Chapter 4*

4. *Dɛm kam tif ɔl mi kɔpɔ.* [They came and took all of my money.]
5. *Im fambul dɛm kam luk am.* [His relatives came to see (about) him.]

Serial Verbs with Initiating Function

The verb *kam*, when followed by another verb often carries the meaning of
[get ready to X] or [starting to X.] There is an obvious potential for ambigu-
ity in these instances since it overlaps with the purposive/sequential function.
However, our analysis suggests that this Initiating Function is only compatible with Present Progressive and the Simple Past tense/aspect markers. The
examples below reveal the Initiating Function:

1. Wi de kam go. [We're getting ready to leave.]
2. A de kam kuk. [I'm getting ready to start cooking.]
3. Nain, di uman kam vɛks. [Then, the woman began to get angry.]
4. A de kam was di plet dɛm jisnɔ. [I'm going to wash the dishes in
   a minute.]
5. Olamide de kam go na makit. [Olamide is about to go to the market.]

Idiomatic Serial Verbs

A subset of serial verbs are idiomatic and, thus, are not generalizable. In other
words, they are stand-alones and cannot be applied to a wider set of other
verbs. They have a unique, special meaning. A few examples have been collected here to demonstrate idiomatic serial verbs:

1. *ɔnkul ɔsɛ de sɛn kɔl di dɔkta.* [Uncle Ose is sending for the doctor.]
2. *We go sidɔm blo lilibit.* [We're going to rest a little while.]
3. *I butu beg am.* [He humbly pleaded with him.]

THE PREPOSITION, *TO*

In the previous chapter, the reader was introduced to locative sentences, using
the verb, *de* "to be at a place," and to a variety of prepositions that indicate
the location of things. In addition to specific prepositions like *bien* [behind]
or *pantap* [on top of], we described the generic preposition, *na*, which is
translated differently, depending upon the qualities of the *non-human object*
it precedes. Here we introduce the reader to another preposition which can
vary in meaning, depending upon the *human object* it precedes. *To* can mean
[to], [at the residence of], or [from]. Observe the variant meanings of *to* in
the following sentences:

Complex Sentences Structures 89

1. *i de to Osɛ.* [He is at Oseh's (house).]
2. *Dɛm nɔ rich to Pa Luwis te ivintɛm.* [They didn't get at Mr. Lewis' house until evening.]
3. *Wi go go ple Lodo to ɛkundayɔ.* [We're going to play Ludo at Ekundayo's (place).]
4. *Udat go kɛr mi trɔsis go to tela?* [Who volunteers to take my pants to the tailor?]
5. *A bay am to mi padi.* [I bought it from my friend.]
6. *i rɔn go to Jɔn wit di alejo.* [He hurried to John's (house) with the good news.]
7. *Ayɔ bin it to mi mama.* [Ayo ate at my mother's (house).]
8. *Di tifman nɔ de to di edman.* [The thief isn't at the edman's house.]

A KRIO SHORT STORY: *AW TUNDE ɛN BƆD NA PADI DɛM*

Wan de ya, wan bɔbɔ bin de we nɛm Tunde. Wan de, Tunde ɛn im padi bin waka go insay dis bush ya, nain, dɛm yeri wan bɔd de ala. We dɛm go niar am, nain dɛm si im fɛda dɛm fasin na wan tik-an. Tunde fil sɔri fɔ di bɔd. i nɔ no wetin fɔ du, so, i rɔn go kɔl im big brɔda na os.

Im big brɔda wɛr im klos kwik-kwik. i sɛn Tunde go na pantri go bring im ɔntin-nɛf. Wen Tunde kɛr di nɛf go gi im brɔda, im brɔda put am insay im ɔntin bag ɛn aks Tunde fɔ go sho am usay di bɔd de. Dɛm rɔn go de ɛn tek tɛm pul di bɔd im fɛda dɛm kɔmɔt na di tik-an.

Wen di bɔd lus, i shek-shek im fɛda dɛm. Nain, i flay go tinap na Tunde im sholda. i nɔ gri kɔmɔt de. Tunde im big brɔda tɛl Tunde se mek i bring di bɔd kam na os. Wen dɛm rich de, dɛm bigin bil kej fɔ di bɔd. Tunde ɛn di bɔd gladi. Frɔm da tɛm de, i ɛn di bɔd de go ɔlsay tugɛda.

Translation

[Once upon a time, there was a boy named Tunde. One day Tunde and his friend were walking in the woods when they heard a bird cawing. When they got closer, they saw his feathers were stuck to a branch. Tunde felt sorry for the bird. He didn't know what to do, so, he ran to get his older brother at home.

His brother got dressed quickly. He sent Tunde to the pantry to get his hunting knife. After Tunde had given his brother the knife, his brother threw his hunting bag over his shoulder and asked Tunde to show him where the bird was. They ran there and carefully pried the bird loose.

90   *Chapter 4*

When the bird was free, he straightened up his feathers and flew up onto Tunde's shoulder and wouldn't leave. Tunde's brother told Tunde to bring the bird home with them. When they arrived home, they immediately started building a bird cage. Tunde and the bird were both happy. From that day forward, whenever you saw Tunde, the bird was there with him.]

DIALOGUE—*GETTING AROUND*

A. *Gud mɔnin, Sa.* [Good morning, Sir.]
B. *Kushɛ-o, Bo aw yu du?* [Hello, how are you doing?]

A. *A wɛl, Sa. Aw di bɔdi?* [I'm fine, Sir. How are you?]
B. *A tɛl Gɔd tɛnki. Usay yu de go so?* [I give thanks to God. Where are you going?]

A. *A wan fɔ go King Jimi Makit, bɔt a nɔ sabi usay i de.* [I want to go to King Jimmy Market, but don't know where it is.] *Aw fɔ rich de?* [How do I get there?]
B. *Yu fɔ pas go dɔng dis trit ya tete yu rich wan big chɔch.* [Go straight down this street until you come to a big church.] *Wɛn yu rich de, yu go bɛn na yu lɛf an.* [Turn left.] *Waka go tri blɔk dɛm.* [Go three blocks.] *Yu go si am na yu rayt an.* [You will see it on right.]

A. *Tɛnki, Sa. A de go, Sa.* [Thank you, Sir. I'm on my way.]
B. *O! Gɔd go wit yu.* [Ok. God speed.]

THE THEMATIC NATURE OF
KRIO: EMPHASIS, FOCUS, CONTRAST

Clifford N. Fyle, the noted Krio scholar, is credited with recognizing that "It is necessary to posit a pre-subject beginning phrase position . . . to account for thematic and other units which precede the subject . . . "[1] What he means by this is that various grammatical devices are available in Krio for signaling the most important element in the sentence to the speaker at that moment. The thematic element can be said to emphasize, place focus on, or contrast the element from other elements in the sentence. Mastering the thematic nature of the language is key to developing a high level of fluency in Krio. Using any of the thematic strategies also adds a level of animation and color to the communication. Krio oral stories accentuate this character of the language by their liberal application of these grammatical devices.

Complex Sentences Structures 91

A number of languages emphasize a noun phrase by stating it first in a sentence. This is an important linguistic strategy in Krio as well. It suggests that the front of a sentence is a privileged position. In Krio, a speaker may shift an element out of its normal position in a sentence, frequently accompanied by the copula verb, *na*, to the front of the sentence. Where Krio distinguishes itself from most other languages is in the fact that Krio speakers can shift almost any element, whether it be *noun, pronoun, prepositional phrase, adjective, adverb,* or *verb,* to the front of the sentence. However, there are rules that must be followed to accomplish this goal.

To facilitate this process, Krio also has a complete set of *Emphatic Pronouns.* In the following sections the rules and procedures for highlighting specific elements of a given sentence will be described in more detail.

Emphatic Pronouns

The Emphatic Pronouns series is presented in table 4.1.

Note that all of these pronouns carry the High Tone, except for *una*, which carries a High-Low Tone. These differ from other pronouns in Krio, all of which begin with Low Tone. Emphatic pronouns may occur in both subject and object positions. When they are used this way they typically denote contrast. For instance, one might say *A nɔ lɛk in, bɔt a lɛk una.* [I don't like him/her, but I like you (Plural).], thereby, making a contrast between *him/her* and *you all.* Otherwise, one would simply say, *A nɔ lɛk am.* Look at the following examples:

1. *Dɛm de go skul.* [*They* are going to school (but not me).]
2. *Mi nɔ go it fufu.* [*I'm* not going to eat any foofoo (but you can).]
3. *Di edmasta nɔ lɛk wi, bɔt i lɛk una.* [The principal doesn't like *us* but she likes *you all.*]
4. *In de na os.* [*He* is in the house (but everyone else is out).]
5. *Una nɔ bigyay lɛk Meri.* [*You all* are not greedy like Mary is.]
6. *Nɔbɔdi nɔ go du natin fɔ wi.* [Nobody's going to do anything for *us.*]

Table 4.1. Set of Emphatic Pronouns

Person	Singular	Tone	Plural	Tone
1st	mi [I]	High	wi [we]	High
2nd	yu [you]	High	una [you all]	High-Low
3rd	in [he, she, it]	High	dɛm [they]	High

92   *Chapter 4*

Emphatic Pronouns in Equational Sentences

Whenever a pronoun functions as the subject of an Equational Sentence, the Emphatic series is required, as seen below:

1. *Mi na ticha.* [I am a teacher.
2. *Wi na treda dɛm.* [We are traders.]
3. *Dɛm na snapa dɛm.* [They are snapper fish.]
4. *In na mi brɔda.* [He is my brother.]
5. *Una na klak dɛm, bɔt wi na fama dɛm.* [You all are clerks, but we are farmers.]

Na and *Nɔto* as Emphatic Markers

In equational sentences, the verb *na* [is/are] and its negative counterpart *nɔto* [is/are not] are the main verb in the sentence. However, *na/nɔto* introduce the emphasized element at the beginning of the sentence, whether the emphasized element is a noun, pronoun, adjective, adverb, or verb. It is the frequency of this pattern that has led to the characterization of Krio as a "thematic language." The following pairs of sentences reveal this emphatic function of *na/nɔto*:

1a.   *Mi mama de kuk fɔl.* [My mother is cooking chicken.] (Non-Emphatic)
1b.   *Na fɔl mi mama de kuk.* [Chicken is what my mother is cooking.] (Emphatic)

2a.   *Dɛm go bit mi sista.* [They're going to spank my sister.]
2b.   *Na mi sista dɛm go bit.* [My sister is the one they're going to spank.]

3a.   *Modupɛ bin it mi rɛs.* [Modupe ate my rice.]
3b.   *Na Modupɛ bin it mi rɛs.* [It was Modupe who ate my rice.]

4a.   *i put di kɔpɔ insay mi pɔkit.* [He put the money in my pocket.]
4b.   *Na insay mi pɔkit i put mi kɔpɔ.* [He put the money right in my pocket.]

5a.   *i sabi drayv.* [She knows how to drive.]
5b.   *Na drayv i sabi drayv.* [She really knows how to drive.]

Complex Sentences Structures 93

Placing the Noun Phrase or Prepositional Phrase into Emphasis Position

Notice that, if the emphasis is on a subject or object noun, the entire NP in which the noun appears is shifted to the front of the sentence after *na/nɔto*. Similarly, if the location is the emphasis, the whole Prep Phrase is moved to the front.

Base Sentence
Di ol uman bin put di it pantap di tebul. [The old woman put the food on the table.]

Emphasizing Subject NP
Na di ol uman bin put di it pantap di tebul. [It was the old woman who put the food on the table.]

Emphasizing Object NP
Na di it di ol uman bin put pantap di tebul. [The food is what the old woman put on the table.]

Emphasizing the Prepositional Phrase
Na pantap di tebul di ol uman bin put di it. [The old woman put the food right on top of the table.]

Emphasizing a Pronoun

When the element being emphasized in a sentence is a pronoun, the *Emphatic Pronoun Series* must be used. Observe that phenomenon in the sentences below:

1. *Na mi de drayv mi mama go tɔn.* [I'm the one who's driving my mother to town.]
2. *Nɔto in di polis bin bit.* [He's not the one the policeman beat.]
3. *Na una di man bin tel.* [You were the ones the man told.]
4. *Na in bin kech da big fish de.* [He is the one who caught that big fish.]
5. *Na dɛm di ticha go tich.* [They are the one's the teacher is going to teach.]

Emphasizing the Verbal Action

If the *verbal action* is the element being emphasized, *a copy of the verb is moved to the front* of the sentence with *na/nɔto, but the original verb is*

94   *Chapter 4*

retained in its normal position. Observe the repetition of the verb in the following sentences and the meaning generated by that process:

1. *Na dans di uman dɛm bin dans so.* [The women danced enthusiastically.]
2. *Na kuk i de kuk.* [She is really enjoying cooking.] or [Cooking is what she is doing.]
3. *Na vɛks di edman bin vɛks.* [The village chief was really angry.]
4. *Na wok dɛm de wok o.* [They are really working hard.]
5. *Nɔto ple i de ple.* [He is really not playing.] or [He is not joking.]
6. *Nɔto bit dɛm go bit wi.* [They're not going to beat us.]

Typical Responses to Substantive Questions Using the Emphatic *na*/nɔto

The topic of Substantive Questions was covered in chapter 2. Remember that such questions begin with a WH-/Question word, like "Who," "What," "Where." The very nature of such questions elicits a response that is specific. Thus, it is to be expected that an emphatic sentence would follow, since emphasis distinguishes the answer from all other answers. Observe the following questions and plausible responses to them:

Q: *Udat bin was di plet dɛm?* [Who washed the dishes?]
A: *Na mi bin was dɛm.* [I am the one who washed them.]

Q: *Wetin na da ting de na yu bag?* [What is that in your purse?]
A: *Na mi nyu ɛnkincha.* [It's my new scarf.]

Q: *Usay yu papa de go so?* [Where is your father going like that?]
A: *Na ɔspitul i de go, Sa.* [The hospital is where he is going.]

Q: *Udat yu mama bin sɛn go na makit?* [Who did your mother send to the market?]
A: *Na Bayo i bin sɛn go de.* [Bayo is the one she sent there.]

Q: *Wetin du yu gladi so?* [Why are you so happy?]
A: *Na bikɔs Joko bin bay nyu drɛs fɔ mi.* [It's because Joko bought me a nyu dress.]

Putting a Noun Phrase in focus without *na*/nɔto

Another thematic strategy in Krio can be carried out without the use of *na*/nɔto. The speaker needs only to state the focal element and then

Complex Sentences Structures 95

referencing that element in its normal place in the sentence, usually as the appropriate pronoun. In the following sentence, *Jɔn* is the focus. That word is placed at the beginning of the sentence. The pronoun reference to him is *am*, the third-person, singular pronoun, which functions in this sentence as the direct object of the verb, *lɛk*.

Jɔn, a nɔ lɛk am. [As for <u>John</u>, I don't like him.]

Other examples show the prevalence of this structure and the closest colloquial translations:

1. *Mi, a nɔ go tɛl am.* [I'm certainly not going to tell her.]
2. *Da uman de, i nɔ go tif natin.* [That woman wouldn't steal anything.]
3. *Modupɛ, in na gud-gud pɔsin.* [Now, Modupe is a very good person.]
4. *Dis mɔtoka ya, i nɔ de rɔn bɛte.* [This car just doesn't run very well.]
5. *Joseph Sekou, in na di bɛs ticha pas ɔl.* [Joseph Sekou is the very best teacher.]

Full Sentence Themes in Krio Discourse

An entire sentence or an extensive proposition can be the focal point in Krio. The entire thematic proposition/sentence is stated first, followed by the main sentence containing *na/nɔto* and the reference to the thematic proposition. The pattern for this kind of emphasis looks like this:

Sentence. + na/nɔto-Main Sentence.

A few examples reveal this complex discourse device:

1. *ɔltɛm Tunde de ambɔg pɔsin. Na in a nɔ lɛk.* [Tunde is always harassing people. That is what I don't like.]
2. *i nɔ tɔk fayn to mi wɛf. Na dat bin mek a vɛks.* [He didn't talk nice to my wife. That is what made me angry.]
3. *Mi bed de na mi rum. Na de a de kam ledɔm.* [My bed is in my room. That is where I am getting ready to lay down/go to sleep.]

The Interplay of Focus, Emphasis, and Contrast

All of the various devices discussed in the sections above can be used in conjunction with each other to create colorful, dynamic pictures in the everyday language of Krio speakers and in the cultural narratives and stories passed

96   *Chapter 4*

on from one generation to another. Here are only slices of the ways in which this occurs:

1. *Mɔnki, na in lan lɛpɛt fɔ jomp.* [The monkey is the one that taught the leopard how to jump.]
2. *Na arata im mɔt, na in sɛl im ed.* [What comes out of rat's mouth is what gets him into trouble.] (Krio Proverb)
3. *Na ramship, na in du mi so.* [It is the Ram that did this to me.]
4. *Dɛm big-big man dɛm na tɔn, na dɛm bin tif mi kɔpɔ.* [Those powerful men in town, they are the ones who stole my money.]

MORE ON TENSE/ASPECT AND COMMANDS

In chapter 3, we introduced the reader to the ways in which Krio speakers represent the concepts of "Present," "Present Progressive," "Past," "Future," "Habitual," and "Completed" action in the Verb Phrase. Indo-European languages typically express such concepts with *suffixes* attached to the end of the verb, *variant forms of the verb root, auxiliary verbs* that precede the verb, *or some combination of these.* By contrast, there are Four Basic Principles that govern the use of tense/aspect concepts in Krio:

1. Krio Verb forms remain constant, regardless of the Tense/Aspect or the Subject NP.
2. All Tense/Aspect markers in Krio are positioned in front of the verb they effect.
3. The form of Krio Tense/Aspect Markers themselves remain constant.
4. Krio Tense/Aspect Markers consistently represent the same meaning.

Tense/Aspect Concepts Expressed with Multiple Markers

Krio possesses the mechanisms to express the full range of Tenses and Aspects found in most other languages. Some of them use a single marker, as we described in chapter 3, while others use multiple markers. Below is a delineation of the tense/aspect concepts in Krio that employ two or more markers in combination, along with sentences that demonstrate their use:

go dɔn [L-H] Future Completive

1. *Dɛm go dɔn kuk wɛn yu rich ya.* [They will have finished cooking by the time you arrive.

Complex Sentences Structures

2. *Deji go dɔn bay os bifo i dɔn rich tati yia.* [Deji will have bought a house before he is 30 years old.]
3. *Modupe go dɔn bil im os bay nɛks yia.* [Modupe will have built his house by next year.]

bin de [L-L] Past Continuous
1. *Dɛm bin de kuk got wɛn yu rich de.* [They were cooking goat when you arrived.]
2. *Di gyal pikin dɛm bin de sing na dɛm papa im chɔch.* [The young girls were singing in their father's church.]
3. *Wan makit uman bin de sɛl kuta.* [One market woman was selling barracuda.]

go de [L-L] Future Continuous
1. *Dɛm go de kuk na di awujɔ.* [They will be cooking at the funeral ceremony.]
2. *Di bɔy pikin dɛm go de ple futbɔl.* [The young boys will be playing soccer.]
3. *Di ticha dɛm go de lan di pikin dɛm aw fɔ rayt.* [The teachers will be teaching the children how to write.]

bin dɔn [L-H] Past Completive
1. *Dɛm bin dɔn kuk bay di tɛm we yu rich de.* [They had prepared the meal by the time you arrived.]
2. *A gladi we Joko bin dɔn bil im os bifo im wɛf bɔn dɛm pikin.* [I am happy that Joko finished building his house before his wife gave birth to their child.]
3. *Ada bin dɔn wɛr im klos bifo di bɔs kam.* [Ada had finished getting dressed before the bus came.]

fɔ [L] Obligative
1. *Wi fɔ kuk plasas tide.* [We should cook plasas today.]
2. *Una fɔ go naw.* [You all should go now.]
3. *Una fɔ it bifo di plasas kol.* [You all should eat before the plasas gets cold.]

bin fɔ [L-L] Past Obligative
1. *Wi bin fɔ kuk ɔlɛlɛ fɔ di trenja.* [We should have cooked a bean dish for the guest.]
2. *Wi bin fɔ go sidɔm saful.* [We should have sat there quietly.]
3. *Di ɔkɔ bin fɔ bay rɔm fɔ di bachilɔz iv fɔ mek di mared swit.* [The groom should have bought alcohol for the Bachelor's Eve to ensure a good marriage.]

98 *Chapter 4*

bin fɔ dɔn [L-L-H] Conditional
1. *Wi bin fɔ dɔn kuk Jɔlɔf rɛs, if wi bin dɔn no se yu go kam.* [We would have cooked Jolof Rice, if we had known you were going to come.]
2. *A bin fɔ dɔn bring mi kɔpɔ kam tide, if a bin no se di skul fi du tide.* [I would have brought my money today, if I had known the school fees were due today.]

Bin dɔn de [L-H-L] Past Perfect Continuous (somewhat archaic)
1. *i tɛl mi se Modu bin dɔn de kuk frɔm we chɔch kɔmɔt.* [He told me that Modu had been cooking since the church service ended.]
2. *ɔlamide bin dɔn de sik frɔm we i lili.* [Olamide had been sickly ever since she was a child.]

Bin fɔ de [L-L-L] Continuous Past Conditional (somewhat archaic)
1. *Yu bin fɔ de kuk wɛn wi bin go fɛn Sisi Kɔbɔla.* [You should have been cooking when we went to visit sister Kobola.]
2. *Udat bin fɔ de kuk da awa de?* [Who would have been cooking at that odd time?]
3. *Wi bin fɔ de kuk wɛn in bin de klin di abule.* [We should have been cooking when he was cleaning the hut.]

Bin fɔ dɔn de [L-L-H-L] Past Perfect Conditional (somewhat archaic)
1. *Yemi tu trangayes. i bin fɔ dɔn de kuk rɛs na di ayɛn pɔt.* [Yemi is very stubborn. She should have been cooking rice in the iron pot.]
2. *Joko bin fɔ dɔn de rid im buk dɛm, bɔt I dɔn let naw. Di tɛs na tumara.* [Joko should have been reading his books, but it's late now. The test is tomorrow.]

Commands

There are various ways to issue a command in Krio. The simplest way is to give a command to an individual is to state the verbal action desired with increased vocal intensity, like the following:

1. *Go!* or *Yu go!* [Go! Or Go away!] (the second-person, singular is usually implied.)
2. *Go kuk dɔn!* [Go finish cooking!]
3. *Kɔmɔt!* [Come out!]
4. *Kɔmɔt na ya!* [Get out of here!]
5. *Kɔmɔt de!* [Come out of there!]
6. *Kɛr da pɔt de go gi Pa Jɔnsin!* [Take that pot to Mr. Johnson!]
7. *Go bruk yu klos dɛm!* [Go wash your clothes!]

Complex Sentences Structures 99

If the target of the command is *plural*, the second-person plural pronoun is required in the subject position:

1. *Una go!* [You all, go!]
2. *Una kɔmɔt!* [You all get out of here!]
3. *Una kɛr da pɔt de go gi Pa Jɔnsin.* [You all take that pot to Mr. Johnson!]

Polite Commands or Appeals

There are various ways of making one's command more polite, softer, or more respectful, especially among peers. See the following options with their subtleties:

1. *Duya, go nɔ!* [Please go!]
2. *Mek yu go nɔ!* [Get on your way, okay!]
3. *Mek wi go nɔ!* [Let's go, okay!]
4. *Lɛ wi go nɔ!* [Let's go, alright.]

Common Expressions

1. *Mi ed de at.* [I have a headache.]
2. *Mi at pwɛl.* [I am very sad/upset/disappointed.]
3. *Mi at tek am.* [I have become very fond of him/her.]
4. *A dɔn bɛl ful.* [I am full/have eaten too much.]

PROVERB

ɔkrɔ nɔba langa pas im masta.
Literal Translation: [Okra never grows taller past its master.]
Broader Meaning: [Children are never out of the control of their parents.] or [Parents should always be able to manage their children.]

CONJUNCTIONS, RELATIVE CLAUSES, INFINITIVE CLAUSES, AND FOCUS

Complex sentences involve the combination or integration of multiple thoughts, or sentences, into one sentence. Krio uses a variety of devices (or structures) for producing complex sentences. The four most commonly occurring complex structures in Krio are formed using:

100   *Chapter 4*

- Conjunctions
- Infinitive Clauses
- Relative Clauses
- Focus Constructions

Sentences with Conjunctions

Two or more simple sentences can be combined using a class of words called conjunctions, *ɛn* [and], *ɔ* [or], *bɔt* but], *bikɔs* [because], or *fɔseka* [because of]. A simple way to show the combination of two (or more) sentences using conjunctions is the following:

Sentence 1 + Conjunction + Sentence 2

Examples of conjoined sentences in Krio are the following:

1. *Kwesi bin kik di bɔl ɛn Ayɔdele bin kech am.* [Kwesi kicked the ball and Ayɔdele caught it.]
2. *Joko go go na makit ɔ im sista go vɛks pan am.* [Joko will go to the market or his sister will be upset with him.]
3. *Fatu dɔn kuk dɔn, bɔt Omeka nɔ bigin kuk yet.* [Fatu has finished cooking, but Omeka has not begun cooking yet.]
4. *Sam nɔ de ple futbɔl wit im brɔda bikɔs i nɔ kɔmɔt skul yet.* [Sam is not playing soccer with his brother because he is still in school.]
5. *Wi nɔ bin go Bo tide fɔseka we mi papa nɔ bin wɛl.* [We didn't go to Bo today due to the fact that my dad has been sick.]

Sentences with Infinitive Clauses

Another kind of complex sentence involves the collaboration between two sentences. The first of those sentences is formed like any other simple sentence. In the second sentence, the Subject NP is understood to be the same as the Subject NP of the first sentence, and, therefore does not need to be repeated. What remains of the second sentence is the Verb Phrase, which is preceded by the Infinitive Maker, *fɔ* [to]. This infinitive and the verbal action that follows usually denotes the 'purpose' for the action expressed in the primary sentence. The chart that represents this structure would look something like figure 4.2:

The sentence generated by this construction appears below:

A bin go na makit fɔ bay plantin. [I went to the market to buy plantain.]

Complex Sentences Structures

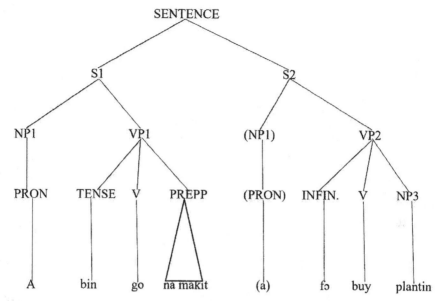

Figure 4.2. Complex Sentence with Infinitive Clause.

Note, again, that the subject is *not* repeated in the second sentence, because the underlying subject in the second sentence is the same as the subject in the initial sentence. In fact, the infinitive connector alleviates the need for a tense/aspect marker.

A few more examples reveal the productivity of this construction:

1. *Sam bin want fɔ drayv im papa im mɔtoka.* [Sam wanted to drive his father's car.]
2. *Eugenia go tray fɔ fɛn banana print klos fɔ im padi.* [Eugenia will try to find a banana print fabric for her friend.]
3. *Di bɔbɔ de rɔn kwiki-kwik fɔ kech di fɔl.* [The boy is running fast to catch the chicken.]

The following two sentences demonstrate that the Subject NP of S2 can be identical to the Direct Object NP in S1. In such cases, the Infinitive Connector makes it unnecessary to repeat that NP in S2. See the examples below:

1. *Modupɛ bin lan im brɔda fɔ rid buk.* [Modupe taught his brother to read.]
   (derived from: *Modupɛ bin lan im brɔda* + (im brɔda) fɔ rid buk.)
2. *Tɔm go kɛr im mama go na makit fɔ go bay pamayn ɛn ɔg fut.* [Tom is going to take his mother to the market to buy palm oil and pig foot.]
   (derived from: *Tɔm go kɛr im mama go makit* + (*im mama*) *go bay pamayn ɛn ɔg fut.*)

102 *Chapter 4*

Sentences with Relative Clauses

Relative clauses further describe or more specifically define a Noun Phrase in a sentence. In their underlying structure, relative clauses are full sentences that contain a Noun Phrase which is identical to a Noun Phrase in the dominant sentence. The Noun Phrase that is being further described by the relative clause can be the Subject, Direct Object, or the Object of a Prepositional Phrase. Rather than adding two or more sentences together, one after another, the Relative Clause sentence is attached to the Noun Phrase in the dominant sentence. On the surface, the identical Noun Phrase in the relative clause is replaced by the word *we* [who, which, or that] at the beginning of the relative clause. One example of a complex sentence that contains a relative clause is the following:

Di ol man we a bin si na di makit dis mɔnin ya de tɔk to Pa Smit.
[The old man who I saw in the market this morning is talking to Mr. Smith.]

Di ol man is the subject of the complex sentence. *We a bin si na di makit dis mɔnin ya* is the relative clause that is inserted into the sentence immediately after the subject to further describe *di ol man*. It answers the question: "What old man are you referring to?"

The remainder of the sentence, *de tɔk to Pa Smit*, is the Verb Phrase of the dominant sentence, indicating what the primary subject is doing.

In other words, the two sentences that have been fused together to create a complex sentence are the following (fig. 4.3):

1. *Di ol man de tɔk to Pa Smit.* +
2. *A bin si di ol man na di makit dis mɔnin ya.*

Notice that one of the characteristics of complex sentences is that there are frequently words in the primary sentence (the independent clause) that do not appear in the secondary sentences (subordinate clauses). We can say that a relative clause is a vehicle for compressing more information into the independent clause without having to use a whole sentence. You saw that in the example above and will see it in the sentences below:

Di bɔbɔ we bin sɛn di ton na mi brɔda.
[The boy who threw the stone is my brother.]

This sentence is comprised of two sentences in which *di bɔbɔ* is the subject NP of both.

Complex Sentences Structures

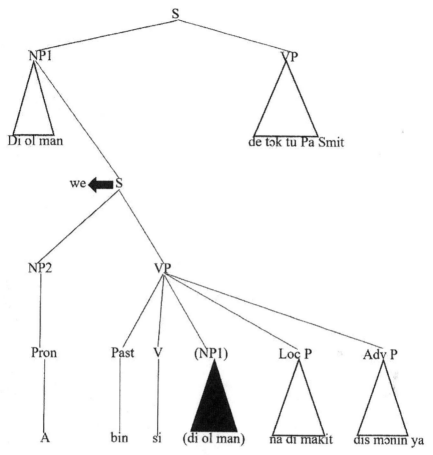

Figure 4.3. Underlying Structure of Relative Clause.

1. *Di bɔbɔ na mi brɔda.* [The boy is my brother.]
2. *Di bɔbɔ bin ib di ton.* [The boy threw the stone.]

A few more examples of complex sentences with relative clauses in Krio will demonstrate how common these sentences are in the Krio community:

1. *Da titi de na di gyal we Joko lɛk.* [That girl is the one who Joko likes.]
2. *Anti Sera na di uman we kin sɛl bonga na King Jimi Makit.* [Auntie Sarah is the woman who usually sells bonga fish at King Jimmy Market.]
3. *Da mared we go swit, na di bachɛlɔz iv yu go si am.* [A marriage which is going to go well can be witnessed on the bachelor's eve.] (Krio parable)
4. *Di it we wi bin it bin swit-o!* [The food that we ate was delicious]

104   *Chapter 4*

5. *Di uman dɛm we wɛr ashɔbi de go na di awujɔ.* [The women wearing the same outfits are going to the celebration.]

Placing Full Sentence in Focus

In Krio, it is possible to focus on an entire sentence proposition by moving it to the front of a sentence and marking it as the focused object of the sentence, using the Emphatic Marker. An example of this can be seen in the sentence below:

Di man nɔ trit im pikin fayn, na in a nɔ lɛk.
[The fact that the man does not treat his child well is what I don't like.]
(Literal: The man NEG treat his child well, it-is it I NEG like.)

This kind of focus sentence is similar to the pattern described in this chapter, which introduced the concept of "thematic sentences." In that instance, the focus was on *one Noun or Noun Phrase*, as in the sentences below:

1. *Jɔn, a nɔ lɛk am.* [John, I don't like.]
2. *Modupe, in na gud-gud pɔsin.* [Modupe, he is a very good person.]

Now we see that a *full sentence*, or proposition, *can be the focus* of another sentence. Further examples of full sentences being the focused items appear below:

1. *Tifman* dɛm bɔku-bɔku na tɔn, na in mek a nɔ lɛk fɔ go de.
   (literally: Thief PLUR many in town, it-is it cause I NEG like INFIN go there.)
   A freer translation is: [*There are too many thieves in town, that is why I don't like to go there.*]
2. *Uman dɛm kin lɛk man we gɛt mɔtoka, na in mek a go bay nyu mɔtoka.*
   (literally: Woman PLUR HAB like man who has car, it-is it cause I go buy new car.)
   A freer translation is: [It is because women like men who have cars that I am going to buy a new car.]

Complexity Compounded

In the real world, Krio speakers combine not only simple sentences with complex sentences, they also combine conjunctions, infinitive clauses, relative clauses, and focus constructions all in the same sentence. Just a few sentences

Complex Sentences Structures   105

demonstrate the capacity of Krio to combine these various structures to communicate with each other on a regular basis:

1. *Di fishaman dεm we de na Godrich Village kin kech big-big fish εn kεr dεm go na makit fɔ sεl.* [Fishermen in Goderich Village catch large fish and take them to the market to sell.]
2. *A de drayv go na da say de we mi mama bin bɔn mi fɔ go luk mi ɔnkul we nɔ wεl.* [I am driving to that area where I was born to look after my uncle who is not feeling well.]
3. *Wεn lεpet si se Bra fɔl de tray fɔ kil am, na in mek lεpet jomp pan am fɔ mek i nɔ ebul fɔ rɔn.* [When Leopard figured out that Chicken was trying to kill him, that made Leopard jump on Chicken so he couldn't run away.]

Sentences like these, and those that are even more textured and colorful, can be heard in everyday speech of Krio speakers and will be seen in the stories, proverbs, and poems presented in later chapters.

DUPLICATION

Every language uses various devices to accomplish the task of communicating ideas as clearly as possible. Krio, like all African languages, uses Duplication effectively to achieve a number of different purposes. In the following pages, the reader will come to appreciate how fundamental duplication is in Krio. Duplication is the practice of repeating the same word or syllable two or more times one right after the other.

Intensification of an Adjective or Adverb

In some languages, intensification of an adjective or adverb is accomplished by using a word which essentially means "very." The examples below show how duplication in Krio can carry this function:

1a. *Di bɔbɔ bin de rɔn kwik.* [The boy was running fast.]
1b. *Di bɔbɔ bin de rɔn kwik-kwik.* [The boy was running very fast.]

2a. *Waka saful.* [Be careful.]
2b. *Waka saful-saful.* [Be very careful.]

106   *Chapter 4*

3a.   *Go tek yu brɔda na skul nɔw.* [Go and pick up your brother
      from school.]
3b.   *Go tek yu brɔda na skul nɔw-nɔw.* [Go pick up your brother from
      school, right this minute.]

4a.   *I gɛt bɔku pikin dɛm.* [He has a lot of children.]
4b.   *I gɛt bɔku-bɔku pikin dɛm.* [He has a whole bunch of kids.]

5a.   *In na big man na Fritɔn.* [He is a big/important man in Freetown.]
5b.   *In na big-big man na Fritɔn.* [He is one of the most powerful people
      in Freetown.'

6a.   *Im wɛf wɛr rɛd klos fɔ go di pati.* [His wife wore a red dress to
      the party.]
6b.   *Im wɛf wɛr rɛd-rɛd klos fɔ go di pati.* [His wife wore a bright red
      dress to the party.]

Changing from One Word Class to Another

Another productive process in Krio is using duplication to change a word
from one word class to another. Frequently the duplication of a verb will
result in the creation of a noun or an adjective with characteristics similar to
the word of origin. While one cannot simply duplicate every verb in Krio to
create another word, the pattern is regular enough to note it here. The following examples demonstrate this phenomenon:

1a.   *Modu de cham im it.* [Modupe is chewing his dinner.]
1b.   *Modu de it im cham-cham.* [Modupe is eating his snacks.]

2a.   *Onikɛ bin chɛr im trɔsis.* [Onike tore his pants.]
2b.   *Onike nɔ gri fɔ wɛr di chɛr-chɛr klos.* [Onike refused to wear the tat-
      tered clothes.]

3a.   *Abi im sista tek nɛf kɔt di klos.* [Abby's sister cut the cloth
      with a knife.]
3b.   *Mama Tunde bin kɔt-kɔt di yabas.* [Mama Tunde diced the onion.]

4a.   *Olu bin aks im padi fɔ krach im bak.* [Olu asked his friend to scratch
      his back.]
4b.   *Di begaman gɛt krach-krach na im fut.* [The begger has skin disease
      on his foot.]

5a. *ɔl man bin want fɔ go na Lɔmli Bich.* [Everybody wanted to go to Lumley Beach.]

5b. *Da bɔbɔ we sidɔn de, i tu want-want.* [That boy sitting there is very greedy.]

6a. *Pa Dɛka sabi mek motoka.* [Mr. Decker knows how to build cars.]

6b. *Bayo na mek-mek pɔsin.* [Bayo is a pretentious person.]

7a. *Sam dɔn brok im mama im fayn chia.* [Sam has broken his mother's beautiful chair.]

7b. *Da wan de na broko-broko os.* [That's a dilapidated house.]

8a. *Olu de pach im trɔsis.* [Olu is patching his pants.]

8b. *Dis wan ya na pach-pach motoka.* [This is a makeshift car.]

9a. *Bo, duya, mek a pas.* [Excuse me, please let me get by.]

9b. *A tink se Fumikɛ tu pas-pas.* [I think Fumike is very promiscuous.]

10a. *Ade dɔn drɔnk.* [Ade is drunk.]

10b. *Im papa na drɔnkɔ-drɔnkɔ.* [His father is an alcoholic.]

11a. *A gɛt wan pikin nɔmɔ.* [I only have one child.]

11b. *A go gi pɛnsul dɛm tu di pikin dɛm wan-wan.* [I will give the children one pencil each.]

Duplication in Ideophones

Ideophones are words that arise in languages, usually as very culture-specific terms, even though they are very often meant to represent the sounds made by a specific thing (e.g. animal, machine, human function, or natural phenomena). One would expect that a speaker of English and a speaker of Yoruba, for instance, would both hear the sound made by chickens the same and would represent that sound with similar sounds in their respective languages. However, the verbal representations of commonly recognized sounds rarely are similar in different languages. And, if languages cannot agree on sounds that you would think they would hear the same, there is little likelihood that they could agree on how to represent a more abstract concept like the level of fullness of bottle of liquid. The exception to this is, of course, in those instances where one language has borrowed the representation directly from another language.

Examples of ideophones that contain only *one syllable* are the following:

108   *Chapter 4*

1. *tek di bia ful the kɔp <u>pim</u>.* [He filled the cup right up *to the brim* with beer.]
2. *Di got nak am na im ed <u>bap</u>.* [The goat butted him on the head, *BAP!*]

Other Krio ideophones are *multi-syllable and duplicative*:

1. *Di got kam, <u>bɔkita-bɔkita-bɔkita</u>.* [The goat came with *hooves pounding on the ground.*]
2. *I cham di kaw bif, <u>krawn-krawn</u>.* [She chewed the beef *with a grisly sound.*]
3. *Wɛn di chɔch kech faya, the pipul dɛm bigin rɔn <u>kitikata-kitikata</u>.* [When the church caught fire, the people ran *helter-skelter.*]

Duplication of Yoruba Origin

There are a significant number of words in Krio that have come into the language from Yoruba, spoken in western Nigeria. It is well documented that nearly two-thirds of the African peoples in the Freetown Colony in 1848 were native Yoruba speakers. So, it is not only reasonable to assume, but also expected, that the Yoruba language would have a profound effect on the Krio Language that was still in its formative stage. The duplicative words identified below are but a few of the many words of Yoruba origin in Krio.

1. *Kalakala* [weak, incompetent, ineffective]
2. *Pɔtɔpɔtɔ* [muddy (road)]
3. *Gɛdɛgɛdɛ* [dregs, sediments]
4. *Fukfuk* as in *fukfuk de bwɛl.* [person getting angry.]
5. *Kpatakpata* [finish or destroy something completely]
6. *Kotokoto* [rocky road]

Much more information about the influence of Yoruba, and other African languages, on Krio will be described in chapter 5.

NOTE

1. Clifford N. Fyle and Eldred D. Jones, *A Krio-English Dictionary* (Oxford: Oxford University Press, in collaboration with the Sierra Leone University Press, 1980), xxiv.

Chapter 5

African Linguistic Foundations in Krio and the Diaspora

In chapter 1, we demonstrated a number of ways in which Sierra Leone Krio language differs from English, the language of the colonial government during the founding of the country. In spite of the claim made by Clifford N. Fyle and Eldred D. Jones's *A Krio-English Dictionary*, that eighty percentage or more of the vocabulary is derived from English, the actual phonological, grammatical, and semantic systems of Krio more closely resemble West African language systems.[1] This has led us to theorize that Krio has an underlying Kwa Language Family substratum overlaid with a veneer of English words. In this chapter, we will provide more extensive evidence to support our claim. More precisely, we will demonstrate that Yoruba has had a dominant, but not exclusive, influence on what became Sierra Leone Krio. These Yoruba features were reinforced very often by consistent or similar patterns, structures, or semantic concepts from other Kwa languages or proximate Sierra Leone languages. In most cases, what was adopted by those who would become native Krio speakers, was adopted in simplified form.

ENGLISH LEXICAL CONTRIBUTIONS TO KRIO

To begin, we will revisit the questions revolving around the massive borrowing of English words into Krio. Were they borrowed wholesale? If not, how do they differ from the English source language? What explains why they function the way they do? If the adopted forms are simplified, in what way(s) are they simplified?

In chapter 1, we observed that even simple English words, like "take" and "come" function differently in Krio than they do in English. While the English word "take" is pronounced the same in Krio, phonetically [tek], it means "take hold/possession of" and does not include the elements of

109

110   *Chapter 5*

"movement" or "directionality" that are inherent in the English word. In addition, a reasonable translation of a sentence like "Take this food to your father" in Krio requires the use of a serial verb construction, which provides the "movement" and "directionality" that is absent in the Krio word [tek].

The English word, "come," when adopted by Krio speakers, is pronounced [kam], not [kəm], as it is in English. We also learned that, while [kam] can appear in some Krio sentences with essentially the same meaning found in English (for example: *Di bɔbɔ go kam.* [The boy will come.]), it also appears in sentences that are totally foreign to English:

1. *A de kam go.* [I am getting ready to go.]
2. *Go kam-o.* [Go in peace, until we meet again.]

So, these examples clearly demonstrate that English words were not adopted into Krio wholesale, but rather were inserted into a lexicon with its own semantic and grammatical features and restrictions.

A number of Krio words that are derived from English are used in idiomatic expressions that do not exist in English. The following example demonstrates this phenomenon:

Di man gɛt swit mɔt.
(Literal: The man has sweet mouth)

Interestingly, this idiomatic expression appears in a number of the African languages that contributed to the formation of Krio. Table 5.1 reveals the same expression in three African languages.

Examples of other expressions that contain words which are clearly derived from English, but carry very different meaning are the following:

do mɔt [entry way] (literal: door-mouth)
do klin [dawn, sunrise] (literal: door clean)
di bɔbɔ gɛt na an. [The boy misbehaves/is unruly] (literal: The boy has LOC hand.)
tranga yes [stubborn, hard-headed] (literal: strong ears)
blo lilibit [rest, catch a breath] (literal: blow a little)

Table 5.1   Commonality of 'sweet mouth' in Three African Languages

Language	Expression	Translation	Literal Meaning
Yoruba	*ɛnu didu*	[persuasive]	mouth-sweet
Ga	*na mo*	[flattery]	sweet mouth
Twi	*ano yɛdɛ*	[flattery]	mouth sweet

an [area from fingers to elbow] (literal: hand)
fut [area from toes to knee] (Literal: foot)

Examples like these lend further credence to the claim that there is a non-English substratum that exists in Krio and provides the framework into which English words were inserted.

AFRICAN LEXICAL CONTRIBUTIONS TO KRIO

The adoption of words from African languages into Krio, as it was developing, was quite different from the adoption of English words into Krio. As Gibril R. Cole points out, "Jones draws attention to the fact that little or no phonetic changes occurred in the transfer of loanwords from African languages to Krio."[2] This was the case, whether the word was of Yoruba, Igbo, Akan origin, or words from one of the languages indigenous to Sierra Leone. Given the impactful history of the Yoruba who settled in Sierra Leone, it is not surprising to find Yoruba words in Krio in a variety of areas associated with religious and ceremonial events, Islamic practices and traditions, the hunting societies, or traditional Yoruba clothing or Yoruba dishes. However, what we find is that Yoruba words and expressions can be found throughout Krio language, indicating the Yoruba influence in almost every aspect of Krio life. Listed below are just a sample of the areas in which Yoruba words are found in everyday Krio speech:

Personal names: *Amina, Adedeji, ɔlabisi, Fumilayo*)
Weather: *agbara* [torrential rain stream]
Sections of a house/building: *aja* [rafters, attic]
Personal character traits: *aroana* [good for nothing]
Condition of the road: *kotokoto* [rough/rocky road]
Cooking utensils: *igbakɔ* [wooden ladle]
Wedding partners: *yawo ɛn ɔkɔ* [bride and groom]
Geology: *akpata* [flat stone usually found near rivers/streams]
Parts of the body: *kpakɔ* [occiput]

According to Cole, loanwords from Mende and Temne, as representatives of local indigenous cultural groups, "include plant names, animal and bird names, and words for cooking utensils, as well as more abstract nouns."[3] It makes perfect sense that the speakers of local languages would have been the ones to contribute the names of animals, plants, and terrain native to their homelands as well as anything associated with them, such as dishes prepared

112

Chapter 5

using them as ingredients. A couple of the nouns identified by Cole that fall outside of those parameters are the following:

kombra [A suckling mother] (source: Temne *kom'*ra)
mum [mute] (source: Mende *mumu*)[4]

Examples of loan words from Mende and Temne retrieved from Fyle and Jones' *Dictionary* reflect an even larger variety of borrowings from those two important local languages:

Mende
blay [round cane basket] (source: *bla*)
bonga [small fish] (source: *bonga*)
bondo [tribal society initiation for girls] (source: *bundu*)
bomboli [kind of ant] (source: *mbomboli*)
bumbu [lift, carry] (source: *mbumbu*)

Temne
awɛfu [half-grown bonga fish] (source: *wɛfu*)
baranta [rebel] (verb) (source: *gbaranta*)
bosbos [trouble, disaster] (source: *gbosgbos*)
bulukɔ [sesamum radiatum tree] (source: *kɔ-bulɔkɔ*)
bunya [little gift or something extra for a customer] (source: *bunya*)

Our close review of the Fyle and Jones' *Dictionary* revealed that many of the entries of African origin that have made their way into the Krio lexicon may have done so because they had multiple sources. Given our theory about the development of Krio, it logically follows that similar or identical words for the same concept from different languages would strengthen the adoptability of the word. We have seen no previous reference to this motivating factor anywhere in the literature on Krio or other creolized languages. This phenomenon deserves further research, but the display in table 5.2 lay the foundation for such research.

COMMON AFRICAN PHONOLOGICAL
PATTERNS AND CONSTRAINTS

Krio words follow a defined set of phonological patterns and constraints. Some of those patterns and constraints are commonly found in many, if not most, African languages. Some of those are identified on the next page.

African Linguistic Foundations in Krio and the Diaspora

Table 5.2 Multiple African Language Sources for Some Krio Words

Krio	Translation	Source Language	Source Word	Meanings
butu	Bend down, stoop	Twi	*butwu*	Turn over
		Ewe	*butu*	Turn upside down
fityay	Insult	Mende	*fityay*	Arrogance, pride
		Twi	*fite*	abuse
fufafu	In vain	Mende	*fufafu*	For nothing
		Mandinka	*fufafu*	For nothing
gbangbaode	Outside, open space	Yoruba	*gbangba-ode*	Wide open/public space
		Limba	*gbangala*	In an open manner
geleng	Ringing of bell	Temne	*a-gbeleng*	bell
		Mende	*gbeleng*	Sound of small bell
kotoku	Money pouch	Twi	*kotoku*	Pocket/pouch
		Ga	*kotoku*	Pocket/pouch

1. The vast majority of Krio words and morphemes follow a C-V-C-V pattern in words. This means that most words contain an alternating sequence of Consonants and Vowels. This is readily apparent in Krio and West African personal names (for example Ama, Deji, Ola, Aminatu, Dayo, Kofi, Modupe, Regina). This pattern is also found in common everyday words. Below are examples from Krio and Yoruba:

> Krio
> *ala* [holler, shout]
> *aja* [attic]
> *bitas* [bitter-leaf soup]
> *falamakata* [copy-cat]
> *bɔbɔ* [boy]
> *arata* [rat]
> *pɛpɛ* [hot pepper]
> *poda-poda* [transport van]
> *abule* [grass hut]
> *waka* [walk]
>
> Yoruba
> *abala* [rice pudding]
> *abata* [marsh, swamp]
> *agbada* [large gown for men]
> *buka* [market stall]
> *abere* [needle]

114   *Chapter 5*

> *ibosi* [cry for help]
> *alu* [fell onto]
> *dudu* [be a dark color]
> *gedɛgɛ* [liquid sediment]
> *alugba* [calabash drummers]
> (gb and kp represent a single sound, although written with two letters.)

2. Clusters of consonants are rarely found in West African languages. Thus, if an English word that contains a consonant cluster is incorporated into a West African language, the number of consonants in the cluster will be reduced, if the cluster is not eliminated. Here are a few examples of that phenomena in Krio:

> stick [stIk] is pronounced [tik] in Krio
> story [stori] is pronounced [tori] in Krio
> bend [bɛnd] is pronounced [bɛn] in Krio
> street [strit] is pronounced [trit] in Krio
> left [lɛft] is pronounced lɛf] in Krio

3. Many of the African languages spoken in the colony of Sierra Leone during the development of Krio are tone languages, including Yoruba, Akan, and Igbo. Thus, it is not surprising to find that tone is also distinctive in Krio, even in words derived from English. Krio has two distinctive tones, High and Low, while Yoruba, Akan, and Igbo all have three distinctive tones. Look at the examples from all four languages:

> Krio
> *Aja* (H-L) [person who has made the pilgrimage to Mecca]
> *aja* (L-H) [attic]
> *afbak* (H-L) [halfback in soccer]
> *afbak* (L-H) [slippers]
> *de* (L) [Present Progressive marker or there]
> *de* (H) [to be at, in location]
>
> *kɔntri* (H-L) [country]
> *kɔntri* (L-H) [countryman]
>
> Yoruba
> *ɔkɔ* (L-L) [spear]
> *ɔkɔ* (M-L) [vehicle]
>
> *bɛɛrɛ* (H-H-H) [type of grass]
> *bɛɛrɛ* (M-M-M) [extensively]

African Linguistic Foundations in Krio and the Diaspora 115

atɛ (M-H) [applause]
atɛ (L-H) [flavorless soup]

ɛwɛ ((L-H) [small particles]
ɛwɛ (L-L) [again]

ti (H) [who/which]
ti (M) [Past tense marker]

Igbo
akwa (H-H) [cry]
akwa (L-H) [egg]

isi (H-L) [smell]
isi (L-H) [to cook]

oke (H-H) [male]
oke (L-H) [rat/mouse]

mma (H-M) [good]
mma (H-L) [knife]

Twi (Akan)
papa (L-H) [father]
papa (L-L) [good]

Ama (M-H) [Girl's name]
ama (L-L) [so that]

kooko (H-H-H) [porridge]
kooko (L-L-H) [hemroid]

dada (H-H) [old]
dada (L-L) [already]

As one would expect, depending upon the tone of a tense/aspect marker in Twi, the meaning of a sentence can be altered significantly, as in the following examples:

Ama da ha. (M-H, H, M) [Ama sleeps here.] (indicating Habitual)
Ama da ha. (M-H, L, M) [Ama is sleeping here.] (indicating Present Progressive)

116   *Chapter 5*

EVIDENCE OF A KWA SUBSTRATUM
AT THE GRAMMATICAL LEVEL

Serial Verb Constructions in Krio, Yoruba, Igbo, Twi, and Akan

As we stated in chapter 1, some of the strongest evidence in support of an African substratum analysis comes from the Krio grammatical system. Serial verb constructions are one of those non-English constructions that stand out.

Serial Verb Constructions in Krio

As described in chapter 4, serial verb constructions can communicate a wide range of meanings that are communicated in English with only one verb. The full range of those meanings were represented in that chapter. The Krio sentence below employs two verbs (sɛn and go):

Dɛm bin sɛn di man go. [They sent the man away.] (Literal: They PAST send the man go.)

The next sentence uses four Krio verbs (*go, fes, kam,* and *gi*) to communicate the message communicated in English with one verb, "bring."

Go fes di fufu kam gi mi. [Bring me the fufu.] (Literal: go get the fufu come give me.)

Serial Verb Constructions in Yoruba

While serial verb constructions are virtually non-existent in English, the rare exception being a sentence like "Go get me something to write with," which is actually just an abbreviated form of "Go and get me something to write with," Yoruba is rich in serial verb constructions. Olasope O. Oyelaran demonstrates the complex array of Serial Verb constructions in Yoruba.[5] Just a few examples that he provides show the similarities between Krio and Yoruba with respect to this linguistic structure:

1. *O sɔrɔ tan.* [He has stopped talking.] (Literal: He talk stop)
2. *Oniwaasu su ire fun wa.* [The preacher gave us a blessing.] (Literal: preacher say blessing give us.)
3. *O ba ɛnu ɔna wo ile.* [He entered the house through the door.] (He use mouth way enter house.)

Serial Verb Constructions in Igbo, Twi, and Akan

It is to be expected, based on the fact that Yoruba is a member of the Kwa Language Family, that we would also find serial verb constructions in other Kwa languages. A few examples of this are presented here:

Igbo
1. *O ji mma bee anu.* [He cut the meat with a knife.] (Literal: He hold knife cut meat.)
2. *O zuru akwukwo nye m.* [She bought a book for me.] (Literal: S/he buy book give me.)
3. *Ada na-ebu nku aga ahia.* [Ada is carrying firewood to the market.] (Literal: Ada PROG-carry firewood go market.)
4. *Ada mere di ya aruo ulo.* [Ada made her husband build a house.] (Literal: Ada cause husband her build house.)
5. *O were ukwu gaa ahia.* [S/he went to the market on foot.] (Literal: S/he take leg go market.)

Twi
1. *ɔ yɛ adwuma ma me.* [He works for me.] (Literal: He does work give me.)
2. *Tɛtɛ baahe wolo yɛ Osu.* [Tete will buy a book at/in Osu.] (Literal: Tɛtɛ FUT-buy book be-at Osu.)

Akan
1. *Kofi de burrow gun sum.* [Kofi pours corn into the water.] (Kofi take corn flows water-in.)

Although serial verb constructions do not appear in English, they do appear in other languages, notably Chinese. However, what is being argued here is not that Kwa languages are the only languages that contain serial verb constructions, but rather that, because of the known history of contact between speakers of Kwa languages and speakers of English during the development of Krio, Kwa languages are the most plausible source of serial verb constructions in Krio. The fact that serial verb constructions in Krio do not contain words from Kwa languages, but English derived words instead, provides evidence that it is the Kwa grammatical structures that form the grammatical substratum of Krio. Kwa is the framework into which English words are inserted. This makes logical sense, since what children learn in interactive, multilingual communities is language patterns. This is true at the phonological, grammatical, and semantic levels.

118   *Chapter 5*

Pre-Verbal Tense/Aspect Markers in Krio, Yoruba, and Igbo

In chapter 1 we introduced the reader to the differences between the way Krio renders concepts of Tense and Aspect. We expanded upon this system in chapters 2 through 4. We noted how distinct the Krio system of Tense/Aspect markers is from the way English handles these concepts. In the following pages, we will demonstrate how similar the Krio examples are to the following Pre-Verbal Tense/Aspect Markers from African languages that are known to have played prominent roles during the Kriolizing period in Sierra Leone.

Tense/Aspect Markers in Yoruba

Present Progressive is indicated by the preverbal marker, *n,* in Yoruba. See the following examples:

Present Progressive, *n*
1. *Olu n jɛun.* [Olu is eating.] (Literal: Olu PRES. PROGR. eat.)
2. *Mo n lɔ.* [I am going.] (Literal: I PRES. PROGR. go.)
3. *Ade n san.* [Ade is sleeping.] (Literal: Ade PRES.PROGR sleep)
4. *ɛyin n jɛ ɛyin* [You all are eating eggs.] (Literal: You-Pl PRES.PROGR eat egg)

Future Tense/Habitual Aspect, *maa*
The marker, *maa,* indicates either Future Tense or Habitual Aspect, as reflected in the sentences below:
1. *Mo maa jɛun.* [I will eat.] (Literal: I FUTURE eat.)
2. *Iwɔ maa lɔ.* [You will go.] (Literal: You FUTURE go.)
3. *Awa maa fɔ ashɔ.* [We will wash clothes.] (Literal: We FUTURE wash clothes.)
4. *A maa si i.* [We will open it.] (Literal: We FUTURE open it.)

Past Tense, *ti*
Just as the other tense/aspect markers above perform in Yoruba, so too does the Past Tense marker, ti:
1. *Mo ti ri ɛ.* [I saw you.] (Literal: I PAST see you.)
2. *O ti ka iwe.* [He read a book.] (Literal: He PAST read book.)
3. *ɛyin ti sise nibi.* [You all worked here.] (Literal: You-PLUR PAST work here.)

African Linguistic Foundations in Krio and the Diaspora 119

Tense/Aspect in Igbo

The literature on Igbo Language refers to the linguistic components that relay tense and aspect as "auxiliary verbs."[6] However, they behave very similar to the pre-verbal tense/aspect markers described in Krio and Yoruba. We believe the difference in terminology (that is, "auxiliary verb" vs. "Tense/Aspect Marker"), along with the Igbo writing convention that separates the "auxiliary verb" from the main verb by a hyphen, masks the remarkable similarities. The examples provided in the next few pages reveal the similarities between tense and aspect in Igbo and those in Krio and Yoruba:

Present Progressive, *na*
1. *ɛze na-abia.* [Eze is coming.] (Literal: Eze PRES.PROGR-come.)
2. *ɔ na-abia.* [He/she is coming.] (Literal: He/she PRES.PROGR–come.)
3. *Unu na-agba ɔsɔ.* [You all are running.] (You-Pl PRES.PROGR-run.)
4. *ɔ na-agu akwukwɔ.* [He/she is reading a book.] (Literal: He/she PRES.PROGR-read book.)

Future Tense, *ga*
1. *ɔ ga azuta anu.* [He/she will buy meat.] (Literal: He/she FUTURE buy meat.)
2. *Ha ga asu akwa.* [They will wash clothes.] (Literal: They FUTURE wash clothes.)
3. *I ga aga ahia.* [You will go to the market.] (Literal: You-Sing. FUTURE go market.)

Further support for considering these Igbo "auxiliary verbs" to be Pre-verbal Tense/Aspect Markers is the fact that, in at least one case, the *Future Progressive*, where the auxiliaries remain constant and appear in the same word order as the corresponding markers do in Krio. While some morphemes in Igbo are sensitive to vowel harmony, based on the word that follows them, that is not the case with Future Progressive. The Future indicator, *ga*, comes first, followed by the Progressive Aspect indicator, *na*, before the main verb. Observe this phenomenon below:

Igbo—Future Progressive [ga + na] in First Person Pl. and Third Person Singular
1. *Anyi ga na-ere ahia.* [We will keep selling.] (Literal: We FUT. PROGRES.-sell.)
2. *Ha ga na-agu akwukwɔ.* [They will keep reading.] (Literal: They FUT. PROGRES.-read.)

120   *Chapter 5*

3. *ɔ ga na-abia.* [He/she will keep coming.] (Literal: He/she FUT.
   PROGRES.-come.)
4. *ɛze ga na-aru oru.* [Eze will continue working.] (Literal: Eze FUT.
   PROGRES.-work.)

These examples of Future Progressive in Igbo demonstrate that, at least in
relation to First Person Plural and Third Person Singular, there are remarkable
similarities with Krio. Look at these Krio examples:

1. *Modupɛ go de sɛl plantin.* [Modupe will be selling plantains.]
   (Literal: Modupe FUT. PROG sell plantain.)
2. *Di titi go de rid buk.* [The girl will be reading a book.] (Literal: The <u>girl</u>
   <u>FUT. PROG</u> read book.)

This is strong evidence to support the claim not only that Igbo, like Krio
and Yoruba, communicates a number of its Tense/Aspects concepts via
immutable pre-verbal markers, but also that those pre-verbal tense/aspect
markers can be used, in prescribed combinations and order, to communicate
complex notions, like "Future Progressive." The fact that not all notions of
tense/aspect in Igbo are communicated with pre-verbal markers does not
diminish the apparent historical and contemporary relationship between Krio,
Yoruba, and Igbo.

Zero Tense/Aspect Marker

Given the regular appearance of Tense/Aspect Markers in Krio, one would
think that a tangible, observable marker had to be present in every sentence.
However, some sentences have no visible pre-verbal marker. The meaning
that is communicated in such cases is just as revealing as the visible markers.
In fact, the following examples show that the absence of a visible marker, or
a ZERO marker, communicates Simple Present or Simple Past:

1. *Di bɔbɔ dɛm ZERO go na di makit.* [The boys go to the market.] OR [The
   boys went to the market.] (Literal: The boy-PL go LOC the market.)
2. *Ayɔ ZERO mɛmba di pikin im nɛm.* [Ayo remembers the child's name.]
   OR [Ayo remembered the child's name.] (Literal: Ayo remember the
   child POSS name.]

If these structures are truly part of an underlying Kwa substratum, we
would expect to find the same or similar phenomena in known Kwa languages. And that is exactly what we found. Another look at Yoruba reveals

African Linguistic Foundations in Krio and the Diaspora

that the Zero Marker, in the context of Action Verbs communicates Simple Past, like the following sentences:

1. *Mo* ZERO *jeun*. [I ate.] (Literal: I eat.)
2. *Mo* ZERO *ra*. [I bought.] Literal: (I buy.)
3. *O* ZERO *fɔ ashɔ*. [He washed clothes.] (Literal: He wash clothes.)
4. *Wɔn* ZERO *jo*. [They danced.] (Liberal: They dance.)

In the context of non-action verbs, Zero Marker communicates either Present or Past. See these examples below:

1. *Mo* ZERO *mɔ*. [I know/I knew.] (Literal: I know.)
2. *O* ZERO *gba*. [You agree/You agreed.] (Literal: You agree.)
3. *Wɔn* ZERO *ri*. [They see/They saw.] (Literal: They see.)
4. *A* ZERO *fɛ*. [We want/We wanted.] (Literal: We want.)

Although we have not conducted an exhaustive study of Tense/Aspect Markers across all West African languages, finding such deep similarities between Krio, Yoruba, Twi, and Igbo in so many areas confirms that our theory about how Kriolization proceeded is accurate.

Locative Prepositions in Krio, Yoruba, and Igbo

Locative Preposition, na, in Krio

Another of the unique features of Sierra Leone Krio is possession of the generic Locative Preposition, *na*. Its meaning can vary, depending upon the inherent semantic characteristics of the noun object that follows it. It can be translated as "at," "in," "on," "near," and is the most widely used preposition in the language. Observe its usage in the following examples:

1. *Di bɔbɔ sidɔm na chia*. [The boy is sitting on the chair.] (Literal: The boy sit LOC chair.)
2. *Di uman dɛm de waka go na tɔng*. [The women are walking to town.] (Literal: The woman-PL PROG walk go LOC town.)
3. *i de na os*. [S/he is in/at the house.] Or [S/he is at home.] (Literal: S/he be-at LOC house.)

Locative Preposition, na, in Igbo

Fyle and Jones credit Portuguese, Igbo, and possibly Maninka with the origin of this preposition.[7] Searches of Portuguese grammars revealed no preposition which resembles the breadth of this preposition or a similar sounding

122   *Chapter 5*

word. However, a review of the literature on Igbo revealed that, according to Michael Widjaja, "In Igbo, there is only one preposition, *na*. When preceding a vowel, it has the tone of that vowel and is written n' instead."[8] Given the examples he provides, it is clear that the [a] in [na] is deleted, when followed by a word that begins with a vowel, allowing the first vowel of the noun that follows to remain intact. If, the noun that follows *na* begins with a consonant, both the preposition and the noun remain intact.

1. *ɔ nɔ n'ulɔ.* [He is in the house.] (Literal: He be-at Prep house.)
2. *ɔ di n'ala.* [It is on the ground.] (Literal: it be-at Prep ground.)
3. *ɔ di na ji.* [It is on the yam.] (It be-at Prep yam.)

This locative preposition in Igbo is used in conjunction with location nouns to more highly specify the location in question. Observe some of the identified location nouns and their merger with *na* (table 5.3).

Sentences that emerge from these prepositionalized nouns are the following:

1. *ɔ di n'enu akpati.* [It is on top of the box.]
2. *ɔ di n'okpuru akpati.* [It is under the box.]
3. *ɔ di n'ime akpati.* [It is inside the box.]
4. *ɔ di n'akuku akpati.* [It is beside the box.]

The preposition, however, appears in its full form when the noun that follows it begins with a consonant, as the next examples show:

1. *Eze bi na Warri.* [Eze lives in Warri.] (Literal: Eze live Prep Warri.)
2. *Amaka nɔ na be Ngozi.* [Amaka is at Ngozi's house.] (Amaka be-at Prep house Ngozi.)

Igbo appears to be the clear source of the generic locative preposition, *na*, in Krio.

Table 5.3 Merger of Igbo Nouns with Preposition, *na*

Igba Location Noun	Meaning	Merger with na	New Meaning
enu	[top]	n'enu	[on top of, up]
okpuru	[underside]	n'okpuru	[under, below]
ime	[interior]	n'ime	[inside]
akuku	[edge]	n'akuku	[beside]

Locative Preposition in Yoruba

While Yoruba does not possess a preposition with the same pronunciation as *na* in either Krio or Igbo, there is a preposition in Yoruba that has some resemblance to this preposition, the word, *ni*, which is translated as 'at' or 'in' and appears in sentences like those below:

1. *O wa n'ile.* [He is at home.] (Literal: He exist LOC house.)
2. *Mo wa ni nun ile naa.* [It was in that house.] (Literal: It exist LOC that house there.)
3. *Ko si n'ile.* [He is not at home.] (Literal: NEG be-at LOC house.)

As was pointed out earlier, features that have become integral to Krio Language often are found to have multiple sources that reinforced their entry into the language. We initially suspected that all of the languages that had contributed to the African substratum of Krio were members of the Kwa Language Family, because many of the prominent Krio features are also prominent in Kwa.

However, based on our research, it is quite clear that one determining factor as to whether a particular language contributed to what became Krio is whether or not that language possessed structures that paralleled, or were very similar to, those found in Kwa languages. In fact, when we probe the structures of languages other than Yoruba, we find that the probability of certain features being adopted into Krio were greatly enhanced if those features existed in multiple languages in the community. The next section reveals this dynamic in relation to local indigenous languages.

LINGUISTIC CONTRIBUTIONS FROM LOCAL INDIGENOUS LANGUAGES: THE TEMNE CASE

In our quest to determine, as accurately as possible, which source language(s) contributed most to the formation of the Krio Language, we should consider languages that were indigenous to the western region of Sierra Leone. Remember that, in order to establish the colony, the colonialists had to purchase land from the Temne. Remember also that Cole and others have argued, convincingly, that some of the local ethnic groups contributed in significant ways to the evolution of the Krio community. Is there evidence of linguistic contributions to Krio beyond a few vocabulary words? Let us take a look at Temne. All examples here were taken from or based on information presented in the *Peace Corps [Sierra Leone]: Temne Language Manual.*[9]

124   *Chapter 5*

Some differences between Temne and Krio are readily obvious. Temne has eight Noun Classes which influence the phonological shape of words related to nouns, like adjectives. Krio does not have classes of nouns. From the examples below we learned that (1) the prefix on the base form of the Temne adjective, *bana* [big] has to agree with the class, to which the noun belongs; and (2) in Temne, the adjective follows the noun, rather than preceding the noun, as it does in Krio:

1. *Aseth abana* [a big house] (Literal: a house big)
2. *ɛseth ɛbana* [big houses] (Literal: houses big)
3. *kəbap kəbana* [a big axe] (Literal: axe big)
4. *Təbap təbana* [big axes] (Literal: axes big)

Similarly, negation in Temne is manifest as a suffix, *-yɛ*, on the basic form of the verb, rather than as a negative marker in front of the verb, as it is in Krio. Look at this phenomenon in Temne:

1. *i kɔ ro Kambia.* [I am going to Kambia.] (Literal: I go to Kambia)
2. *i kɔ-yɛ ro Kambia.* [I am not going to Kambia.] [Literal: I go-Neg to Kambia)
3. *Sə di ɛmuna.* [We eat potatoes.] (Literal: We eat potatoes)
4. *Sə di-yɛ ɛmuna.* [We don't eat potatoes.] (Literal: We eat-Neg potatoes)

These few examples demonstrate some of the ways in which Temne differs from Krio.

Tense/Aspect in Temne

However, there are a number of features in Temne that parallel substantive features in Krio. One such feature is the use of pre-verbal Tense/Aspect markers, so reminiscent of Krio. Although there is research that demonstrates subtle changes in these markers, with respect to stress and tone, based on the subject noun being singular or plural and definite or indefinite, these markers are remarkably constant.[10] Observe these examples:

Future Tense, *tə*
1. *i tə di.* [I will eat.] (Literal: I FUT eat)
2. *ɔ tə kɔ.* [He/she will go.] (Literal: He/she FUT go)
3. *aŋ tə der.* [They will come.] (Literal: They FUT come)

Present Perfect/Past, *po*
1. *i po di.* [I have eaten.] (Literal: I Pres Perf eat)

2. *ɔ po wai.* [He/she has eaten.] (Literal: He/she Pres Perf buy)
3. *sə po fɔf.* [We have spoken.] (Literal: We PresPerf speak)

Somewhat surprisingly, Temne, like Krio, has a *Zero* marker, which can indicate Simple Present Tense or Past Tense, depending upon the context in which it is used. The next few examples demonstrate this marker:

Simple Present/Past Tense, ZERO
1. *i di.* [I eat.] (Literal: I ZERO eat)
2. *i di dis.* [I ate yesterday.] (Literal: I ZERO eat yesterday)
3. *Sə fɔf.* [We speak.] (Literal: We ZERO speak)
4. *Sə fɔf ɔwoni.* [We spoke for a long time.] (Literal: We ZERO speak long time)

Locative Preposition, *ro*

While we did not find evidence of some of the prominent linguistic features found in Krio, like serial verb constructions or the Thematic nature of Krio that allows the speaker to place emphasis on any aspect of a sentence by moving the element to the front of the sentence, we did find a near parallel generic Locative Preposition that carries different interpretations based on the semantic characteristics of the noun that follows it. That preposition, [ro], is demonstrated below:

1. *Aŋ kɔ ro Amɛriko.* [They are going to America.] (Literal: They go LOC America)
2. *Aŋ di ro Masongbo.* [They ate in Masongbo.] (Literal: They eat LOC Masongbo)
3. *i kɔ ro seth.* [I am going home.] (Literal: I go LOC house)
4. *Sə wur ro Yoni.* [He is from Yoni.] (Literal: He be-from LOC Yoni)

From our limited review of Temne language, we conclude that Temne did not have the same level of influence on the formation of Krio as did, say Yoruba, Igbo, or Akan, but it does contain a number of core features which align with the structures found in Krio. We contend that it was exactly in those areas of alignment that Temne reinforced the adoption of those features or structures into Krio. Thus, there is linguistic evidence to demonstrate that the Temne people contributed more to the development of Krio language than just the names of plants, animals, food dishes, and geographic landmarks. It contributed by reinforcing linguistic patterns that were part of the linguistic makeup of the multi-ethnic community that forged Krio.

126   *Chapter 5*

AFRICAN LINGUISTIC FEATURES AND STRUCTURES IN DIASPORAN LANGUAGES

Sierra Leone Krio is an archetype for African diasporan languages that have developed throughout the trans-Atlantic as a consequence of the long history of African enslavement by European powers. Our analysis of Krio should assist us in identifying the African sources of linguistic phenomena in other creolized languages. Although a creolized language has developed in almost every British, French, Portuguese, and Dutch colony, we will focus our attention on the commonalities, identifiable sources, and direct linkages between Krio and Jamaican Creole. We have selected Jamaica for three reasons: (1) both were colonized by the British in the eighteenth century; (2) two of the settler groups in Sierra Leone lived in Jamaica before taking residence in Sierra Leone; and (3) we can document the sources of the largest groups of enslaved Africans in Jamaica.

Remember that Jamaica was a large sugar cane factory. The island depended on a constant flow of enslaved Africans from up and down the west coast of Africa, but especially those from the Windward Coast and the Gold Coast (modern day Ghana). Jamaican planters had a strong preference for Akan people (Ashanti, Fanti, Coromantee) until near the end of the eighteenth century. So, the Maroons who were expelled from Jamaica and settled in Freetown in 1795 must have spoken a variety of Jamaican Creole and been shaped, in large part, by the Akan people. The fact that the Maroons resisted British rule in Jamaica for nearly a century demonstrates that the Akan had a forceful ethnic character and would most likely have played a major role in determining the shape of Jamaican Creole.

Tense/Aspect in Jamaican Creole

As we have seen in Krio, Jamaican Creole has adopted the base form of verbs, which are largely derived from English. Instead of using auxiliary verbs, suffixes, or changing the morphological shape of the base forms of verbs to communicate Tense and Aspect, verbs in Jamaican Creole are preceded by Pre-Verbal Tense/Aspect markers. Although L. Emile Adams identifies more variation among the pre-verbal markers in Jamaican Creole than is the case in Krio, we are using the forms that appear to be the most conservative. The following are examples of sentences that would be generated by Adams' analysis:[11]

Present Progressive in Jamaican Creole, *a*
1. *Im a se.* [He/she is saying.] (Literal: he/she Pres Prg say)
2. *Im a go.* [He/she is going.] (Literal: he/she PresPrg go)

African Linguistic Foundations in Krio and the Diaspora　　127

3. *Dɛm a go.* [They are going.] (Literal: they PresPrg go)
4. *Yu a go.* [You are going.] (Literal: You PresPrg go)

Past in Jamaican Creole, *ɛn*
1. *Im ɛn se.* [He/she said.] (Literal: He/she Past say)
2. *Wi ɛn go.* [We went.] (Literal: We Past go)
3. *Uno ɛn kəm.* [You all came.] (Literal: You-Pl Past come)
4. *Dɛm ɛn kəm.* [They came.] (Literal: They Past come)

Future in Jamaican Creole, *a + go*
1. *Im a go se.* [He/she is going to say.] (Literal: He/she Prog Fut say)
2. *Dɛm a go hit.* [They are going to eat.] (Literal: They Prog Fut eat)
3. *Yu a go hit.* [You are going to eat.] (Literal: You Prog Fut eat)

Negative Present Progressive, *no + a = na*
1. *Im na se.* [He/she is not saying.] (Literal: He/she Neg + Prog se)
2. *Uno na kəm.* [You all are not coming.] (Literal: You-Pl Neg + Prog come)

Negative Past, *no + ɛn = nɛn*
1. *Im nɛn se.* [He/she did not say.] (Literal: He/she Neg + Past say)
2. *Wi nɛn go.* [We didn't go.] (Literal: We Neg + Past go)

Like Krio, these Tense/Aspect markers can occur singularly or in combination to express more complex states, such as Conditional, Past Conditional, Future Conditional.

Locative Sentences with the Verb, *de*

Jamaican Creole possesses a Locative Verb, *de*, sometimes pronounced as *di*, which accepts all of the Tense/Aspect markers like other verbs, to indicate the position or location of a person or object. Examples of this are below:

1. *Dɛm de ɛnai hos.* [They are in the house.] (Literal: They LOC in house)
2. *Dɛm no de ya.* [They are not here.] (Literal: They Neg LOC here)
3. *Im de pan tebul.* [It is on the table.] (Literal: It LOC ontop table)
4. *Uno go di de.* [You all will be there.] (Literal: You-Pl Fut LOC there)
5. *Uno na go di de.* [You all won't be there.] (Literal: You-Pl NEG LOC there)
6. *We uno de?* [Where are you all?] (Literal: Where you-Pl LOC)

Notice that, like Krio, the word for 'here' is *ya* and the word for 'there' is *de*.

128 *Chapter 5*

Equational Sentences with Copula Verb, *a*

Equational sentences in Jamaican Creole also operate as they do in Krio. Instead of the verb, *na*, in Krio, we find the verb, *a*, in Jamaican Creole. In the following sentences, you will see the use of *a* in the Present and Past forms:

1. *Bunny a di lida.* [Bunny is the leader.] (Literal: Bunny Equat. the leader)
2. *Meri a wan fama.* [Mary is a farmer.] (Literal: Mary Equat. one farmer)
3. *Mi dadi a ɛn tela.* [My dad was a tailor.] (Literal: My dad Equat. Past tailor)

Notice that in Krio the Past marker in an Equational sentence follows the Equational verb, *na*, just as the Past marker follows *a* in Jamaican Creole (for example, Mi dadi na bin ticha. [My dad was a teacher.]).

Thematic Nature of Jamaican Creole

In Krio we observed the capacity of the language to emphasize virtually any element of a sentence by relocating that element to the front of the sentence, along with the Equational Verb, na. Just as a reminder, a simple sentence, like the following:

Mi mama bin bit mi. [My mother spanked me.]

could be transformed into a focused sentence like this:

Na mi, mi mama bin bit. [I am the one who my mother spanked.]

Although the verb of the sentence can receive the same kind of focus, it requires the verb to be retained in its normal place in the sentence, as well as being highlighted in the front:

Na bit, mi mama bin bit mi. [My mother really gave me a sound spanking.]

Let's see how this phenomenon presents itself in Jamaican Creole:

1. *Dem a tɔk a wi.* [They are talking to us.] (Literal: They Pres Prog talk to we)
2. *A wi dɛm a tɔk.* [It is us they are talking to.] (Literal: Equat. we they Pres Prog talk)
3. *A no wi dɛm a tɔk.* [It isn't us they are talking to.] (Literal: Equat. Neg we they Pres Prog talk)

African Linguistic Foundations in Krio and the Diaspora

4. *A rɔn dɛm a rɔn.* [They are really running.] (Literal: Equat. run they Pres Prog run)
5. *A jok dɛm a jok.* [They're just joking.] (Literal: Equat. joke they Pres Prog joke)

Serial Verb Constructions in Jamaican Creole

Of all of the linguistic features that appear in Atlantic creolized languages, none of them are more definitively African than serial verb constructions. We have witnessed them in Krio and have demonstrated the parallels in Yoruba, Akan, and Igbo. Finding serial verb constructions in Jamaican Creole is not only strong evidence of an African substratum but will very likely direct us to the primary source language for Jamaican Creole. Let us, first, see the evidence of serial verb constructions in Jamaican Creole. The following examples were found in Adams:

1. *Kyai go bring kəm.* [Go fetch/spread gossip] (Literal: carry go bring come)[12]
2. *Di rakston we im tek lIk mi.* [the stone that he hit me with] (Literal: the stone that he hit me)[13]

A more extensive set of examples were found in Nicole Arsenec's 2020 study, titled "Serial Verbs in Jamaican and Martinican." They demonstrate a wider range of serial verbs in Jamaican Creole and the variety of functions serial verbs carry out.[14] View them below:

1. *Mi a rɔn go a shap.* [I'm running to the shop.] (Literal: I PresProg run go LOC shop)
2. *Mi waak trii mayl go a makit.* [I walked three miles to the market.] (Literal: I walk 3 miles go LOC market)
3. *Im rɔn kɔm.* [He ran toward me.] (Literal: He run come)
4. *Mi a go beg im a lif.* [I'm going to ask him for a ride.] (Literal: I Prog Fut beg him for ride)
5. *Kyai kɔm gi mi.* [Bring it for/to me.] (Literal: Carry come give me)
6. *Im tek nayf kɔt di brɛd.* [She cut the bread with a knife.] (Literal: She take knife cut the bread)

The parallel of these serial verb constructions to those found in Krio, Yoruba, Igbo, and Akan are remarkable. This leads us to conclude that languages in the Kwa sub-family of Niger-Congo are the source of these serial verb constructions and probably most of the other features described above.

130   *Chapter 5*

We can say with confidence that the commonalities in Yoruba, Igbo, and Akan led to the realization of serial verb constructions and a number of other features in Sierra Leone Krio, because we have documentation that speakers of all three languages were members of the community that developed Krio. Can we say, with any degree of certainty, which of the Kwa languages contributed to those features in Jamaican Creole? History tells us that there were large numbers of enslaved Africans from the Gold Coast working in the sugar cane plantations in Jamaica. We also know that the Jamaican planters had a strong preference for Akan people. Furthermore, the Jamaican Maroons, who led the anti-slavery movement for nearly one hundred years on the island were Akan and, therefore, would have had a strong influence on the language that developed among the Africans in that setting. It is safe to say that Akan is the primary source language for serial verbs in Jamaican Creole. If there were other Kwa languages prominent in Jamaica, their language(s) would have reinforced that structure in the creole that developed.

EVIDENCE OF MORE CONNECTIONS

Other linguistic evidence supports the contention that Akan was a strong contributor to the African substratum of Jamaican Creole. Remember that Krio possesses a set of Mental Verbs that require a following complementary clause that begins with the word [*se*] "say/that." This was described in chapter 4 and generates sentences like the following:

1. *A bin mɛmba se Ama go kam.* [I thought that Ama was going to come.] (Literal: I PAST think SAY Ama FUT come)
2. *i go tɛl am se i nɔ fɔ kam.* [She will tell her not to come.] (Literal: She FUT tell her SAY she NEG OBLIG kam)

Twi, *sɛ*, with Mental Verbs

A review of Jamaican Creole reveals a parallel structure in that language, requiring the word [*se*], with the same meaning:[15]

1. *Im tɛl wi se im bɛx.* [He told us that he is angry.] (Literal: He tell us SAY he angry)
2. *Yu no se dɛm dɛd?* [Do you know that they are dead?] (Literal: You know SAY they die?)
3. *Yu no tink se me fi dwi?* [Don't you think I should do it?] (Literal: You NEG think SAY I OBLIG do-it?)

African Linguistic Foundations in Krio and the Diaspora   131

As we conducted our research for this chapter, we discovered that Twi has a morpheme, [sɛ], that functions in the same way that *se* functions in Krio. Florence Abena Dolphyne offers the sentences below to demonstrate how this morpheme functions in Twi:[16]

1. *Mepɛ sɛ mekɔ.* [I want to go.] (Literal: I want that I go)
2. *ɔkaa sɛ ɔbɛba.* [S/he said that he will come.] (Literal: S/he said that she/he-FUT-come)
3. *ɛyɛ me sɛ ɔbɛba.* [I think s/he will come.] (Literal: I think that s/he-FUT-come)
4. *Menim sɛ ɔbɛyɛ.* [I know that s/he will do it.] (Literal: I-know that s/he-FUT-do)

It appears that this word was close enough in meaning, function, and pronunciation to reinforce the adoption of the English word 'say' into Krio and Jamaican Creole.

Igbo Source of Second-Person Plural Pronouns

We have noted in our review of Krio and Kwa languages that they both make a distinction between second-person singular and second-person plural pronouns, different from English where "you" is either singular or plural. The phonological shape of these words in the relevant languages is very revealing. See table 5.4.

Of the three African languages most likely to have contributed the second person plural forms to Krio and Jamaican Creole, Igbo is clearly the one, based on linguistic data. The fact that the second person plural form in Gullah is [*unu*][17] suggests that Igbo may have had a stronger influence on the formation of creole languages in the African diaspora than it has been given credit for.

We would be remiss if we did not acknowledge the degree to which many of the same languages that we have discussed here have contributed to other African diasporan languages, even at the very end of the diaspora in North America. Gullah, through the groundbreaking research of Lorenzo Dow

Table 5.4   Second Person Pronouns in Five Languages

Language	2nd Person Singular	2nd Person Plural
Yoruba	[o]	[ɛyin]
Twi	[wo]	[mo]
Igbo	[I] or [gI]	[unu]
Krio	[yu]	[una]
Jamaican Creole	[yu]	[uno]

132   *Chapter 5*

Turner, in his *Africanisms in the Gullah Dialect,* has probably received more attention than any other African diasporan language in North America. He identified hundreds of personal names among the Gullahs which he was able to trace back to African linguistic groups across west and central Africa. But, as we have pointed out in this book, the most solid evidence of African origin of a language rests in the grammatical and semantic systems. Turner identified numerous, systematic grammatical patterns and morphemes that mirror what we have described in Krio and Jamaican Creole, notably serial verb constructions, adjectival verbs, tense/aspect markers operating in tandem with unchanging verb forms, and intonation alone differentiating declarative sentences from yes/no questions. In other words, Gullah has all of the markings of a language with a West African substratum. Although a full description and discussion of Gullah and its cousin, African American Language (AAL), would take us too far away from the central purpose of this book, we highly recommend a paper written by Selase W. Williams, titled "The African Character of African American Language: Insights from the Creole Connection," in which he not only describes phonological, syntactic, and semantic features of AAL and identifies possible African linguistic sources for these features, but also provides an explanation for unusual African American names which are readily associated with their ethnic/racial background.[18]

CONCLUSION

We believe there are important conclusions from this chapter. The first conclusion is that Sierra Leone Krio and other languages like it should not be considered "English-based" creoles. Even at the word level, we have provided evidence that demonstrate that English words that have made their way into Krio were only derived from English, but were not borrowed wholesale. Instead, those words have been fitted into an ethno-linguistic grid that matched the language structures of contributing African languages.

We have also concluded that Krio did not develop out of a set of universal characteristics of creolized language. Instead, the Krio language was formulated out of the linguistic material that was actively being used in the kriolizing community. By this we mean that the words, phonological, grammatical, and semantic systems that constituted the individual languages of the people who lived in that community was the material from which Krio was constructed. We contend that much more attention has to be paid to learning the specific languages spoken at the sites where creolized languages develop.

Finally, it is pretty clear from the evidence presented in this chapter that a particular linguistic feature or structure was most likely to be incorporated into

Krio if that feature or structure was found in more than one language spoken in the community. Common features across a number of languages reinforced their adoptability into Krio. This is evident in pre-verbal Tense/Aspect markers, serial verb constructions, distinctions between singular and plural words for "you," and the presence of a verb meaning "to be at a place." In this way, Krio may have benefitted as much from Temne as it has from Yoruba.

NOTES

1. *A Krio-English Dictionary*, ed. Clifford N. Fyle and Eldred D. Jones (Oxford: Oxford University Press, in collaboration with the Sierra Leone University Press, 1980), x.

2. Gibril R. Cole, *The Krio of West Africa: Islam, Culture, Creolization, and Colonialism in the Nineteenth Century* (Athens: Ohio University Press, 2013), 51.

3. Cole, *Krio of West Africa*, 50.

4. Cole, *Krio of West Africa*, 50.

5. Olasope O. Oyelaran, "On the Scope of the Serial Verb Construction in Yoruba," *Studies in African Linguistics*13, no. 2 (1982): 109–46. https://www.academia.edu /75193726/On_the_scope_of_the_serial_verb_construction_in_Yoruba (accessed February 2, 2024).

6. Elisha O. Ogbonna, *Comprehensive Igbo Language* (Las Vegas: Prinoelio Press, 2020), 41–90.

7. Fyle and Jones, *Krio-English Dictionary*, 255.

8. Michael Widjaja, "Igbo Culture/Igbo Language," *IboGuide.org*, 2000–2020, https://www.IgboGuide.org (accessed February 7, 2024).

9. A. K. Turay, *Peace Corps [Sierra Leone]: Temne Language Manual*, https://fsi-languages.yojik.eu/languages/PeaceCorps/Temne/Peace%20Corps %20Temne%20Language%20Manual.pdf (accessed February 2, 2024).

10. See Indiana University, Center for Language Technology, "Temne Language Portal, Indiana University" (audio recorded tutorials), 2024, https://celt.indiana.edu/ portal/Temne/index.html (accessed February 2, 2024).

11. L. Emile Adams, *Understanding Jamaican Patois: An Introduction to Afro-Jamaican Grammar* (Kingston, Jamaica: LMH Publishing, 1994), 26–28.

12. Adams, *Understanding Jamaican Patois*, 34.

13. Adams, *Understanding Jamaican Patois*, 24.

14. Nicole Arsenec, "Serial Verbs in Jamaican and Martinican," *HAL Open Science*. January 8, 2020, https://hal.science/hal-02910343 (accessed February 2, 2024).

15. Adams, *Understanding Jamaican Patois*, 25

16. Florence Abena Dolphyne, *A Comprehensive Course in Twi (Asante)* (Accra: Ghana Universities Press, 1996), 41.

17. Lorenzo Dow Turner, *Africanisms in the Gullah Dialect* (Chicago: University of Chicago Press, 1949; 3rd printing, Columbia: University of South Carolina Press, 2002), 175.

134   *Chapter 5*

18. Selase W. Williams, "The African Character of African American Language: Insights from the Creole Connection," in *Africanisms in American Culture*, 2nd ed., ed. Joseph E. Holloway (Bloomington: Indiana University Press, 2005), 397–426.

PART III

Krio Culture and Traditions

Chapter 6

Elements of Krio Culture

LƐ WI TƆK BƆT KRIO KƆLCHƆ
[LET US TALK ABOUT KRIO CULTURE]

As we have established in various sections of this book, the early Krio community comprised groups of "returnees" from various areas like Jamaica, Nova Scotia, the United Kingdom, Nigeria, and Sierra Leone. The "Settlers" (descendants of freed slaves from England, Nova Scotia, and Jamaica), as they were called, eventually became the early nucleus of a Krio society, who benefited from the blend of religion, cultures, and traditions they infused into the Krio community. Here were Africans, some of whom had been enslaved in these regions and others who had been rescued from slaving ships before they reached their plantation destinations, coming together to forge a new society in Freetown and its surrounding villages.

Many in the group, like the Jamaican Maroons, brought back to their homeland what Kenneth Bilby astutely called "a robust Afro-creole culture their ancestors had forged in Jamaica."[1] A notable example of this culture is the *gumbe* drum and dance which the Maroons brought with them just as Freetown was beginning to emerge into an organized community in the early 1800s. More will be said about the *gumbe* drum and dance later in this chapter. In addition to *gumbe*, Akintola J. G. Wyse reports that the settlers popularized a ceremonial feast called *bamchu* which again was very similar to what we know today as the *awujoh* [a ceremonial feast] in Krio culture.[2] Arthur T. Porter further explains the similarities and differences between *bamchu* and *awujoh*. Both were "ceremonial feasts in which all the ancestors were believed to participate. But the settler feast called *Bamchu*, started at dusk and ended, passover-like, before dawn. . . . The Liberated-African feast . . . was celebrated during the day and consisted of a meal of African foodstuffs."[3]

138   *Chapter 6*

The Settlers also brought with them the *talla* dance, a form of dance that required intricate movements, similar to the *gumbe* dance that was popular in Freetown and parts of West and Central Africa. They were also credited with introducing traditional dresses like the *print* and the *kabaslɔt* that we will discuss more fully in this chapter. Thus, we can conclude that some of the cultural contributions identified and described here are African cultural survivals that Settler ancestors had modified throughout the period of enslavement.

By far, the greater proportion of contributions to Krio culture came from the Liberated Africans who, as we know, were rescued from slave ships bound for the Americas and the Caribbean and brought back to Freetown. They were predominantly of Yoruba origins, although there was an appreciable number of Fante, Ewe, Mende, Vai, Temne, Limba, and Soso in the group. From this group, we get a prolific set of customs and rituals such as ceremonies honoring the dead, the birth of babies, and the celebration of marriages, foods like *jollof rice, krenkren, bitas,* and *bɔlɔgi,* secret societies like the *ɔntin* [hunting] society, *gɛlɛdɛ,* and *ɔjɛ,* belief systems, and elements of the Krio language itself, specifically grammatical structures and lexicography.

In the early 1800s, it was clearly evident that both groups, the Settlers and the Liberated Africans, would need to systematize Krio culture and language for their collective survival. On the one hand, by the time they arrived in Freetown, the Maroons and the Nova Scotians were already familiar with English although they spoke different variations. The Liberated Africans, on the other hand, had had limited contacts with the language outside their interaction with slavers, missionaries, and British authorities who rescued them from the slave ships. As these two groups moved closer together through the enticement of religion and their common mercantilist interests, mutually intelligible communication became a powerful imperative in developing a society and a language they could call their own. The syncretic elements they brought to bear upon this process became the building blocks of Krio language and culture. Words, sounds, and gesticulations became the mediating processes through which they painted pictures, educated each other, interpreted history, reinforced cosmological beliefs, and socialized the young. In short, developing this kind of communicative competence helped them open new and vital links to their collective social and cultural existence.

Let us now examine some of the more specific elements of Krio culture that have been developed and expanded over the years.

Elements of Krio Culture

RELIGION

Christianity Among the Krio

Religion was a driving force in the evolution of Krio society starting in the eighteenth century when groups of repatriated enslaved Africans, notably the Black Poor, the Maroons, and the Nova Scotians, arrived in Freetown with an unbridled commitment to the Christian faith. Porter informs us that "The settlers themselves had been conversant with the Gospel message before their arrival in the Colony, and had subsequently established their own churches and chapels."[4] Gibril R. Cole perceptively described it this way: "Christianity was not simply an external imposition but part of an identity that has been forged in the crucible of Atlantic enslavement, resistance, and freedom."[5] Over time, various Christian missionaries, mostly from the United Kingdom, established missionary programs and activities through, for example, the Church Missionary Society (CMS) and the Methodist Church. Porter and Wyse variously reported that the CMS, for example, administered "parish systems" for Liberated Africans in villages like Gloucester [St. Andrews' Parish], Bathurst [St. James' Parish], York [St. Henry's Parish], Waterloo [St. Michael's Parish], and Hastings [St. Thomas' Parish], between 1812 and 1819. Many of the early Krios embraced Christianity so thoroughly that they became purveyors of the religion up and down the West African coast while simultaneously spreading Western values and lifestyles. Even the much-publicized Niger Delta Mission, Wyse added, "was run almost exclusively by Krio clergymen, including Samuel Ajayi Crowther, an enslaved boy, who in 1864 became the first African bishop."[6]

In addition to church and worship activities, parochial schools were set up especially for children of church members. These schools were not simply learning institutions, they were extensions of the church; institutions in which religious education and Western ideals are a key part of the curriculum. Notable among these schools were the CMS Grammar School for Boys established in 1845, and its sister institution, the Annie Walsh Memorial School (AWMS), established in 1849. Both were founded by the CMS. The Methodist Mission founded its own parochial schools as well: the Methodist Boys High School (MBHS) in 1874, and the Methodist Girls High School (MGHS), in 1880. Christian teachings and the Bible were key components of the curriculum for virtually all these parochial schools. Students had to pray in assembly halls before classes began, Bible studies were required at lower grades before pupils chose a special focus in arts or sciences at the higher grade levels. Finally, memorization of the *collect* (a prayer meant to bring church goers together) for the week was a mandatory activity in many of these parochial schools.

140   *Chapter 6*

For many Krios who are Christians, going to church (morning prayer, martins, and evensong), participating in Sunday school classes, youth fellowship programs, singing in the choir, and attending Mother's Union meetings, as appropriate, were a regular and uncompromising part of their weekly life. Special dresses and suits (*sɔndeklos*) and shoes were purchased for wear exclusively on Sundays. Dressing for church usually happens after families have had their *Sɔnde mɔnin kol fufu or kol rɛs* [traditional meal of left-over fufu or rice and heated-up vegetable soup, both cooked the previous day and eaten on Sunday mornings].

Here is an example of a typical Conversation:

Aunty Oju: *Jabɛz, usay yu de go dis ali-ali mɔnin insay yu sɔndeklos?*
             [Jabez, where are you going this early morning dressed in your church clothes?]

Jabɛz: *Na mɔnin preya a de go wit grani, ma.* [I am going to morning prayer with my grandmother, ma'am.]

Aunty Oju: *Yu dɔn it?* [Have you eaten yet?]

Jabez: *Yɛs, ma. Grani bin wam sɔm kol fufu fɔ mi, ma, we a mɔndɔ kwik-kwik so wi nɔ go let, ma.* [Yes, ma'am. Grandmother warmed some left over fufu and soup for me which I ate hurriedly so we will not be late for church.]

Aunty Oju: *ɔrayt. Sidɔm saful na chɔch-o.* [Okay. Sit quietly at church, you hear?]

Jabɛz: *Yɛs ma.* [Yes, ma'am.]

Islam and Krio Society

Many of the Liberated Africans, who were rescued from slave ships bound for America and the Caribbean, were avid practicing Muslims. But the colonialists applied relentless pressure for them to convert to Christianity, no doubt selling the benefits not only of the Christian religion but also of infinite possibilities of gainful employment and a better life while under British protection. Some of the Liberated Africans succumbed to the pressures of the colonial authorities to convert to Christianity and thus contributed to the advancement of Christendom in the emerging Krio society. Many among this group were enticed by the opportunity to participate in business and in the social atmosphere that was evolving in Freetown.

The great majority who resisted conversion incurred the displeasure of the colonial administration and the missionaries whose incipient goal was to Christianize Freetown and sell it as a successful model for the rest of West and East Africa. The resistant Liberated Africans group was further ostracized through the Colonial Administration's *Tribal Administration (Freetown)*

Elements of Krio Culture   141

Ordinance of 1905, an *Act* which Cole tells us was meant to "marginalize all non-Christians, who henceforth were 'tribalized' and excluded from the mainstream of Freetown colonial politics."[7] This group was branded as "Aku Mohammedans" in the Krio community and settled to the east of Freetown in areas known as Fullah Town, Fourah Bay, and Magazine Cut, where Islam was gradually spreading partly through trade with the Mandes from the north. Other Liberated Africans were settled in nearby villages like Hastings, Wellington, and Waterloo.

Some Christian Krios in the past, especially the affluent and the religiously dedicated, may not have recognized the obvious fact that the Krio community was religiously heterogeneous, since Muslim and Christian Krios have coexisted peacefully for a very long time. Both have intimate and familial relationships across the religious divide. It is not uncommon to see members of a Krio family with both Muslim and Christian relatives as well as Muslim and Christian names. In addition, both groups celebrate each other's holidays. The Christians would celebrate the end of the fasting period for Muslims by sharing food, notably *fura* [sweetmeat made from rice] and *rɛs pap* [rice pudding], and by participating in the traditional lantern parade. Muslims would also help Christians celebrate Easter and Christmas holidays. They share membership in cultural and secret societies like hunting, *egwugwu*, and *ɔjɛ*. In spite of all this, further education is needed for all Krios, especially the Christian Krios, to understand that the Liberated Africans who remained loyal to Islam are bona fide Krios, and their contributions to Krio society are substantial. In recent times, however, progress has been made in this area with the publication of Cole's *The Krio of West Africa*, and the manuscript he edited with Mac Dixon-Fyle, *New Perspectives on the Sierra Leone Krio*.

KRIO CULTURAL BELIEFS

Below are some specific and long-standing cultural beliefs and practices in Krio society that parents and grandparents have passed down to the young ones:

1. *Bɛrin Grɔn* [Cemetery]: Krios see the cemetery as a mysterious and sacred place. In the old days, you must not linger around cemeteries, especially at night. It is believed that spirits are very active at night and their world is not far removed from ours. Many African traditions share this belief that death is only a transition from the physical to the spiritual world and that spirits do function in some capacity in both worlds; a tradition that Krios got from the Liberated Africans, many of

whom were Yorubas or from related ethnicities. About this tradition, Kemi Adamolekun had this to say: "Yoruba belief [is] that death does not break the communication line between ancestors and descendants if the descendants continue to address the dead and ask for their support and protection."[8] In honor of this close relation between the spirit and physical worlds, graves of loved ones are cleared of brush once or twice a year, preferably before major holidays like Christmas or New Year. In addition, when relatives do visit the grave site, they would take cooked food, water, kola nuts, and the favorite drinks of the deceased. They would "share" the meal while talking to their loved ones as if they were sitting there right next to them. Thus, Krio people have this parable: *Nɔ tek bad yay luk bɛrin grɔn, wi ɔl gɛ fɔ de go wan de.* ["Don't look at the cemetery with contempt or fear because we all have to end up there someday."]

2. *i dɔn lo* [she is low]: When it is evident that a person is close to death, she is moved from her bed and placed on the floor next to the bed frame. When that happens, the Krio say, "Da mami dɔn lo- o" ["Grandma is close to death."]

3. *Snɛk* [snake]: Children are warned not to call a snake by its name, particularly at night, because Krios believe it will appear before them in an aggressive manner. What should they call the snake at night? *langalanga*. Also, if a snake appears in your dream, it means a baby is on its way within the family.

4. *Wisul* [whistling]: Children are strictly warned not to whistle at night or inside the house because by doing so, you may be invoking evil spirits to come out and possibly harm you.

5. *Yay de krach* [itchy eyes]: If your eyes are itchy, it means somebody is calling your name.

6. *An dɛm de krach* [hands are itchy]: If the center of your right hand is itchy, that means that you are going to come into some money. But you must relieve the itch with a silver or gold coin. If the center of your left hand is itchy, then you are going to be giving money to someone.

7. *Bad Dreams*: Many Krios believe that if you have bad dreams at night, you should put a bible under your pillow and open it to the 23rd Psalm.

8. *Bɔk-fut* [stub one's toe]: If you hit your left toe while walking, it is a sign of bad luck for you.

9. *ɔnda mi rayt fut de krach* [under my right foot is itchy]: Unexpected/ possible travel.

10. *Put brum bien frɔnt ɛn bak do* [placing a broom behind the front and back door]: This is believed to ward off witches and thieves.

Elements of Krio Culture 143

11. *Bag na grɔn* [putting your purse on the floor]: Krios believe that it is bad luck for a woman to put her purse on the floor. If she does, she would lose money.

12. *Munin* [mourning]: The wife and daughters of the deceased wear black, navy blue, or white (only solid colors) for varying periods of time ranging from forty days, three months, to a year, in honor of the departed relative. This tradition is rapidly disappearing. Many choose not to wear black or any of these colors at all, or they may do so for a very short time.

13. *ɔspitul nɔ fɔ dischaj yu Satide* [Hospital should not discharge a patient on a Saturday]: Krios believe that a patient in a hospital should never be discharged on a Saturday. The reason? You will go home with the same ailment you came into the hospital with.

14. *Nɔ muf Satide.* [Don't move to a new house on a Saturday]: The belief is that you will have to move again soon.

15. *Pas bebi oba im mama in kɔfin* [Passing a baby over the coffin of her mother]: If the baby's mom dies, the baby is passed over her coffin for protection of the child so that the departed spirit does not come back for her.

16. *Pikin de ikɔp* [a child is experiencing hiccups]: Take a piece of white thread from her clothes roll it into a circle and put it on her head. Krios believe it would cure the hiccups and most of the time it does.

17. *Bele uman fɔ ɔlwez ol pen nef en ston* [a pregnant woman must always carry a small knife and a stone]: It is believed that these items would protect her from harm and danger.

18. *Pikin dem we bɔn bifo dem mama mared nɔ fɔ go dem mama in mared.* [The children a women had before she got married should not go to her wedding]: Besides it being seen as bad luck, having children out of wedlock in the old days was frowned upon and therefore these children were barred from attending their mother's wedding.

19. *Mami nɔ de go pikin berin.* [A mother does not attend the funeral of any of her deceased children]: Krios endorsed this practice because they strongly believe that "*na pikin fɔ ber im mami nɔto mami fɔ ber pikin.*" ["it is the children who should bury their parents, not the other way around."]

20. *Bele uman nɔ fɔ waka na trit na net.* [A pregnant woman should never walk the streets at night. It is believed that evil spirits will steal her baby if she does.

21. *Nɔ gi emti pɔs as prezent* [When you give a purse as a gift, always put something in it.]: It is impolite and an element of bad luck when you give an empty purse as a gift.

144   *Chapter 6*

22. *Yu bɛt yu tɔng.* [You bit your tongue.]: If you bite your tongue accidentally, it means someone is calling your name.

23. *Nɔ trowe yu ia ɛni say afta yu lus ɔ kɔt am.* [Don't just throw your cut or loose hair anywhere.]: To do this will bring bad luck to you.

24. *Nɔ so klos wɛn you wɛr am na yu bɔdi.* [Don't sew a dress while you have it on.] This can be dangerous and ill-fated.

25. *If yu drim se yu nekɛd bad ting dɛm go apin to yu.* [If you dream that you are naked, bad things will happen to you.]

26. *ɔkɔ nɔ fɔ si in yawo bifo di mared.* [The groom cannot see his bride before the day of wedding.]: It is bad luck to see your bride before the wedding.

27. *Bɛlɛ uman nɔ fɔ sidɔm na fana.* [A pregnant woman should not seat on a winnower.]: To do so would bring bad luck to the baby.

28. *Nɔ put pikin pantap tebul fɔ sidɔm bikɔs i go bi tifman we i big.* [Don't sit a child on a table otherwise he will grow up to be a thief.]

29. *If yu tek fufu tik bit man, i go tɔn okobo.* [If you strike a man with the stick for stirring fufu, he will become impotent.]

30. *If bɔku-bɔku pipul na wan ples ɔl tap fɔ tɔk wan tɛm, Krio pipul dɛm kin se "spirit pas."* [If a lot of people together in one place stopped talking at the same time, the Krios would say, "spirit pass."]

31. *If yu jomp dɔg pis yu go get ronin.* [If you jump over dog's urine, you will get gonorrhea.]

32. *If yu drim se yu de flay, bɛtɛ go fala yu.* [If you dream that you are flying, something good will come through for you.]

33. *If yu drim bɔt mared, na bɛrin de kam.* [If you dream about a wedding, it means a funeral is on the way.]

34. *Di de we uman de mared, i nɔ fɔ was insɛf, na in mami, in grani, ɔ in anti, fɔ was am.* [On the day of a lady's wedding, she should not bathe herself. Her mother, grandmother, or aunt should bathe her.]

35. *Tu bɛlɛ uman dɛm nɔ fɔ tap na di sem os pas tete dɛm rɛdi fɔ bɔn.* [Two pregnant women should not stay in the same house until they are ready to give birth.]

KRIO DRESSES

There are two main Krio traditional dresses whose history and development are closely linked: the more formal *kaba slɔt* and the *print* dress.

Kaba Slɔt

The *kaba slɔt* is a traditional Krio dress that was popularized by the Liberated Africans who were brought to Freetown after being rescued from slave ships bound for the Americas and the Caribbean. Upon arrival in Freetown, they were all given Western clothing which turned out to be what the English called *cover slut*; a long loose and sometimes flowing dress that was worn by women mostly during the Victorian era in Britain and elsewhere in Europe. The Liberated Africans did not like this type of clothing because it was made of thick material and extremely uncomfortable. In the hands of the Krio, specifically the Liberated Africans, the *cover slut* was thoroughly Africanized so that it reflected the emerging Krio culture as well as meet the challenging demands of the tropical weather of Western Africa. In short, as Betty M. Wass and S. Modupe Broderick observed, the *kaba slɔt* afforded "the African dressmaker a great deal of creative freedom."[9] To make the *kaba slɔt*, the Liberated Africans chose light print materials instead of the heavy canvas of the *cover slut*, cleverly employing patterns that show variegated flower, fruit, and animal designs. The *kaba slɔt* did not lose the elegance of the *cover slut* since it continued to be worn on mostly formal occasions. Part of the ritual of wearing the *kaba slɔt* is to proudly and elegantly raise the skirt to expose the intricately embroidered petticoat.

Other accoutrements that must go with the *kaba slɔt* dress are, (1) the *ashɔkɛ*, otherwise known as *oku lapa*, (2) *kotoku*, (3) *ɛnkincha*, (4) *abana/gras at*, and (5) *kapɛt slipas*. These are described in more detail below:

Ashɔkɛ/Oku-Lapa

Ashɔkɛ, or *oku lapa*, is another Yoruba addition to Krio culture. It is a piece of meticulously folded and elongated fabric material that hangs loosely over the right or left shoulders of *kabaslɔt* wearers. If it is resting on the left shoulder, as it is worn in Yoruba culture, that indicates that that person is married; if on the right shoulder, she is single. Wass and Broderick observe that this marriage identification tradition "demonstrated the strong influence of Yoruba culture in Krio society."[10] In the old days when Krio society was quite conservative, marriage identification was valuable information to have because married women could not be approached or talked to in a casual manner.

Kotoku

British and European women who were dressed in *cover slut* used to store items they might need in a pouch. The Krio, however, modified that pouch for their *kaba slɔt* dress by developing what they called the *kotoku*, a popular

Figure 6.1. The kaba slɔt (traditional Krio dress), modeled by Mrs. Milbank Rowe. *Photograph courtesy of Mrs. Milbank Rosetta Rowe.*

term for a pouch or money bag whose linguistic origins are from the Twi and Ga of Ghana. The *kotoku* is designed with very colorful materials, quite often materials that match the color and floral patterns of the *kaba slɔt*. It is worn by tying it around the waist area of *kaba slɔt* or left hanging loosely on the lady's arm. It is frequently used to store cosmetics, money, keys, and the like.

ɛnkincha

The *ɛnkincha* is a piece of print material that is used to cover the hair. In early Krio society, a woman's hair cannot be freely exposed so the *ɛnkincha* served a useful role in providing cover. It is tied around the head, usually in a variety of styles. The creativity of Krio women as they constantly produce ingenious or creative ways to tie the *ɛnkincha* is another evidence of the influence of Yoruba culture in Krio society.

Abana or Gras At

For the *kaba slɔt,* an additional cover known as the *abana* or *gras at* [straw hat] is worn to give more formality to the head gear.

Figure 6.2. Kapɛt slipas (carpet slippers).

Kapɛt Slipas (Carpet Slippers)

Carpet slippers are soft shoes made up of wool which has been knitted into canvas. Like the print dress patterns, patterns for carpet slippers have endless varieties that reflect trees, animals, flowers, games, as well as other elements of the environment around them. Since this is a competitive business, carpet slippers makers must draw from their imagination to create designs that are immediately attractive to their customers. There are times when they would be commissioned by groups, such as *ashoebi* groups [groups wearing the same traditional outfits during cultural events like weddings and engagement ceremonies] and, to create uniform designs that complement their *print* dresses or the *kabaslɔt ɛn kotoku* dresses. Bright colors are regularly used because they draw attention to the product.

In early Krio society, only elderly Krio women wear *kabaslɔt*. However, things are much different today. It is now very common to see *kabaslɔt* worn by young Krio women and in less formal events.

Print

The *Print* dress is the second of the main traditional dresses worn by Krio women. Unlike the *kabaslɔt,* which is a long flowing dress, the *Print* dress has been modified into a shorter and more stylish dress to meet modern fashion trends. It has a remarkably interesting history. Some of the repatriated Africans from Jamaica and Nova Scotia arrived in Freetown with craft-making skills that they used in numerous ways. Some made patterns for *kapɛt slipas* which are worn with the Krio *Print*. Others focused on developing patterns for print fabrics. Many of the designs used for the *kabaslɔt* were adapted for the print dresses as well. Patterns may be fruits like papaya, banana, *kushu* [cashew], *black tɔmbla* [tamarinds], mango, orange, or vegetables like okra, cabbage, onions. These patterns would be block-printed and stamped into the print fabric repeatedly (see photo examples below).

The same pattern would be reproduced for yards and yards of materials. Later, the Krio developed knowledge of mixing patterns although the single pattern was still preferred because the uniformity made it easier to select printed fabrics for cultural and religious events in which *ashoɛbi* [the uniform dress for a group or family] is required. The *Print* fabric became so popular that the rights to the manufacturing of this fabric was purchased in Britain. Today, Krio *print* fabrics are being manufactured in places like China and Indonesia, although many local people still prefer the original Krio print.

Figure 6.3. Example 1 of fabric print dress.

Figure 6.4. Example 2 of fabric print dress, modeled by Dr. Princess Dougan. Photograph courtesy of Dr. Princess Dougan.

NYANYAM (FOOD)

The foods most popular in Krio culture are not much different from many you would find in the rest of the continent or the African Diaspora. For example, you would find a lot of common dishes prepared with cassava, yams, rice, plantains, and a variety of grains and vegetables. What is different is the history of these foods in Krio society, their preparation, cultural significance in Krio communities, and their availability and consumption.

Foods like cassava, yams, and rice have been readily available in the West African region for centuries. For most people in this region, these are staple foods whose cultivation has been written into their cultural arsenal. A Krio house usually has fruit and vegetable gardens at the side or the back of these houses. The matriarch or other senior women in a household will decide which vegetable and/or roots would be prepared for that day. The young ones in the family would be tasked to get these from their garden. Boys or helping hands will get the firewood and start the fire. In the old days, the food would be prepared in big pots placed over a three-stone fireplace.

Below are a variety of dishes and snacks that will regularly be on the list when we talk about Krio food culture:

Sawa-Sawa (Sorrel)

Sawa-Sawa is made from the leaves of the sorrel plant which is part of the *hibiscus sabdariffa* plant family. The leaves are picked from the stems, thoroughly washed, and sliced into smaller pieces in preparation for cooking. See figures 6.5 and 6.6.

Krenkren

The leaves of this brambly plant are exclusively used as a vegetable in soup. When cooked, the leaves become very slippery. Variants of this green leafy vegetable can be found in many West African countries and as far away as Congo in Central Africa, and the Philippines. See figure 6.7.

Figure 6.5. Sawa-Sawa (sorrel) leaves.

Figure 6.6. Sawa-Sawa (sorrel) cooked.

Jɔlɔf Rɛs (Jollof Rice)

Jollof Rice is a rice dish that is very common all over West Africa, most notably, Sierra Leone, Senegal, Ghana, Nigeria, and The Gambia, where it is locally known as *bɛnichi*. These countries have engaged in endless arguments about who makes the best jollof rice; an indication of how passionate people can be about this particular food item. Jollof rice is cooked in a rich sauce made with oil, fresh tomatoes, tomato paste, onions, garlic peppers and different spices including thyme, and bay leaves, to give a rich aroma. This admixture is slowly cooked to a golden-brown color. Sometimes it is served with a stew of chicken, beef, pork, or fish, and at other times, it is eaten as is without any stew. See figure 6.8.

152   *Chapter 6*

Figure 6.7. Krenkren (brambly plant) cooked.

Bitas (Bitter Leaves; Vernonia Amygdalina)

Bitas [Bitter leaves] Bitter leaves come from a shrub with bitter barks and leaves (*Veronia amiygdalina*). Bitter leaves are used as a vegetable in *bitalif sup*. The leaves are so bitter they have to be pounded and soaked in water for a long time to get the bitter taste out. It is important to note here that bitter leaves have been found to have medicinal value.

Once the bitter leaf sauce has been prepared, it is preferably eaten with *fufu* which is made from soaked, fermented, cassava that is then pounded, sieved, and allowed to settle. Once it is settled, it is then cooked in a deep and round pot while it is constantly stirred with a *fufu tik* [slender stick used for stirring the fufu]. In other West African countries like Ghana and Nigeria,

Elements of Krio Culture

Figure 6.8. Jɔlɔf Rɛs (Jollof Rice).

they make their fufu out of yams or plantains. Krios love their *bitas ɛn fufu*. It is a favorite Saturday dish and some even have it two or three times a week. See figure 6.9.

Kasada (Cassava Root)

Various foods made from cassava include *fufu, kasada bred, gari, kanya.*

Kasada [Cassava]: *Kasada* is a versatile and popular food item in Krio cuisine. Once the skin is shed, it can then be boiled and eaten with any soup; it can also be fermented, pounded, and cooked, into a starchy consistency that

Figure 6.9. Bitas (bitter leaves; Vernonia Amygdalina).

Krios call *kasada fufu* which can be eaten with sauces like *bitas, krenken,* and *ɔkrɔ sup*. Finally, *kasada* can be grated into fine pieces and baked into a flat round bread called *kasada bred* [cassava bread] that is usually eaten with *frayfis* [fried fish]. In addition, the leaves of the cassava plant are a popular vegetable for the famous *kasada lif sup* [cassava leaf soup].

Kasada Lif Sup (Cassava Leaf Soup)

To prepare cassava leaf soup, fresh and tender leaves are selected, thoroughly washed, and grounded into a fine consistency. The sauce is then prepared with water, grated onions, pepper, palm oil or coconut oil, and pinch of groundnut paste. Meat, pork, and/or fish will be added, as needed, before the cassava leaves broth is carefully spread among the other ingredients in the pot. Allow the mix to cook for about forty-five minutes in medium heat.

Cassava Root

Figure 6.10. Kasada (cassava root).

Fufu

Figure 6.11. Fufu (Foofoo).

Cassava Bread

Figure 6.12. Kasada bred (Cassava bread).

Kola Nut

Kola nut comes in red and white colors and is used both as food and at ceremonial events. It is bitter in taste and has an appreciably high caffeine content. As food, some people chew kola nuts to stave off hunger. Others, notably college students, use it as a stimulant to stay up late as they study for exams.

However, its ceremonial uses are far more significant in Krio communities everywhere. Primarily, kola is a symbol of peace and reconciliation. It is used in many African cultures to foster community and collective well-being. After praying for peace or adjudicating difficult family or community situations, elders would take a bite out of a kola nut that they would pass around

Figure 6.13. Kola nɔt (Kola nut).

for every adult in the group to take a bite of as well. This is an indication that all agree with and accept the decisions that have been reached. In the old days, refusal to take a bite out of a kola nut that was circling the group, is a sign of disrespect and a challenge to the community efforts for peace and reconciliation.

Kola nuts are also used to invoke and communicate with the ancestors. In all formal or traditional ceremonies, the ancestors are called upon not only to witness the event, but to approve the decisions made and the prayers offered. Krios do this through what is known as the "kola ritual." Two kola nuts, one white and one red are split open. The diviner would take all four pieces, wash them, and shake them within his closed hands, while calling upon the ancestors to come and answer their prayers. He or she would pour the ancestors' favorite drinks before throwing all four pieces on the ground to ascertain that the ancestors have answered their call. One red and one white piece of the kola must turn upward, and one red and one white must face down. Any other combination means that the ancestors are not readily satisfied with the entreaties of the diviner. So, he or she would try again, or pass the kola nuts to another elder who would repeat the same ritual to "convince" the ancestors to come down and bless the efforts of the family. That elder would try even harder to persuade the ancestors. If she/he hits the right combination, then Krios would excitedly shout out, "*dɛn dɔn tek am!*" meaning, "they have accepted our calls and entreaties." After that, the elder who "reached" the ancestors would take a bite on one piece of the kola nut which she/he would pass around the group, as we saw before. What is left over of the water and the alcoholic beverages must also be consumed or disposed of to close the ceremony.

SNACKS

Kanya

Kanya is a snack made from pounded roasted peanuts, sugar, and finely sieved *gari* [dried cassava]. In some cases, pounded rice is substituted for *gari*. It is an immensely popular snack at parties and traditional ceremonies.

Figure 6.14. Kanya (snack of peanuts and sugar).

Jinja Kek (Ginger Cake)

Ginger cake is baked hard until light brown. It is a much sought after snack especially during holidays such as Christmas and Easter, as well as celebratory functions such as 40-day, *bɛrin chɔch* [memorial service for the departed], birthdays, and one-year remembrance events.

Figure 6.15. Ginija kek (Ginger cake).

Figure 6.16. Kɔngu (snack of peanut butter rolled into rings or balls).

Kɔngu

Kɔngu is a Krio snack made with a mixture of peanut butter paste, flour, sugar, rolled into rings or made into balls.

Rayz Bred (Rice Bread)

Rayz Bred is a Krio staple that is readily found in unique events like weddings, repasts, and birthday parties. The main ingredients of this delicacy are rice flour, banana, and sugar. Below is a quick recipe for *rayz bred* from Desiree's kitchen.[11]

   4 cups of rice flour
   8 cups of crushed ripe bananas
   1 cup of sugar
   1 cup of oil
   1 teaspoon of grated nutmegs

Mix all thoroughly.

Bake in the oven at 300 degrees for one hour

Figure 6.17. Rayz bred (rice bread).

Then, turn temperature down to 250 degrees
Bake for another hour until brown.

KRIO MUSIC/DANCE

Music and dance in Krio culture as with most traditional African cultures, play an especially important part in the daily lives of the people. Besides their entertainment value for which they are well known, Krio music and dance tell stories about relationships, provide historical details about families and communities, and celebrate births, weddings, and funerals. Among the pacesetters who enriched traditional Krio music and dance are Ebenezar

Calendar, the Rokel River Boys, Dr. Oloh, and Peter na Lepet. There were other Krio musicians who performed in bands that played only Western music at formal dance parties ("dignity balls") in various dance halls like the famed Wilberforce Hall in the center of Freetown. Dignity balls attracted mostly the affluent and well-educated Krios whereas traditional music and dance like *gumbe* and *marimba* music tended to be popular among the rank-and-file Krio. Over time, *gumbe* music became the most popular genre in Krio communities all around the colony, and we will see why below.

Gumbe Music and Dance

Several researchers have proffered information about the origins of Gumbe music and dance. John Collins argues that *gumbe* originated from West Africa and was brought to the Americas by enslaved Africans.[12] According to David Buisseret et al., the origins of *gumbe* is closely tied to the tonal elements of the Kwa language group of West Africa, providing the linguistic and sonorous basis for the "West African drum and dance tradition in which the drummer and dancer appear to be engaged in a storytelling session."[13]

It may be worth exploring a possible Bantu origin of the *gumbe* as the Kicongo group in Central Africa use the term "Ngkumbi" to mean a "drum" that comes with a dance of the same name. Jean Rouch and Enrico Fulchignoni's account about the origin of the drum also situates it in the African continent. They believe that *gumbe* is of Mandingo origins, although we cannot find conclusive evidence that it is.[14] Rachel Jackson weighs in on these theories of *gumbe* origins and sees some plausibility for the argument that the *gumbe* drum may have existed in Africa before slavery. "Since the escaped slaves were Africans," she conjectures, "it is safe to assume that the *gumbe* was modelled on various pre-slavery African drums."[15] In acknowledging the influence of *gumbe* [goombay] in the Bahamas, the Bahamas government's website stated that the "derivation of the word is West African, from an African drum called 'goom-ba.' This early style of music was typical for both song and dance."[16]

Thus, it is quite evident that the pre-slavery origins of *gumbe* cannot be easily established, and we believe that this is so because this type of drum and dance has existed, perhaps simultaneously, in various parts of the continent.

The drum itself is either square or rectangular with a flat surface covered with rawhide like goatskin or sheepskin which is held together by a complex knot of ropes tightened to produce the exact sounds the players want to get out of it. Most *gumbe* drums in Sierra Leone are played with the hands while the player is sitting upon it; however, others, more smaller drums, may be played with specially cut and smoothed sticks while the drum is slouching around the neck of the player or firmly locked under his arms.

164   *Chapter 6*

The history of *gumbe* drum and dance in Sierra Leone is closely associated with the Maroons of Jamaica. In Freetown, they joined other repatriated Africans, the Black Poor from England, African Americans from Nova Scotia who fought on the side of the British in the American War of Independence, and the Liberated Africans who had been rescued from slave ships bound for slavery in the Americas and the Caribbean. This motley collection of immigrants interacted to some extent with the local inhabitants such as the Thaimne (Temne), Bullom, Mende, Loko, and the Limba. As Jackson astutely observes, "Freetown quickly became a melting pot of ethnicities and nationalities."[17] It was in this setting that the Maroons built their *gumbe* drums and the ensuing *gumbe* culture. Having mastered the art of carpentry in Jamaica, it was not long before they made *gumbe* drums popular in Freetown and the surrounding villages.

Over the years, *gumbe* music thrived and came to be championed by a celebrated gumbe artist, Dr. Oloh. He was born Israel Olufemi Cole, and hails from the village of Leicester. His musical interests started at a very young age when he began to experiment with homemade instruments like empty milk cans, old saws, tiny stones, and makeshift boxes, that were initially used for sitting purposes. These homemade instruments when syncopated gave the sound and rhythm of *gumbe* music which the Jamaican Maroons had made popular in Freetown. Dr. Oloh continued to hone this music and eventually made *gumbe* music one of the most popular musical genres not only among the Krios in Freetown but in many parts of the country, and even as far away as the Gambia, Senegal, Liberia, Ivory Coast, and Fernando Po. The creative musician that he was, Dr. Oloh mixed *maringa music* forms, made popular by Ebenezer Calendar, with gumbe rhythms to create a more contemporary sound of the *gumbe* drum. Now, *gumbe's* popularity has expanded rapidly in West Africa and the African diaspora and the genre has influenced popular music in these regions as well. A Krio wedding, birthday party, or holiday celebrations, without gumbe music is unimaginable. In short, as Jackson concludes, "*Gumbe*'s survival in Sierra Leone is linked to its standing as a powerful signifier of a shared Creole identity."[18]

It is very clear now that scholars from various parts of the world are recognizing the cultural, linguistic, and historical connections that tie *gumbe* to West and Central Africa, and the Caribbean.

We now know that *gumbe* (or its idea and forms) was preserved by enslaved Africans in Jamaica and later spread to other islands like Trinidad and Tobago, Dominica, Guyana, and Suriname. The Jamaican Maroons brought it (back) to Sierra Leone in the late 1800s and early1900s.

NOTES

1. Kenneth Bilby, "Africa's Creole Drum: The Gumbe Vector and Signifier of Trans-Atlantic Creolization," in *Creolization as Cultural Creativity*, ed Robert Baron and Ana C. Cara (Jackson: University of Mississippi Press, 2011), 312.

2. Akintola J. G. Wyse, *The Krio of Sierra Leone: An Interpretive History* (London: C. Hurst, 1989).

3. Arthur T. Porter, "Religious Affiliation in Freetown, Sierra Leone," *Africa: Journal of the International Journal Institute*23, no. 1 (1953): 11, https://doi.org/10.2307/1156028.

4. Porter, "Religious Affiliation in Freetown," 6.

5. Gibril R. Cole, *The Krios of West Africa, Culture, Creolization, and Colonialism in the Nineteenth Century* (Athens: Ohio University Press, 2013),4.

6. Wyse, *Krio of Sierra Leone*.

7. Cole, *Krios of West Africa*, 8.

8. Kemi Adamolekun, "Survivors' Motives for Extravagant Funerals Among the Yorubas of Western Nigeria," *Death Studies* 25, no. 7 (2001): 609–19.

9. Betty M. Wass and S. Modupe Broderick, "The Kaba Sloht," *African Arts* 12, no. 3 (1979): 62, https://doi.org/10.2307/3335581.

10. Wass and Broderick, "Kaba Sloht," 62.

11. Desiree Spencer-Walters, from her personal collection of recipes for Krio dishes.

12. John Collins, "The Early History of West African Highlife Music," *Popular Music* 8, no. 3 (1989): 221–30, https://doi.org/10.1017/S0261143000003524.

13. Tom Spencer-Walters, "Creolization and Kriodom: (Re)Visioning the "Sierra Leone Experiment," in *New Perspectives on the Sierra Leone Krio*, edited by Mac Dixon-Fyle and Gibril Cole (New York: Peter Lang, 2006), 249.

14. Jean Rouch and Enrico Fulchignoni, "Cine Ethnography: Jean Rouch with Enrico Fulchignoni," in *Ciné-Ethnography*, ed. and trans. Steven Feld (Minneapolis: University of Minnesota Press, 2003), 147–87.

15. Rachel Jackson, "The Transatlantic Journey of *Gumbé*: Where and How Has It Survived?" *Journal of International Library of African Music* 9, no. 2 (2012): 128, https://core.ac.uk/download/pdf/230340048.pdf (accessed February 2, 2024).

16. Government of The Bahamas, "Origins of Goombay Music," https://www.bahamas.gov.bs. See https://www.bahamas.gov.bs/wps/portal/public/Culture/Performing%20Arts/ (accessed February 2, 2024).

17. Jackson, "Transatlantic Journey of *Gumbé*," 134.

18. Jackson, "Transatlantic Journey of *Gumbé*," 126.

Chapter 7

Krio Traditions

DƐN TRADISHƆN WE WI PIPUL DƐN, MƆNIN-MƆNIN, LƐF GI WI. [TRADITIONS OUR ANCESTORS LEFT FOR US LONG AGO.]

Folk traditions in many parts of the world anchor people solidly to their cultural and linguistic environments. Customs, cultural practices, stories that our elders and senior family members tell us, naming ceremonies, and the like, are traditions that enhance our sense of self and bring us closer to others within our communities. Frank Sonnenberg aptly summarized traditions this way:

> They remind us that we are part of a history that defines our past, shapes who we are today and who we are likely to become. Once we ignore the meaning of our traditions, we're in danger of damaging the underpinning of our identity.[1]

Among the Krios, traditions have helped to solidify a syncretic culture that has existed now for several centuries. As the various strands of cultural and linguistic artifacts come together, Krio families began to see and experience the things that bind them together as a community. It does not matter if the source of a cultural practice, for example, is of Yoruba, Akan, or Mende origins. Over time, such practices became integral components of Krio culture. A few of these traditions discussed in this chapter are: the practice of dedicating a new-born baby to the world; the act of and the reason for having an elaborate and family-oriented engagement ceremony; ceremonies to honor and/or celebrate the deceased; secret cultural societies; and traditions of architecture that are closely related to history and class structure among the Krio. Most of

168   *Chapter 7*

these traditions are of Yoruba derivation except for the architectural tradition which is credited to the Nova Scotians and the Maroons from Jamaica.

PULNADO/KƆMƆJADE

Pulnado/Kɔmɔjade, which means "Take outside" is a ceremony for dedicating the new-born to the world. Seven days after a child is born (eight days for girls), the baby is dressed up for this important ceremony. The oldest and most respected female relative will get up to the acclamation of the invited guests seated in the living room. She will carefully pick up the baby and head for the doorway with the invited guests following closely behind. She will walk out of the house with the baby into the open, as it were, for the dedication ceremony. First, libations will be poured for the ancestors to solemnly invoke their presence as witnesses to the dedication of the child to the world. The elder will then point the baby to the sky, the trees, the stream, and the road, all elements of a life the child is expected to encounter as they grow up. The female elder will pray to God and the ancestors to shield the child from all harm and danger so that the child may grow up to protect their own mother, father, and siblings. Other elders will also offer prayers for the child, following which the parents would go through the process of naming the child.

NAMING TRADITION AMONG THE KRIO

The Krio people say *Luk os bifo yu gi pikin nem.* [Think about your family history and traditions before naming a child.]. Names in Krio societies are not given because they sound good or because they are popular. Names are given because they are usually connected to circumstances surrounding the birth of the child [for example, *Adebayɔ,* meaning, "He came at a joyful time"], significant events in the family [for example, *Oluwɔle,* meaning, "The Lord has entered this house"]; or, fulfillment of wishes of a deceased relative [for example, Adebimpe, 'The crown gave me my birth and did a finished job of it"]; or, the day of the week the child is born [for example, *Esi,* "girl born on Sunday," or *Kwame,* "boy born on Saturday"]; or, naming a child as a result of a striking resemblance to a deceased relative whose memory nostalgically lingers in the minds of family who do not wish to forget him or her [for example, *Tunde,* "Father returns"]; or, a child born after a family loss or tragedy [*ɛkundayɔ,* "Weeping becomes joy"]. In early Krio society, these names would be kept secret until the *pulnado* ceremony. More Krio names and their meanings can be found in the Glossary.

Once prayers and naming of the child have been completed, the actual dedication ceremony will begin. The elder conducting the ceremony will then lightly touch the lips of the child with four life-affirming elements:

1. Water: because it is believed to sustain life, purity, and renewal.
2. Salt: provides food for the earth as well as wisdom for humankind.
3. Honey: brings joy, good health, and prosperity.
4. Hot Pepper: believed to give strength and help life to persevere.

Once the entire ceremony is over, the group excitedly goes back into the house in eager anticipation of delectable traditional food and drinks for everyone to partake in.

PUT STƆP

Put Stɔp means "putting a stop to dating once a couple commit to one another." It is a dramatic and exciting ceremony to celebrate one's intention to get married. Getting married in traditional Krio society is a very elaborate and complicated process. Once an intention to marry is declared, the man must write a letter to the lady's family explicitly declaring his intentions for the girl. Her family, in turn, will launch investigations into the young man's family to establish there are no health or mental issues, that the man's family is from a reputable family tree, and that there are no criminal issues or embarrassing scandals associated with that family. The man's family will investigate as well but not always as vigorously as the lady's family. Equally important, these investigations are meant to ascertain that there are no direct blood relations between the two families. Once the lady's family is satisfied, they will respond to the letter and both families, or representatives thereof, will meet to get acquainted. It is noteworthy that although the girl's consent would be sought, it is the family's decision that will be paramount in this case.

The date is then set for the elaborate and dramatic engagement ceremony, *Put Stɔp*. This ceremony makes the relationship official and binding. In short, the man has been approved by the lady's family and therefore she is now said to be "marked" out. No more dating of other men or, in the case of the man, other women. The lady would wear her head tie [*ɛnkincha*] in a way that would indicate that she now has an *intended* boyfriend who plans to marry her.

The following is an abbreviated version of the actual *Put Stɔp* ceremony taken from a play written by Tom Spencer-Walters:[2]

170   *Chapter 7*

PUT STƆP, THE PLAY

[In the home of Bisi, the lady who is about to be engaged. The door is locked solidly, and everybody waits tensely. After a while, a knock is heard. The knock is repeated several times.]

Adeshɔla (Spokesperson for the lady)
Udat da wan de we de kan nak na mi do dis let-let awa? [Who is that knocking at my door this late?]

Sɔni (Spokesperson for the man)
Bo, na mi, Sɔni. ["Oh, it's me, Soni."]

Adeshɔla
Udat? Sony Ayenbolt? [in jest] *Bra, wi nɔ gɛt nɔ ayɛn bolt fɔ mɛlt-o. Tray wi neba.* [Who? Soni Ironbolt? Brother, we do not have any iron to smelt in this house. Why don't you try our neighbor?]

Sɔni
Nɔ-o, nɔto dat wi kam fɔ. Na siriɔs biznɛs bring wi kan na ya dis ivin. ["No, that's not why we are here. It's a very important business that brought us here this evening."]

Adeshɔla
Bra, dis tin ya nɔ go wet te tumara? [Brother, can't this wait until tomorrow?]

Sɔni
We yu si man lɛf in os dis awa we otutu de waya so, yu tink se na fɔ natin. Wi pipul dɛm kin se we yu si ɔkpɔlɔ tinap na fɛnch, no se gron wam. Na sɔntin wi si na yu gadin we wi want bad-bad. So, duya lɛ wi kan insay. [When you see a man leaves his house and ventures into this bitingly cold weather at this time, it is for something serious. Our people have this parable: when a frog must leap up the fence, know that the ground is very hot. We saw something in your rose garden that we desperately want. So, please let us in.]

Adeshɔla
Bra, uskayn ojukokoro dis. ɔrayt, una kan insay nɔ. Bɔt una nɔ te tumɔs-o. Wi wan go nak bɔdi. [Brother, what kind of envy is this? Ok, you can come in. But don't stay too long because we want to go to bed.]

[He opens the door. Sɔni and his group, which includes a young girl carrying a covered basket, walk in. They exchange greetings with Sɔni's group who offered them seats in the room.]

Adeshɔla
Una kabɔ-o. Una dɔn fos-fos wi tete wi dɔn opin di do fɔ una. So lɛ wi yɛri bɔt dis alejo ya so we bring una kam. [Welcome to you all. You were very insistent,

Krio Traditions

171

so we had to open our doors to you. Now, let's hear this great news that brought you here today.]

Soni

We wi de pas na fo rod nain wi si una fayn-fayn rozis gadin. A min, a nɔ wande si da kanaba gadin de. Yu tɔn ya, yu si rɛd rosis; yu smɛl am, i smɛl swit. Yu tɔn yanda, yu si yala rosis; yu smɛl am, i smɛl lɛk tin fɔ it. Du ya wi want wan pan yu rosis dɛm fɔ go plant na wi yon gadin. [While walking in the streets, we saw your magnificent rose garden. It is really an incredible garden. I have never seen such a beautiful garden. You look over here, there are red roses, you smell them and they smell so sweet. You look in another area, you see yellow roses, you smell them and they smell like a delicious dish. Please, we would like to ask for one of your roses to plant in our garden.]

Adeshɔla

Wi gladi fɔ yɛri dat. ɛnti yu nɔ chuk wan na yu pɔkit de? [We are happy to hear that. I hope you didn't pick one and hid it in your pocket.]

Soni

Nɔ-o. Na wan pan dɛm rosis ya so we wi si we wi nɔ ebul pul yay pan. If yu si we i rɔju, na kyapin bɛlɛmantande nɔmɔ kin diskrayb am. [Oh, no. It's one of these roses that we saw and couldn't take our eyes off. It is so beautiful; only Captain Belematande could describe its beauty.]

Adeshɔla

ɔrayt bra, i du so. Fambul dɛm, na di wɔd dis ya so we Bra Soni dɔn bring kam-o. [Ok, Brother Soni, that is enough. My family, this is the news that Brother Soni as brought us.]

Sisi Mɔkɛ (Adeshɔla's wife)

Bra Soni, yusɛf yu get liba-o. Wi dɔn plant dis rozis ya naw fɔ ɔmɔs yia. Wi de wach ɛn wata-ram kɛlɛ-kɛlɛ. Naw we i dɔn gro fayn-fayn, yu se yu want am? [Brother Soni, you're so bold. We planted this rose for so many years. Patiently caring for it. Now that it's grown to be so beautiful, you want us to give it to you?]

Soni

ee! Sisi Mɔkɛ, if wi gɛt da wan rosis de, i go shek ɔp ɔl dɛm fɛkɛ-fɛkɛ rosis na mi gadin. ɛn da rosis de dɔn mek una gadin fayn, duya lɛ wi sɛf ɛnjɔy am lilibit, nɔ? [Please Ms. Mokeh, if we can secure that one rose from your garden, it would rejuvenate all the withering roses in ours. Most of all that rose has beautified your garden, please let us enjoy it too.]

Adeshɔla

Wel, mi nɔ no uswan pan wi bɔku rozis dɛm yu de tɔk. Sisi Biɔla, du ma, yu no us rozis Bra Soni de tɔk bɔt? [Well, we don't know which one of our many roses you're talking about. Ms. Biola, do you know which rose Brother Soni is talking about?]

172   *Chapter 7*

Sisi Biɔla (Adeshɔla's sister)
A nɔ tink so-o. Pas wi pul dɛm wan bay wan. [I don't think so. We will have to bring out each one to find out.]

Adeshɔla
Misɛf tink se na dat wi fɔ du. [I also think that's what we should do.]

[Sisi Biɔla goes into a room and returns with a beautiful lady, one of the "roses."]

Adeshɔla
Dis wan ya naim wi call wi kɔnyɔ- kɔnyɔ rozis. As yu tɔch am so, i tan lɛk se i go mɛlt na yu an. Nain im yu se yu want? [This one is a calm and lethargic rose. As soon as you touch it, it becomes very coy. Is it what you want?]

Sɔni
Mi dadi, i fayn-o. Luk we i de mara. Bɔt nɔto im wi want. i nɔ te na di gadin yet. Gi am tu-tri yia, wi go kan bak fɔ insɛf. [My friend, she is beautiful. Look at how coy she is. But she is not our choice. She hasn't been in the garden too long. Give her a few more years and we will be back to ask for her.]

Adeshɔla
Ojare! Sisi Mɔkɛ, du ya go tray bak, nɔ. [Yes-o! Ms. Mokeh, could you please get another of the roses?]

[Sisi Biɔla goes into the room and returns with another lady, much older than the first].

Adeshɔla
Dis ya nain wi kɔl wi "nɛva day rozis." Ren ɔ shayn, de ɔ nɛt, na in lif dɛm de pul kɔla. Dis mɔs bi di rozis we una kan fɔ. [This rose is called "never-die" rose. Rain or shine, day or night, her petals always bring joy and acclamation. This must be the rose you came for.]

Sɔni
Mama yaa! Dis insɛf fayn-o! Bɔt oya, nɔto in wi de luk fɔ. [Wow! This too is very pretty! But, alas, it is not what we are looking for."]

Adeshɔla:
Bra wisɛf dɔn de taya-o. Sɔntɛm una dɔn mis rod. Sisi Mɔkɛ lɛ wi jɛs bring wan mɔ rozis nɔmɔ. If nɔto im dɛm want, dɛn go gɛ fɔ go ɔda say. ["Brother, we are getting tired. Mabe you're in the wrong place. Ms. Mokeh, let's bring out only one more rose. If it is not the one they want, they would have to look elsewhere.]

[Sisi Biɔla goes to the room one last time and emerged with a stunningly beautiful girl.]

Krio Traditions

Soni

Wetin dat!!! enheee! Na naw wi de tɔk! Na dis na di rozis we bring wi kan na ya tide. If una gi wi dis rozis, ed sef nɔ go at am. We i de waka so, anch dɛm sef go giam rod mek i pas. [Wow! Yesss!!! Now we're talking! This is the rose that brought us here tonight. If you give us this rose, we will take exceptional care of it. When she walks, even the ants will move out of the way for her to pass.]

Adeshɔla

ɔrayt, bra. Wi pipul den kin se, fayn wɔd pul kola. Una si dis rozis ya so, na wi bɔl yay. So wi nɔ de giwe am fɔ natin-o. Aw una kam? [Ok, brother. Our people used to say, positive words bring out positive responses. This rose you're asking for is the apple of our eye. So, we are not giving her away without anything in return. What did you bring us?]

Soni

Wi pipul dɛm kin se, if yu sabi was yu an, yu go it with dɛm agba dɛm. So wi bring dis shuku blay wit bɔku-bɔku prɛzent dɛm fɔ yu ɛn yu fambul dɛm. [Our ancestors used to say, if you wash your hands properly you can eat with kings. So, we brought you this basket with a lot of gifts for you and your family.]

[Soni leads the little girl with the basket on her head to Adeshɔla's family members].

If una tek am, wi wan mak wi fayn-fayn rozis wantem-wantem. [If you accept of gift, we want to "mark" our roses right away.]

Adeshɔla

Wi dɔn yɛri una wɔd. Bifo wi ansa, wi fambul dɛn gɛ fɔ go luk insay dis shuku blay fɔs dɛn dɛn go eng ed ɛn tɛl wi if wi fɔ gi una wi fayn-fayn rozis. [We have heard what you have to say. Before we give you our answer, family members must inspect the basket first, after which they would meet to decide whether we can release our beautiful rose to your family.]

The basket will be covered with a white and pink cloth. The white symbolizes purity, and the pink symbolizes peace and love. The contents are symbolic gifts to the bride-to-be's family. In this basket (or *shuku blay*), the following items are a must. The explanation of their importance is provided next to the items:

- Money: It is more like the dowry [amount is selected based on your financial worth and your commitment to the girl's family.]
- Bible: Signifies peace and blessings.
- The Ring: Tying the knot.
- Lime, sugar, kola, bitter kola: sweet and sour times in life.
- Salt: For flavor.

174   Chapter 7

- Alligator pepper [pod must remain closed]: Hot and hidden surprises. Don't go looking for what is hidden from you. Could mean trouble.
- Rice: For fertility.
- Needle and thread: Mending bad situations and making good ones.
- Clothing material: To make dresses when necessary.
- Pin: Not just for making dresses, but just so that you *can't* say: "*i nɔ gi mi pin frɔm we wi mit/mared.*" ["He did not give me anything, not even a pin, since we met or got married."]
- Icons of her profession: If she is a nurse, a thermometer would be added. If a doctor, a stethoscope; and if a teacher, a piece of chalk or red and blue pens, etc.

After a while, the group will emerge from the room with the bride-to-be. If their decision is positive, they will come out singing: *Yawo mami dɔn ansa yɛs-o, Dɔn ansa yɛs-o, Yawo mami dɔn ansa yɛs-o.* [The mother of the bride has answered "yes"; has answered "yes"].

[The bride-to-be will come out wearing the engagement ring which she will proudly display to everyone at the event].

If the woman's family is not satisfied with the contents of basket, the spokespersons for both families will go into negotiation mode immediately.

CELEBRATION AND REMEMBRANCE OF THE DEAD

Immediately after a Krio person dies, especially in the villages, all window blinds are taken down and replaced with white blinds or white sheets to signal the passing of someone in that house. As soon as neighbors or passers-by see the white blinds, they would go directly into the house to find out who died and to offer their sympathies. The adults will immediately rub ashes on the children's forehead so that when the spirit begins to travel it will not take the children with it. The deceased is usually celebrated and remembered at intervals of 7 days, 40 days, and one year among Krios who are Christians.

The 7-Day Event

For the 7-day event, a glass of cold water is placed on the center table in the house to honor the dead. The next morning, the elder members of the family would take that glass of water to the front door to communicate with the dead relative. They would ask for protection: "*du ya nɔ lɛf wi-o. Beg Papa Gɔd mek i opin rod fɔ wi we lɛf oba ya*" ["Please, don't forget us. Intercede with the almighty to make opportunities available to us on this side"], while sprinkling some of the water on the front steps. The 7-Day ceremony is becoming increasingly rare, partly because the funerals are taking much longer these days as family, friends, and acquaintances have to travel from various parts of the country or the globe to reach the deceased's home. Another reason is that in the old days when refrigeration was not easily available or accessible, burials took place quickly; so, it made sense to have a 7-day ceremony. Nowadays, corpses can be kept for long periods of time because refrigeration is widely available, and because burial plans are more elaborate and involving. Thus, more and more people are focusing on the next levels of remembrance, the 40-day and the one-year ceremonies.

The 40-Day/One Year Event

Unlike the 7-Day event, the 40-day and the one-year ceremonies are a bit more elaborate. Water would be put on the center table as before. But the family would do a ceremonial cook traditionally known as the *awujɔ*. It has been consistently used to honor the dead and to ask for their presence and support of important family functions like a wedding, key birthdays, and other significant accomplishments. All kinds of *plasas* [vegetable soups] including *bitas* and *krenkren* are prepared. In addition, other dishes such as *binch* [black-eyed peas], boiled or cooked with palm oil, fried plantains, and potatoes, *binch akara* [fried beans made out of black-eyed peas]; and *rɛs akara* [made with rice flour], will be on hand to enrich the variety of *awujɔ* foods. Portions of these foods become part of the *Nyɔle* ceremony that usually takes place in the morning and is conducted by senior members of the family.

The *Nyɔlɛ*

The *Nyɔle* is another symbolic way to acknowledge the presence of the deceased and to honor their memory principally during the 40-day event. It is a tradition that the Yoruba contingent of the Liberated Africans brought with them to Freetown that has now evolved into a staple in Krio culture. Once the cooking for the 40-day *awujɔ* is virtually complete, samples of that food is taken to a designated place in the backyard of the house for the *Nyɔle* ceremony. According to tradition, the food for the *Nyɔle* must have no salt added to it. It is not clear why salt is taboo to *Nyɔle* food. To perform the *Nyɔle* ceremony, one or two holes are dug in the backyard and parcels of the prepared food, water, and the favorite drink(s) of the departed are placed in these holes. Libations would begin with invocations of the ancestors and entreaties to the recently departed. One red and one white kola nuts are washed and split open into four pieces in all. Just as we pointed out earlier in our discussion of the

176   *Chapter 7*

kola nut, the most senior family member would throw the kola nuts on the
ground, and the way you know the departed have responded positively to
your message is one white and one red kola nut would be facing up and one
red and one white facing down. Once that happens everyone, especially the
children, would be ecstatic because now they can look forward to devouring
the delectable dishes that have been prepared. Everyone would then rush into
the house to partake of the *awujɔ.*

SECRET SOCIETIES

As we have established in other areas of this book, Muslim Krios who lived
in Fula Town, Fourah Bay, and Magazine Cut, were primarily members
of Yoruba groups among the Liberated Africans who were settled in what
became Freetown. This group was very passionate about preserving and
practicing Islam, as much as they were committed to keeping key elements
of Yoruba culture and traditions alive; and sometimes they did just that even
over the objections of the colonial authorities in Freetown.

One such Yoruba tradition that they maintained faithfully throughout are
secret societies. While secret societies are common in many parts of Africa,
including Sierra Leone, most require strict membership guidelines. Gibril
R. Cole agrees that "membership was tightly controlled and restricted to
those who had undergone the requisite rituals that were known only to the
initiated."[3] A loyalty oath was also required from members to never to divulge
the secrets or activities of the group or face serious, even fatal consequences.

Each of these secret societies have their own masquerades that Sierra
Leoneans refer to as *"debul."* A masquerader, Nathaniel King observes, is
a "mask-wearing figure that symbolizes the spirit and essence of a secret
society and leads it public performance."[4] When masqueraders perform in
public, such performances are usually accompanied by songs and dances that
are mainly of Yoruba origins. "Therefore," King concludes, "masqueraders
are a nexus of visible and invisible powers and urban secret societies' public
performances."[5]

Three of the most common secret societies in early Muslim Krio community in Fullah Town, Fourah Bay, and surrounding Liberated Africans villages
are the following.

The *ɔjɛ* [*ɛgwugwu*]

This organization took hold in the early nineteenth century when the
Liberated Africans not only in Fula Town and Fourah Bay communities
but also in nearby villages of Hastings, Waterloo, Benguema, and Orogun,

Krio Traditions 177

participated in preserving this secret society. The predominant Yoruba groups in Hastings, were the Okus and the Egbas. Each established communities at opposite ends of the village primarily to preserve the nuances of their culture and language. However, both nurtured the *ɔjɛ* society in strict adherence to established rituals. The organization has a number of masqueraders whose dress and function in public are different. *Alarugbe,* colorfully dressed in beaded gowns, is usually calm around people, but the *gbegi* masquerader is very agile and can become rather aggressive when excited. Young people like to tease him in order to get him to chase them. Whoever he catches up with will get a crack of his cane. These and a few other masqueraders come out in public on special occasions such as holidays. When they do, they sometimes incur the displeasure of the some Christian Krios who view the *ɔjɛ* masqueraders as evil or satanic. Some Christian Krios would remember growing up when they were strictly forbidden from having anything to do with these *dɛbul dɛm* [masqueraders] because they are anti-Christian and/or satanic. Over time however, both Muslim and Christian Krios became more comfortable with the *ɔjɛ* as an integral part of Krio culture.

The *ɔntin* Society

The *ɔntin* society also has its roots in Yorubaland and was brought over to Freetown by the Liberated Africans in the mid-nineteenth century. Its initial focus was hunting wild animals, which it still does today. However, it is now a more rigidly organized secret society like the *ɔjɛ* society. Women's participation in this society is limited. They cannot go on hunting expeditions with the men. In addition, while the hunters are away in the bush, women will prepare meals for their return, since the hunt may take the better part of a whole day. Hunters are not expected to come back empty handed, so they will keep hunting for as long as it takes to get a kill. Their return to the village is a festive occasion which brings people out into the streets, singing and dancing with the hunters. The *ɔntin* Society masquerader, the *ɔdɛ,* and his handlers, will lead the pack through the village to the designated house for the continuation of the hunting celebration. The *ɔntin* Society has arguably done more for social integration among the Krio and other ethnic groups in Sierra Leone than any of the other Yoruba-derived secret societies. Today, membership is more ethnically integrated, and *ɔntin* Society groups are invited to perform at weddings and other special events. Some of their more popular songs have become musical icons at parties and other social events.

When someone passes away, particularly if that person is a member of the *ɔntin* Society, a lead member of that society will blow their characteristic horn, commonly known as the *(a)fere* walking around the village or town and immediately the people will know that someone has passed away.

178   *Chapter 7*

Gɛlɛdɛ

The *gelede,* like the other secret societies we discussed, is of Yoruba origins
and demands strict membership rituals. Its masquerader is tall with a long
neck and often dresses like a mature woman whose face is a carved wooden
mask, supposed to be that of the spirit that the masquerader represents.

There are all kinds of folk stories associated with this masquerader. One is
that if a child's head is constantly unsteady, it is known as a *gelede nɛk,* and it
is believed to be caused by a mother looking directly at a *gelede* masquerade
when she was pregnant.

ARCHITECTURAL TRADITIONS

Beginning in the early nineteenth century, wooden houses, which the Krio
called *bod os*, were being constructed in many areas of Freetown. These
wooden houses were designed after the traditional colonial board houses
that were popular on the east coast of the United States in the eighteenth
century, and in prominent islands in the Caribbean, like Jamaica, Trinidad
and Tobago, and Suriname. The origin of these houses in Freetown is closely
tied to the history of enslavement in the eighteenth and nineteenth centuries.
Africans who were repatriated from Nova Scotia to Freetown, which included
free blacks from the east coast of the United States and the Maroons from
Jamaica, were already familiar with traditional colonial board houses. They
were, in most cases, forcibly recruited by the colonial authorities to build
these houses in Freetown and the surrounding villages like Regent, York, and
Wilberforce; thus, the Settler population was instrumental in the design and
construction of *bod os*.

The two *bod os* in the pictures below have somewhat similar architectural
designs except that one was built near a range of mountains and, therefore,
has a strong concrete base partly to support the wooden structure during the
heavy rains (figure 7.1). Freetown and its environs have some of the heavi-
est rainfall in the country. The other bod os is typically found in urban areas
(figure 7.2).

The houses are designed to have one main entrance which is directly
through the front porch. It is a much more acceptable cultural practice for vis-
itors to enter into the house only through this porch even though the house's
back door entrance is also available. The front porch also serves a strategic
and interesting purpose. It is where fathers and other senior male members of
the family sit to monitor all the traffic to and from the house especially in the
evenings; a time when boys are looking for ways to get around this restricted
area to visit their girlfriends or female friends in the house. Because of this

Figure 7.1. Example 1 of bod os (wood plank house with mountain view in background).

seemingly impenetrable "porch obstacle," the young men resort to whistling codes that would signal to the girls that they are around their house. But fathers, older brothers, and uncles, eventually mastered these as well.

Many of the currently existing board houses in Freetown were built as far back as the 1800s and early 1900s. So, it is not surprising that they are rapidly

Figure 7.2. Example 2 of bod os (wood plank house in an urban setting).

deteriorating from neglect, urbanization, lack of resources, and competition with newer stone and concrete designs which Krios call *ton os* ["concrete houses"]. The picture of the *ton os*, has a balcony on the side of the front entrance (fig. 7.3). Many use it to entertain as well as converse with neighbors and people walking along in the street below.

Over the years, concrete houses became not just a more durable architectural design but clear symbols of wealth, power, and status. Many of the educated and well-to-do increasingly opt for concrete houses while giving little thought to the preservation of the *bod os* as a vital component of Krio and, indeed, Sierra Leone history.

Today, with very minimal resources, the Monuments and Relics Commission and the Architectural Field Office, a non-profit organization, are working fervently to preserve what is left of the board houses as part of Freetown's architectural and freed slaves resettlement history. Sounding the alarm for what the disappearance of these monuments of history would mean for the Krio and for Sierra Leone history, Isatu Smith, Chair of the Monuments and

Relics Committee, had this to say: "If we cannot protect these houses, it will be a major part of our history and our heritage erased. They are a testament to the resilience of people who came from slavery to found this city. They're iconic."[6]

Figure 7.3.   Example of ton os (concrete houses).

In short, traditions enrich the culture of a people as they have done for Krio people for centuries. By strengthening the values and belief structures of Krio society, traditions are essentially giving the people tools and resources to honor and respect their past while leaving rich legacies for generations to come.

NOTES

1. Frank Sonnenberg, "Reasons Why Traditions Are So Important," *Weebly*, June 30, 2015, https://selatmeigs.weebly.com/uploads/9/3/2/7/9327727/7_reasons_why _traditions_are_so_important.pdf (accessed February 2, 2024).

2. Tom Spencer-Walters, *Put Stɔp*, Unpublished play (1977).

3. Gibril R. Cole, *The Krio of West Africa: Islam, Culture, Creolization, and Colonialism in the Nineteenth Century* (Athens: Ohio University Press, 2013), 161.

4. Nathaniel King, "Freetown's Yoruba-Modelled Secret Societies as Transnational and Transethnic Mechanisms for Social Integration," in *The Upper Guinea Coast in Global Perspective*, ed. Jacqueline Knörr and Christoph Kohl (New York: Berghahn Books, 1987; 2016), 60.

5. King, "Freetown's Yoruba-Modelled Secret Societies," 60.

6. Isatu Smith, quote in Tommy Trenchard, "Part of Sierra Leone's History Is Being Dismantled Board by Board," *New York Times*, January 20, 2016, https://www .nytimes.com/2016/01/20/world/africa/freetown-sierra-leone-board-houses.html (accessed February 2, 2024).

Chapter 8

Krio Folk Wisdom

Parables and Riddles

Krio folktales and riddles are organic components of Krio oral literature. They are focal elements in social interaction across Krio communities and they enhance cultural continuity while at the same time providing a strong basis for educating young people. The elders insist on cultural mastery of proverbs and riddles through oral participation partly because it is a natural way to pass knowledge of the culture and the language from one generation to the next. It is important to understand that the process of using proverbs and riddles in social situations is not punitive or dogmatic. Rather, it is spontaneous, exuberant, and entertaining, but firm. Below is a list of proverbs with explanations and some scenarios to demonstrate how these proverbs can be used in contextual situations. Following that is a collection of riddles and puzzles that are popular in Krio culture. Answers to these riddles and puzzles can be found in the Appendix at the end of the book.

PARABLES
LƐ WI KAN PUL PAREBUL.
["LET US TALK ABOUT PROVERBS."]

Parebul [Proverbs] are didactic sayings, often couched in figurative language that sets the tone to moralize or to speak of general truths in very concise language. They enrich the language by transforming ordinary experiences and linguistic expressions into meaningful interpretations in the lives of individuals or the community. Many of these proverbs quickly gain currency in the language. The Krio *parebul* is an integral part of communication among the Krio community of speakers. It is very common in everyday conversations.

184   *Chapter 8*

The *parebul*, like the *nansi tori* which will be discussed later, plays a significant role in raising children. In Krio society, just as in most African communities, elders use key elements from the environment, the language, and
nature, to educate the young. The house, trees, the forests, the animals, even
traditional cooking utensils find their way into the Krio *parebul*. As they
instruct and educate, these *parebuls* also help to anchor the young to their
environment while exposing them to higher levels of sophisticated uses of
Krio. Thus, they offer Krio speakers unlimited opportunities to be creative
and artful with the use of the language.

For example, to teach our young people about the benefits of generosity
and of reciprocity, you would often hear many parents and adults say:

"Fɔdɔm fɔ mi a fɔdɔm fɔ yu." [*Fall down for me and I will fall down*
   for you.]
Meaning: "If you give me a hand, I will return the favor."

Another proverb in this same vein is: *"An go an kam"* [*hand go, hand come*]
Meaning: "If you share with other people, you will receive more in return."

There are many variants of these proverbs in Sierra Leone Krio and African
Diaspora Creoles in North and South America and the Caribbean. For example, Jamaican Patois which shares many linguistic and cultural features with
Sierra Leone Krio, has a proverb that is almost identical to the Krio proverb,
An go an kam. It reads: *"Han' go, packy come,"* which essentially means
the same in Krio: share what you have and you will receive more in return.
In Susu, a major language spoken in Sierra Leone and Guinea, this adage is
also very evident and popular. Often you would hear adult speakers of Susu
say: *"Badyka seeka, badyka fa,"* meaning, "one good turn deserves another."

In the following pages, the presentation of Krio parables will be organized
in four dimensions: (a) the *parebul* itself, (b) its literal meaning, (c) its figurative meaning, and then, (d) a scenario in which this parable might be used.

Young people everywhere are adventurous and curious. Sometimes this
curiosity lands them in trouble, especially the kind from which they have
difficulty extricating themselves. Thus, to guide young people away from
trouble or difficult situations, certain Krio proverbs or wise sayings are often
used in conversations with the youth:

Parebul 1
Da fɔl we nɔ yɛri shi, na ston i go yɛri [The chicken who fails to go away
   with a gentle nudge will do so with a stone.]
Meaning: Do not ignore subtle warnings in life; if you do, dire consequences can result.

Scenario:

Ola: *Modu, a dɔn wɔn yu se lɛ yu lɛf fɔ fala bad kɔmpin. Dɛn go put yu pan bibig wahala. Bɔt yu nɔ de yɛri wɔd. A de wɔn yu egen-o. Yu grani kin se, "Da fɔl we nɔ yɛri shi, i go yɛri ston. Lonta"*

English translation

[Ola: Modu, I have warned you about associating with bad kids. They will get you into a lot of trouble. However, you don't listen. I am warning you again. Your grandmother used to say, "The chicken that does not heed a gentle nudge, will get something more severe. Period!"]

Parebul 2

Da pikin we wan wɛr in dadi in trɔsis, na rop go it in wes. [The child who insists on wearing his father's pants, the rope belt would damage his waist.]

Meaning: Don't try to be what you're not. It can lead to dire consequences.

Scenario:

Amina: *Dis bɔbɔ ya tu fityay ɛn bigman. i tink se da lili buk we i dɔn lan, nain mek an man.*

Peter: *So wetin yu tɛl am se?*

Amina: *Wetin yu tink? A jes pul dis parebul pan am: "Da pikin we wan wɛr in dadi in trɔsis, na rop go it in wes."*

English translation

[Amina: This boy is too arrogant and bigheaded. He thinks that the little knowledge he has acquired makes him a man.

Peter: So, what did you tell him?

Amina: What do you think? I just recited this parable to him: "The child who insists on wearing his father's pants, the rope belt would damage his waist."]

Parebul 3

If yu trowe asis, asis go fɔdɔm bak pan you. [If you throw ash, some of it would end up on your own skin.]

Meaning: You would reap whatsoever you sow.

Scenario:

Yetunde*: Wetin da uman du yu we yu de kɔs am so?*

Oyɛmi*: Yu nɔ yɛri we i de kongosa mi? If a kech am, i nɔ go du am to nɔbɔdi egen.*

Yetunde*: Oyɛmi, na fɔ kɛlɛ-kɛlɛ-o. ɛnti yusɛf no,* if yu trowe asis, asis go fɔdɔm bak pan you.

English translation

[Yetunde: What did that lady do to you that you are abusing her so much?

Oyemi: Didn't you hear her spewing gossip about me? If I get hold of her, she would never do this to anyone again.

Yetunde: Oyemi, you should calm down and take it easy. You know what they say, "If you throw ash, some of it would certainly end up on you."]

The value of hard work is something parents and communities across Africa teach the young ones. This imperative is solidly etched in their cultures as it is in the realization of the many challenges facing the continent. Among the Krio as well, hard work is perceived as the engine of success. What better way to impart that in the young ones than through the artful uses of the proverbs.

Parebul 4

If yu tek tɛm kil anch, yu go si in gɔt. [If you are very careful in dissecting the ant, you will see its entrails.]

Meaning: If you are very diligent and careful in what you do, you will be successful.

Scenario:

Kojo: *Mama, a dɔn lan mi mat sɔm dɛm soteee, bɔt a stil nɔ ɔndastan.*

Mama: *Kojo aw yu kin lan dɛm?*

Kojo: *A kin luk di ɛgzampul we ticha gi wi, dɔn, a kin wok dɛm fas-fas.*

Mama: *Yu fɔ tek dɛm wan bay wan tete yu dɔn ɔl. Yu mɛmba wetin wi pipul dɛn kin se: If yu tek tɛm kil anch, yu go si in gɔt.*

Kojo: *ɔrayt ma.*

English translation

[Kojo: Mama, I have studied my math problems for a long time, but I still don't get.

Mama: Kojo, how do you approach these problems?

Kojo: I study the examples the teacher gave us, then I go through the problems very quickly.

Mama: You should work on each problem separately until you finish all of them. Do you remember what people used to say? If you are very diligent and careful in what you do, you will be successful.]

Parebul 5

Saful-saful kech mɔnki. [Moving softly, softly, helps you catch a monkey.] Or, "*Jɛntri nɔ kam bay takiti.*" [You do not acquire wealth by sudden, unplanned activity; you must work hard at it.]

Meaning: Diligence and hard work will certainly pay off.

Scenario:

Krio Folk Wisdom

Soni: *Na mi gɛt di wahala fɔ kech di rɛd kak we wi wan kuk fɔ wi Sɔnde fray sup. Da kak de at fɔ kech bikɔs i fas lɛk dia.*

Kɔle: *Wetin yu fɔ du, tu-tri de bifo yu rɛdi fɔ kech am, yu fɔ de fid am wit rɛs sid tri tɛm fɔ de so wɛnɛba i si yu, i go rɔn kan to you fɔ rɛs sid. i go mek an izi fɔ kech am. Saful-Saful kech mɔnki.*

Soni: *Mi brɔda a go tray dat ɛn si. Tɛnkya.*

Kɔle: *No wahala.*

English translation

[Soni: I have the challenging task of catching the red cock that we will be preparing for our Sunday stew. That cock is very difficult to catch because it is as fast as a deer.

Kɔle: This is what you should do. About three days before you are ready to catch it, give it rice seeds three times a day, so that whenever it sees you, it will run over to you for more rice seeds. That will make it easy for you to catch it. "Moving carefully helps you catch the monkey more readily."

Soni: My brother, I'll try that method. Thank you.

Kɔle: No problem.]

Parebul 6

Yanga na pen. [Beauty is pain.]

Meaning: One must endure pain to look pretty.

Scenario:

Nansi: *Alaba, stɛdi nɔ we a de plant yu ia.*

Alaba: *Sisi, yu de mek di kɔn ro tu tayt, ma. I de at me ed.*

Nansi: *Wɛl, mi pikin, ɛnti yu sɛf no, if yu wan luk rɔju, yu gɛ fɔ memba se, yanga na pen.*

English translation

[Nansi: Alaba, keep still while I am braiding your hair.

Alaba: Ma'am, you're making the corn rows too tight. It's hurting my head.

Nansi: Well, my child, you know if you want to look pretty, you have to endure the pain that comes with it.]

A common feature in human interactions is the desire to seem brave and fearless in the face of challenges or impending danger. Young people especially tend to display these feats of bravery or boastfulness in front of their peers or people they want to impress or, alternatively, are afraid of. Krio culture has incorporated several parables to objectify this idea. Here are some of them:

Parebul 7

Fɔ mas agidi go gi lɛpɛt nɔto ɛnitin. na udat fɔ go gi am nain na di wahala.
[Crushing and mixing the ground corn to give to the leopard is nothing.
Who should deliver it to that leopard, that is the question.]

Meaning: People will boast, threaten, and show bravado, but when it's time
to act, they are nowhere to be found or do not have the heart to take the
challenge.

Scenario:

Olu: *Na Dele de kan kuk di jɔlɔf rɛs fɔ di awujɔ.*

Sera: *Na da laylondo de yu aks fɔ kan du dat? i lay ɛn kongosa i kayn nɔ
de. If i se wan wɔd bɔt mi fambul, a go kɔs am pik pɔkit.*

ɔmɔ: *Misɛf na ya. A dɔn rɛdi fɔ-r-am. Mek a yɛri wan wɔd bɔt mi pipul dɛm,
i nɔ go kongosa nɔbɔdi egen.*

kɔn kɔn kɔn [knock at the door]

Olu: *Udat da wan de?*

Dele: *Na mi Dele-O.*

Olu: *Kan insay. Dis na mi padi dem, Sera ɛn in sista, ɔmɔ.*

Dele: *ee! ee! a no dɛm. Nɔto una dadi bin de pan da vawchaget wahala?
Wetin apin afta dat? Dɛn lɔk an ɔp, ehn?*

(*Di ples mek yeng. Nɔbɔdi nɔ se natin.*)

English translation

[Olu: Dele is coming to cook the jollof rice for the ceremonial feast.

Sera: You asked that notorious liar to do that for you? She is a liar and a
scandalous gossiper, the likes of whom you've never seen. If she says
anything about my family, I will curse her profusely.

ɔmɔ: Me too. I am ready for her. Let me hear a word from her about my
family and she will never disrespect anyone again.

[Knock at the door]

Olu: Who is there?

Dele: It's me, Dele.

Olu: Please come in. These are my friends, Sarah and her sister, Omoh.

Dele: Eeee! I know them very well. Wasn't it your dad who was involved
in the vouchergate scandal? What happened in the end? Was he thrown
in jail?]

(There was silence. No one said anything.)

Parebul 8

If yu yams wayt, kɔba-r- am. [If your yam is white, cover it.] Or, *If yu koko
ros, sidɔm na kɔna ɛn it am saful.* [If your cocoa yam is nicely roasted,
sit in a corner and eat it quietly.]

Meaning: When peeled or cut, the whiter the yam looks on the inside, the
healthier and more delectable it is. Or, A nicely roasted cocoa yam is a
desiring treat. Thus, the meaning: Do not be boastful, pretentious, cocky.

Krio Folk Wisdom 189

Scenario:

Tobi: *Bɔbɔ, a tek fɔs pan ɔl mi sɔbjɛk dɛm. A tink se a sabi buk pas ɔl man na di klas.*

Ade: *Bra, if yu yams wayt, kɔba am-o.*

English Translation

[Tobi: You know, I came first in all my subjects. I must be the smartest person in the class.

Ade: Brother, do not be boastful, pretentious, or cocky.]

In Krio culture, living honestly, religiously, and successfully are paramount. Parents take this notion seriously because failure to adhere to a righteous life reflects negatively not only on the individual but on their families. Thus, parents and elders in the culture made sure they add appropriate proverbs and wise sayings in their communicative arsenal that would constantly remind the youth of their responsibilities not to let themselves or their families down.

Parebul 9

Shɔt at man nɔ de joyn kaka dɛbul. [A man with a hasty temper does not join a fiery masked devil group.]

Meaning: Know your limits and make prudent decisions about your well-being.

Scenario:

Sally: *ɔsɛ, bo kan fala mi go kɔl dɛt, nɔ?*

ɔsɛ: *Udat yu wan go kɔl dɛt pan?*

Sally: *A de go kɔl dɛt pan Kɔle we de dɔng di trit.*

ɔsɛ: *Aah Mi mami! Mi ɛn da man de nɔ gri-o. From we i lɛnt mi nayn lion, te tide i nɔ pe mi bak. A nɔ wan trɔbul bikɔs if a ol da wande, na kɔnsibul dɛn go kɔl pan mi. ɛnti yu sɛf no se mi na shɔt at man, so a nɔ tink se a go fala yu go de.*

English translation

[Sally: ɔsɛ, please, can you accompany me to retrieve money that is owed me?

ɔsɛ: Who owes you money?

Sally: Kɔle, who is just down the street.

ɔsɛ: Ah! My friend! That man and I are sworn enemies. Ever since he borrowed nine leones from me, he has never paid me back. I don't want any trouble because if I confront him for my money, they will have to call the police on me. You know how I have a hasty temper, so I don't think I should accompany you.]

Parebul 10

190   *Chapter 8*

We yu ɛn ɔntin man nɔ gri na tɔng, nɔ fala-r-am go insay bus. [If you
and the hunter have noticeable differences in town, don't go hunting
with him.]

Meaning: Know your limits and make thoughtful decisions when faced
with overwhelming odds.

Scenario:

Joya: *Wetin yu de du dis Satide ivin?*

Dele: *A wan go Count Down, dans lilibit, ɛn drink tu-tri bia.*

Joya: *Udat yu de go wit?*

Dele: *A de go wit mi padi, Joe.*

Dele: *Da drɔnkɔ-drɔnkɔ de we bin de put yay pan yu uman. If yu nɔ tek tɛm,
i go put yu pan ɔl kayn wahala.*

English translation

[Joya: What are your plans for this Saturday evening?

Dele: I want to go the Club Countdown to dance and drink a few beers.

Joya: Who will you be going with?

Dele: I am going with my friend, Joe.

Joya: That drunkard who has been eyeing your girlfriend? If you're not
careful, he'll get you into all kinds of trouble.]

Krio proverbs are frequently used to caution people to avoid getting
involved in needless conflicts or being overly trusting. Conflicts can compro-
mise your integrity and bring disrepute to your family; similarly, openly trusting people with some of your most intimate secrets can leave you exposed to
blackmail, ridicule, and sometimes exploitation.

Parebul 11

Trɔbul ledɔn saful de slip, yanga go wek am [Trouble lay sleeping peacefully, and vanity went and woke him up.]

Figurative Meaning: Opening up a can of worms. In other words, let sleeping dogs lie.

Scenario:

Kwesi: *Duni, duya we da bɔbɔ we nɔba laf. I dɔn blo fɔ ambɔg, ɛn?*

Duni: *Udat, Kɔle? I de biɛn yad de rid in buk. Tide na bɛtɛ de fɔ-r-am.*

Kwesi: *mek a go tɛl am adu.*

Duni: *A nɔ no-o, bɔt tray.*

Kwesi: *Kɔle! Kɔle! Bo aw yu du tide?*

Kɔle: *Udat dawande?*

Kwesi: *Na mi, Kwesi*

Kɔle: *Wetin yu want? A bizi. A nɔ gɛt tɛm fɔ tɔk to yu. Aw yu tot yu tumɔt
tɔk kan na ya, na so yu go tot am go usay yu kɔmɔt.*

English translation

[Kwesi: Duni, where is that boy who never smiles? Has he stopped getting into trouble?

Duni: Who, Kɔle? He is in the backyard reading a book. Today is a good day for him.

Kwesi: Let me go say hello to him.

Duni: I don't know if it's a good idea, but you can try.

Kwesi: Kɔle! Kɔle! How are you today?

Kɔle: Who is that?

Kwesi: It's me, Kwesi.

Kɔle: What do you want? I am busy. I don't have time to talk to you. So, take your deceitful talk back where you came from.]

Parebul 12

Pit wet pit, lεf bad blɔd na belε [When you spit, be sure your spit is white, but leave the bad blood in your stomach.]

Figurative Meaning: Keep your deep secrets well hidden.

Scenario:

Okabi: *A si yu fambul na makit tide.*

Remi: *Udat? Bayɔ?*

Okabi: *Naim-o. I bin de aks mi aw wi de du. εn i se in yεri se mi εn mi wεf bin gεt lili chamot. Aw i sabi dis, na Gɔd wangren no.*

Remi: *Eeee dεm bisabɔdi-odofo ya so. Wetin yu tεl am?*

Okabi: *A tεl am se wi ɔrayt εn di fambul dεm ɔl de du wεl.*

Remi: *i bεtε we yu nɔ tεl am bɔt di mɔni plaba bekɔs yu nɔ no usay i go εnd.*

English translation

[Okabi: I saw your relative in the market today.

Remi: Who, Bayo?

Okabi: Yes. He asked me how you're doing. He also said he heard through the grapevine that my wife and I had a little disagreement. Only God knows how he knew this.

Remi: These busybodies! What did you tell him?

Okabi: I told him we are fine, and the rest of the family members are doing well.

Remi: I am glad you did not tell him about your financial woes because you don't know how far he would have spread that information.]

Parebul 13

Kakroch nɔ gε nɔ biznεs pan fɔl fεt. [*The* cockroach has no business getting involved in chicken fights.]

Figurative Meaning: Don't get involved in conflicts that could be your undoing.

192   *Chapter 8*

Scenario:

Lara: *Bisi ɛn Tayo, wetin mek ɔltɛm una de mek plaba. Una nɔ de taya for fɛt?*

Bisi: *Uswan na yu yon de?*

Tayo: *U mek yu jɔj?*

Bisi: *Tel am fɔ mi. Go mayn yu os we ɔl kayn tings dɔn de apin de, bifo yuk kan put mɔt pan wi biznɛs.*

English translation

[Lara: Bisi and Tayo, why are you always quarreling? Don't you get tired of fighting?

Bisi: Why are you getting involved in this?

Tayo: Who made you judge?

Bisi: Yea, who? Go put your own house in order where all kinds of shady things are going on, before you start delving into our business.]

Life itself is central to Krio thought and philosophy. It is celebrated, cherished, protected, and nurtured in all aspects of Krio language and culture. People even believe that what we know as the afterlife is life transformed into an ethereal dimension. Thus, elaborate ceremonies and rituals are constructed to talk to, drink with, and feed those in this netherworld. Therefore, it is not surprising that several Krio proverbs have emerged that are meant to impress upon the community the sanctity of life and its unpredictable nature.

Parabul 14

Yu si tide yu nɔ si tumara. [You see today but you haven't seen tomorrow.]

Figurative Meaning: Life can be unpredictable.

Scenario:

Francis: *Dɛn kin se, yu si tide yu nɔ si tumara.*

Olu: *Wetin mek yu de pul da parebul de?*

Francis: *Da bɔbɔ, trade-trade ya we nɔ gri lan buk ɛn we bin de fala ɔl dɛm bad kɔmpin, nain de mɛn pipul dɛm na ɔspitul so.*

Olu: *Na tru-o. Udat bin no se i go cheng so kwik-kwik ɛn go lan buk na kɔlɛj.*

English translation

[Francis: People say, you've seen today but you haven't seen tomorrow yet.

Olu: Why are you reciting that parable?

Francis: That boy, who not very long ago refused to take his studies seriously while hanging out with the wrong crowds, is now a doctor in the hospital.

Olu: That is so true. Who would have guessed that he will reform so quickly and go get a college education.]

Krio Folk Wisdom

193

Parebul 15

Da ed we kan fɔ tot ston, if you put biva at de, i go fɔdɔm. [The head that is made to carry stone, if you put a beaver hat on it, it will fall. down]

Figurative Meaning: Destiny determines what kind of profession you have been earmarked to pursue. Forcing someone into any other professional direction will not work at all.

Scenario:

Mami Esther: *Tu pan Pa John in pikin dɛm go kɔlej ɛn lan buk gud-gud. Di gyal wan na inginia na relway; di bɔy wan na akawntant na Bruwi.*

Bɔla: *We di las wan, wetin in du?*

Mami Esther: *Da lili wan de, nain tawa. I se in nɔ wan go kɔlej. Kɔlej nɔto fɔ-r-am. I go du tredin. Tide i gɛ in yon shap ɛn i de du wɛl.*

English translation

[Mami Esther: Two of John's children went to college and were very successful. The girl is an engineer at Railway, and the boy is an accountant at the Brewery.

Bɔla: What about the last child, what did she do?

Mami Esther: That little one is persistent. She says she doesn't want to go to college. College is not her forte. She went into trading. Today she has her own shop and is doing well.]

Parebul 16

Na wan pɔsin de bɔn pikin bɔt nɔto wan pɔsin de mɛn am [Only one person gives birth to a baby, but more than one person must be engaged in the rearing of that baby.]

Figurative Meaning: Raising a child is a collective effort.

Scenario:

Joya: *Sisi Dowu, aw tings de go fɔ di pul na do?*

Sisi Dowu: *A dɔn gɛt pipul fɔ kuk di jɔlɔf and bek di rayz bred. Bɔt wi gɛt bɔku-bɔku ɔda tings dem fɔ du.*

Joya: *Nɔ wɔri. Wi de ya fɔ ɛp yu. Mi ɛn Jowo go du di bitas ɛn di krenken. Yu neba, Pita, se mek a tɛl yu se in go bring di plet ɛn drink dɛm. Dɛn a yeri se kɔzin Ayɔ de mek sɔm kpekpekpe we pipul dɛn go it fɔs.*

English translation

[Joya: Ms. Dowu, how are the plans coming along for the dedication-of-the-child ceremony?

Sisi Dowu: I already have volunteers to prepare the jollof rice and bake the rice bread. But we have a lot of other things yet to do.

Joya: Don't worry. We are here to help you. Jowo and I would prepare the *krenkren* and *bitas.* Your neighbor, Peter, asked me to tell you that he is bringing the plates and drinks. Then I heard that Cousin Ayo will prepare some snacks for people to munch on first.]

194 Chapter 8

Below are additional *Parebuls* to increase your repertoire, but without scenarios:

Parebul 17
Agbara nɔ de run pas wan man domɔt. [Heavy rainfall water does not flow past only one's man door.]
Figurative Meaning: Everyone is susceptible to some kind of misfortune or danger.

Parebul 18
Da briz we blow mataodo, nɔto fana i go lɛf. [The wind that blows a mortar away will not spare the winnower.]
Figurative Meaning: No one is safe from impending disaster.

Parebul 19
Bɔd wan flay yu go shek tik. [The bird wants to fly away, and you made it easy for it by shaking the tree.]
Figurative Meaning: Your action has created a predictable outcome.

Parebul 20
Kɔtintri fɔdɔm so te, i ay pas gras [A fallen cotton tree is still taller than the grass beneath it.]
Figurative Meaning: It doesn't matter how educated or rich you are, people who are older than you are still wiser and more experienced.

Parebul 21
Ekuru dɔg naim kin kil lɛpɛt [A diseased dog can easily kill a leopard.]
Figurative Meaning: Skill and cunning are better than brawn.

Parebul 22
Os tayt so te, fɔl go le eg. [No matter how packed a house is, the chicken will find somewhere to lay her eggs.]
Figurative Meaning: No matter how difficult a situation is, there is always a way out.

Parabul 23
ɔl kondo le bɛlɛ na grɔn bɔt yu nɔ no uswan in bɛlɛ de at. [All lizards crawl on their stomach but you don't know which one has a stomachache.]
Figurative Meaning: Appearances can be deceiving.

Parebul 24

Da fɔl we nɔ yɛri shi, na ston i go yɛri [The chicken who fails to go away with a gentle nudging will do so with a stone.]
Figurative Meaning: Do not ignore subtle warnings in life; if you do, dire consequences can result.

Parebul 25
Kakroch nɔ gɛ rɛspɛkt na fɔl kɔntri. [A cockroach does not have any respect in chicken country.]
Figurative Meaning: Know your place.

Parebul 26
Int no in masta, kabaslɔt no in misis. [Hint knows its carrier just as the traditional print dress knows its owner.]
Figurative Meaning: It is clear who the hint is directed toward.

Parebul 27
Put yams na faya, tek yay fɛn nɛf. [Leave the yams cooking and take your time to look for a knife.]
Figurative Meaning: Take what you have until you get what you need.

Parebul 28
Yu tek rop drɔ bush naw bush dɔn kan na tɔn. [You used a rope to pull the forest, now the forest is in town.]
Figurative Meaning: Don't go looking for trouble because you may not like the outcome. Or, be careful what you ask for.

Parebul 29
If yu yams wayt, kɔba am. [If your yam is white, cover it.]
Figurative Meaning: Do not be boastful, pretentious, cocky.

Parebul 30
Bad bus nɔ de fɔ trowe bad pikin. [There is no bad bush to throw away a bad child.]
Figurative Meaning: Do not disown a troublesome child; find a way to change his behavior.

Parebul 31
If mi yes nɔ yɛri, mi at nɔ go pwɛl [If my ears do not hear, my heart will not be sad.]
Figurative Meaning: What you don't know won't hurt.

Parebul 32

196   *Chapter 8*

Kɔmiɛl nɔ gɛt bɔks, bɔt i de chenj klos. Figurative [The chameleon does not
  have a suitcase, but he changes clothes readily.]
Figurative Meaning: Like the chameleon, adjust your style or behavior to
  suit situations you are confronted with.

Parebul 33
Bɛlɛ nɔ gɛt lukin glas. [Stomach does not have a mirror.]
Figurative Meaning: No one will know what you eat or what else is going
  on in your stomach.

Parebul 34
Gud wɔd pul kola. [Good word brings out the kola nut.]
Figurative Meaning: Positive words bring out positive responses.

Parebul 35
Kakroch nɔ gɛt nɔ biznɛs pan fɔl fɛt. [The cockroach has no business in the
  fight between two chickens.]
Figurative Meaning: Don't meddle in things that do not concern you.

Parebul 36
Wahala nɔ de blo bigul wɛn i de kam. [Trouble does not announce when
  it is coming.]
Figurative Meaning: Problems can be unpredictable.

Parebul 37
Nɔ blem dɔg, blem u gi am bon. [Don't blame the dog, blame the person
  who gave it a bone.]
Figurative Meaning: Don't hold the recipient of a tempting gift responsible, hold the giver.

Parebul 38
Yu de mɛn dɔg fɔ gɔvmɛnt. [You are taking care of the dog for the
  government.]
Figurative Meaning: You are engaging in a fruitless effort for someone who
  is unappreciative.

Parebul 39
Nɔ ab op pan dayman sus. [Do not put all your hopes on the shoes of the
  deceased.]
Figurative Meaning: Do not depend on wealth or resources you cannot
  own or acquire.

Parebul 40

Awuf nɔ gɛ bon. [Free things have no bones.]

Figurative Meaning: Things that you obtain that you don't have to pay for are nice to enjoy.

Parebul 41

Fri po bɛtɛ pas tayt gɛntri.[Free poverty is better than restricted riches.]

Figurative Meaning: Poverty with freedom is better than riches without.

Parebul 42

Da gladi we de pan sapo nɔto in de pan krɔ-krɔ. [The joy that a sponge shows is not shared by an itchy skin.]

Figurative Meaning: What makes somebody happy may make someone else terrified, miserable, or afraid.

Parebul 43

Da ren we bit shugaken sote i swit, nain bit bitalif sote i bita. [The rain that watered the sugar cane to be sweet is the same rain that watered the bitter leaves to turn out bitter.]

Figurative Meaning: Opportunities for growth do not discriminate. Therefore, we must strive not to discriminate in our choices to help others reach their separate and desired outcomes.

Parebul 44

Wɛn lɛpɛt tit de at am, nain mɔnki kin go kɔl dɛt. [When a leopard has a tooth ache, that's when the monkey chooses to collect his debt.]

Figurative meaning: People will choose to confront a stronger and more powerful enemy when that enemy is at its most vulnerable state.

RIDDLES AND PUZZLES
LƐ WI KAN PLE GEM DƐM. [LET'S PLAY GAMES.]

Some of the most popular forms of amusement and entertainment in Krio culture are riddles and other puzzles. Riddles are questions that may be difficult to unravel or statements that are often confusing or mystifying. Riddles are like social aptitude tests, that require quick thinking, practical knowledge about various aspects of language and culture, and, of course, conciseness. They are sometimes expressed in metaphysical or onomatopoeic terms, and predominantly used for children's and adults' entertainment. However, the entertainment value of riddles does not obscure the didactic roles they are meant to play in the culture. In Krio culture, a Krio is forced to eschew

198   *Chapter 8*

the values of humility, respect for elders, and generally, knowledge of their culture out of which riddles are constructed. At the same time, many will enjoy the freedom and flexibility to engage in critical thinking that riddles accord them.

Below are examples of Krio riddles that will give you insight into how prolific this cultural artifact is. They are divided into two categories. Answers to the riddles are in the Appendix.

Mystifying Puzzles

These are riddles that employ questions of a metaphorical type in which things that seem to be unrelated are compared in order to ask the question. Here are some examples:

a. a go insay wayt, a kɔmɔt malata. [I went in white and came out mulatto.]

b. Wetin de slip na de tɛm ɛn waka na nɛt? [What sleeps during the day and wakes up at night?]

c. Da Inglan uman wit wan yay. [The English woman with one eye.]

d. Di man we mek am nɔ want am; di man we bay am insɛf nɔ want am; di man we de yuz am nɔ ivin no se i de yuz am. Mi na wetin? [The person who made it doesn't want it; the one who purchased it don't want it either; the person who is using it doesn't even know he's using it. What am I?]

e. A gɛt wan fes ɛn tu an bɔt a nɔ gɛt fut dɛm. Mi na wetin? [I have one face, and two hands but I don't have any feet. What am I?]

f. Wetin gɛt nɛk bɔt nɔ gɛt ed? [What has a neck but no head?]

g. Wetin ɔlwez de go ɔp bɔt nɔ wande kan dɔng? [What always goes up but has never come down.]

h. Wetin gɛt an dɛm bɔt nɔ ebul for klap. [What have hands but is unable to clap?]

i. If yu chɛr mi skin a nɔ go kray, bɔt yu go kray. Mi na wetin? [If you tear my skin, I wouldn't cry, but you will. What am I?]

j. Tri-fut tin tinap na tri fut tin de wet for wan fut tin. Mi na wetin? [A three-footed thing is standing on three-legged thing, waiting for a one-legged thing. What am I?]

k. Na wetin siks si pan sɛvun we mek et twis so, nain nain si bien tɛn we mek ilɛvun skata. [What six sees in seven that makes eight so twisted, is what nine sees behind ten that makes eleven scatter.]

l. Tin we de bien wan, we big pas tu, na da sem tin de sɛvun si bien siks we mek et twis so. [The thing behind one which is bigger than two, is the same thing that seven sees behind six which makes eight twisted.]

Krio Folk Wisdom

m. 4-fut tin tinap na 4-fut tin de wait for 4-fut tin. [A four-legged thing is standing on a four-legged thing waiting for a four-legged thing.]

Culturally Related Riddles

These are riddles that require knowledge of various aspects of Krio culture. Examples follow:

a. *Wetin mek wi pipul dem kin put brum tik biɛn domɔt?* [Why do Krio people put a broom behind the door step?]
b. *Wetin mek wi pipul dem kin put brum ɔnda bebi dɛn pila?* [Why do people put a broom under babies' pillow?]
c. *ɔnda mi rayt fut de krach* [Under my right foot is itching. What does that mean?]
d. *Mi rayt an de krach* [My right hand is itching. What does that mean?]
e. *Mi lɛf an de krach* [My left hand is itching. What does that mean?]
f. *Wetin dɛm kin kɔl snɛk na nɛt? Wetin du?* [What do they call a snake at night? Why?]
g. *Na us fish Krio pipul dɛm kɔl "di children ɔf Izrɛl"?* [What type of fish do people call "the children of Israel"?]
h. *Karozin ɛn damzin, na us kayn frut dɛm da wan de na Salon?* [Kerosene and damzin are from what type of fruit in Sierra Leone?]
i. *"Wɛn it opin yay pan yu,"* wetin dat min? ["When food opens its eyes on you." What does that mean?]
j. *Ple ple kil bɔd . . .* [Complete the following: Play play kills bird...]
k. *Tu kik, wan bɔks, wetin dat min?* ["Two kicks and one hit." What does that mean?]
l. *Wetin mek pipul dɛn kin sok rɔ bɔl fufu fɔ lɔng tɛm bifo dɛm kuk am?* [Why do people soak raw ball foofoo for a long time before cooking it?]

Chapter 9

Krio Stories and Trickster Narratives

NANSI TORIZ [ANANSE STORIES]

Picture yourself in the evening in a dimly lit room where the silhouette faces of eight or nine youngsters appear to be shining with anxious expectancy and youthful enthusiasm, eyes all glued on the storyteller, who could be any older relative such as a grandmother, grandfather, uncle or aunt, an older brother or older sister. The youngsters find the storyteller's dramatic skills so engaging, endearing, and exciting, that sometimes they forget these stories have been told several times before. Douglas Odom observes that the storyteller must be exceptionally adept at theatrical renderings for a successful story-telling session:

> Storytelling is not a skill that any unpracticed individual could attempt, which is why talented story-tellers are so venerated in each of the African, Caribbean, and African-American societies. . . . The storyteller *must* have the skill of reading his or her audience members so that the story can be manipulated in such a way that the audience remains engaged.[1]

Nansi toris originated from the animal story trope, *Ananse*, the spider, credited to the Akan people of Ghana. This storytelling tradition made its way to Freetown as a result of the trans-Atlantic slave trade. Enslaved Africans originally from the Akan ethnic groups in Ghana worked in plantations in the Caribbean, primarily Jamaica. They never gave up their storytelling traditions and so when they were repatriated to Freetown, the trope was expanded to include Bra Fox, Bra Lepet, Bra kakroch, and Bra Spider, to name but a few. In addition, types of stories also expanded. We began to see didactic and

202   *Chapter 9*

etiological stories, such as why Bra Spider' middle is so small, added to the storytelling regimen in Krio society.

Nansi toris serve a very important function in Krio society. The creative dramatization of these stories helps to develop positive values in children. It forces young people to be equally creative in responding to repeat stories. *Nansi toris* also serve to entertain and educate. The stories may be mythological, mystical, or trickster-oriented, but one structural and cultural commonality among them is the deep moralizing nature of the endings. For example, we must listen to and inculcate the wisdom of our elders and avoid nurturing hostile or destructive feelings for others. The young ones are taught to be responsible citizens who strive to be loving and compassionate to others.

In short, *nansi toris* provide a wide latitude for comprehending human experiences, animal behaviors, and enhancing theatrical skills. All our social obligations become dependent upon our understanding and interpretation of oral traditions. Although this cultural artifact is diffused from one generation to another, it is not static or banal because the energy, the drive, and the creative expressions of Krio culture accelerate and accentuate the dynamism in the society so much so that for over two hundred years, *nansi toris* still remain a delectable cultural experience.

Nansi toris are also an interactive experience. It is spontaneously participatory in all its components. The introductory formula, [storyteller]: Il!!! and the audience response, Aw!!! is an indication that the story is about to begin and the audience must be ready to participate in this communal experience. For example, when songs are introduced in stories, the audience is expected to participate in choruses. Since these are stories that have been told many times before, the audience will have no problem singing along with the storyteller.

The closing formula: "stori go, stori kam, i lɛf pan yu" ["Stories come and go, now it is your turn"] signals the end of the story and an invitation to the next storyteller to step up. These rituals are not mere embellishments, they are an integral part of cultural education among the Krio.

Here are some trickster stories with various animal characters that our family and friends tell all the time. These stories are popular in Krio folk tale traditions, with the complete English translation following each one:

BRA FƆL ƐN BRA KAKROCH [THE CHICKEN AND THE COCKROACH]

IL!. . . . .AW!

Bra Fɔl ɛn Bra Kakroch na bin tu gud-gud padi. Dɛn ɔl tu bin gɛt wan fam.
So ɔl tɛm we fɔ go klin dis fam, bra kakroch kin se in sik. I kin go rap

Krio Stories and Trickster Narratives 203

ɔnda blankit de slip. So, na bra fɔl in wan gren go go kiln di fam. Wɛn i bring yayam kan om, bra kakroch kin se in fil bɛtɛ. So dɛn ɔl tu go it di it. Wɛn dɛn dɔn it dɔn, bra fɔl tɛl bra kakroch se,
"Bo, ɔltɛm we fɔ go klin di fam yu se yu sik. Wetin du?"
Sɔmbɔdi bin dɔn tɛl bra fɔl se ɔltɛm we i kin go klin di fam, bra kakroch kin bigin sing dis sing ya so:
A mek fɔl ful -o
kongosa
Se a sik -o
kongosa
Sik mi nɔ sik-0
Kongosa
So, Bra Fɔl taym am. As Bra Fɔl kan mit Bra Kakroch, i se:
"Bo kan lɛ wi go klin di fam nɔ?"
Naim Bra Kakroch se:
"Bo, a nɔ wɛl, bo. Yu nɔ si we a rap insay mi blankit."
Nain Bra Fɔl go ayd na wan kɔna de wach am. We Bra Kakroch kam, I bigin sing:
A mek fɔl ful -o
kongosa
Se a sik -o
kongosa
Sik mi nɔ sik-0
Kongosa
Nain Bra Fɔl es in ed ɛn si am de sing. I rɔnata Bra Kakroch fɔ go chuk am. Bɔt Bra Kakroch rɔn go ayd ɔnda sɔm wud dɛm. Naim mek ɔltɛm we Fɔl si Kakroch, i go rɔnata-r-am ɛn if i kech am, i go it am.

Stori go stori kam i lɛf pan yu.

ENGLISH TRANSLATION OF BRA FƆL ƐN BRA KAKROCH

The chicken and the cockroach were two good friends.
Both had one farm.
Whenever they are ready to clear the farm of weeds, Cockroach would claim that he is ill.
He will wrap himself under the blanket and fall asleep.
Thus, Chicken would go to the farm and clear it all by himself.
Whenever Chicken brings food home, Cockroach would say he now feels better.

So, they would both sit down and eat.

When they have finished eating, Chicken would say to Cockroach, "You know, whenever it's time to clear the farm, you always say you're sick. Why?"

Someone had informed Chicken that whenever he goes to the farm, Cockroach will start singing this this song:

I duped Chicken-o
Kongosa!
Claimed I was sick-o
Kongosa
I was never even sick-o
Kongosa

So, Chicken set a trap for Cockroach.

As soon as he saw Cockroach, he said, "Let us go clear the farm, please."

Cockroach would reply: "You know, I am not feeling well. Can't you see how I am all wrapped up in my blanket?"

So, Chicken went and hid in a corner out of sight watching Cockroach. When Cockroach came out, he started singing:

I duped Chicken-o
Kongosa!
Claimed I was sick-o
Kongosa
I was never even sick-o
Kongosa

Chicken raised his head and saw Cockroach singing.

He ran after Cockroach with the intention to hurt him.

But Cockroach ran and hid under some boards.

That's why whenever the chicken sees the cockroach, he will run after her furiously and if he catches him will devour him.

Stories go and stories come. Now it's your turn.

OJUKOKORO [ENVY]

Il . . .
Aw . . .

Wan de ya, Bra Ram Ship ɛn Bra Ram Got na bin neba. Bra Ram Ship gɛt wan lili konko, ɛn Bra Ran Got in gɛt wan lili abule dɔn di trit, nia samba gɔta. ɛnitɛm we dɛm brakɛt na trit, na so ram ship kin de luk ram got bad yay. I tan lɛk fɔ se i de jɛlɔs am fɔ im bi ɔn.

Krio Stories and Trickster Narratives

205

Wan de, ram ship nɔ ebul bia egen. We dɛm brakɛt na forod, naim i bigin ala:

"Yu ran got! Yu ran got! Da yu ɔn de, a want am wantɛm-wantɛm. Ustɛm yu go gi mi?"

Ran got insɛf se, "Bra dawande nɔ to wahala. A go gi yu mi fayn-fayn ɔn if a mis yu tri tɛm ɛn gɛt yu tri tɛm."

"ɔrayt, bra. So ustɛm yu wan du dat?" Ram ship aks ran got.

"Lɛ wi du am Satide, na Rɛcri; Satide na Rɛcri. Tɛl ɔlman mek dɛm kan wach we a de gi yu mi ɔn."

"ɔrayt, wi go si Satide na Rɛkri."

Bra ram ship waka ɔlɔbɔt de tɛl pipul dɛm mek dɛm go rɛkri Satide fɔ go si we in de tek ram got in ɔn. Yu si Mami Jɔku de kɔmɔt makit, so i tɛl: "Jɔku, du ya kan na Rɛkri Satide, kan si we a de tek ran got in ɔn. Mami Jɔku wɔn am bɔt i nɔ lisin. Bifo jako kɔt yay, di alejo dɔn go ɔlɔbɔt na di tɔn. Pa Salakɔ ɛn in neba sɛf de tɔk bɔt dis:

"Wetin dɔn go na ram ship in ed?

"Mi dadi, ɔlman dɔn tɔk to ram ship, bɔt na man we trangayes baad. I nɔ de lisin to advays."

Satide kam. Na so rɛkri dɔn ful. Pipul dɛm de ɔlɔbɔt. Bra ram ship ɛn Bra ran got kan insay. Wan go na wan say pan di fil, dɛn di ɔda wan go na di ɔda say pan di fil. Naim ran got de tɛl ram ship se mek i fiks in ed gud bikɔs in de kam mis am tri tɛm ɛn gɛt am tri tɛm. Bra ram ship se, "Bra, kan nɔmɔ, a dɔn redi fɔ yu."

So, naim Ran Got go chuk spid, i kan, kiti-kata, kiti-kata, ɛn bɔt Ram Ship na in ed. Ram Ship tɔnɔbɔ tu tɛm. Dɛn, Ran Got go tek flo ɛn kam back egen, kiti-kata, kiti-kata, he wap Ram Ship at-at wan. Ram Ship ala: "Woyooo! Woyooo! Bifo i mekɔp, Ran Got kam bak egen ɛn bang Bra Ram Ship na in ed. Blɔd bigin rɔn ɔl oba in ed, in yay, in mɔt.

Nain Bra Ran Got tɛl Bra Ram ship se: "a dɔn mis yu tri tɛm. Fiks yu ed gud bikɔs now a de kan gɛt yu tri tɛm bifo a gi yu mi ɔn."

We Bra Ran Ship yɛri dat, naim i se, "if na mis tan so, aw gɛt in go tan? In ed dɔn krak opin; wan pan in fut dɔn brok, in yay dɔn de sɛt. Nain i tɛtɛ te i rich om. We in pikin ɛn granpikin dɛm si an, dɛm bigin kray: "ee, papa wetin apin." "Eeee granpa udat du dis to yu."

Nain Ram Ship tɛl dɛn se, "na Ran Got du dis to mi. Frɔm dis de, a de put ɛnmiti bitwin in sid ɛn mi sid. Una nɔ fɔ gɛ natin fɔ du wit dɛm." nain i fɔdɔm ɛn day.

Naim mek wi pipul dɛm kin se, ojukokoro nɔ gud. Nɔ milɛ ɔda pipul dɛm fɔ wetin dɛm gɛt.

Stori go, stori kam i lɛf pan yu.

ENGLISH TRANSLATION OF *OJUKOKORO*

Once upon a time, a ram sheep and a ram goat were neighbors.

Ram sheep owns a very small house and ram goat has a little hut down the street close to Samba Gutter.

Anytime they see each other in the street, ram sheep would look at ram goat with anger and jealousy.

It looks like ram sheep is jealous of ram goat's big horns.

One day, ram sheep couldn't take it anymore. So, when they met in the street, he started yelling:

"Ram goat! You Ram goat! I want your big horns right now! When are you going to give them to me?"

Ram goat replied: "Brother, that's not a problem. I will give you my beautiful horns if you allow me to miss hitting you three times and then actually hitting you three times."

"Alright brother," Ram sheep said. "So, when do you want to do that?"

"Let's do it on Saturday at the recreation grounds. Tell everybody to go there and watch me give you my horns," Ram goat said.

"Ok. I'll see you at the recreation grounds on Saturday," Ram sheep replied.

So, Ram sheep walks around town telling everybody to come to the recreation grounds on Saturday to watch him take Ram goat's horns.

He saw Mama Joko heading home from the market, so he told her: "Mama Joko, please come to the recreations grounds Saturday to watch me take Ram goat's horns."

Mama Joko warned him about this but he did not listen.

In no time, the news has traveled all over town.

Mr. Salako and his neighbors were talking about this as well. "What has gone into Ram sheep's head?"

"My friend, everyone has talked to Ram sheep but he is very stubborn He never listens to advice," Mr. Coker added.

It was Saturday. The recreation grounds was full to capacity. There were people everywhere.

Ram goat and Ram sheep entered the arena. One went to one side of the grounds and the other went to the opposite end.

Then, Ram goat asked Ram sheep to fix his head properly because he is coming to miss hitting three times and then actually hitting him three times.

Ram Sheep said, "Come on, brother, I am ready for you."

So, Ram goat took a few steps back and then galloped at high speed and hit Ram sheep hard on his head.

Krio Stories and Trickster Narratives 207

Ram sheep toppled over twice.

Then Ram goat went back again to pick up speed and galloped full force and hit Ram sheep very hard.

Ram sheep screamed: "oooooohhhhh!!!"

Before he knew what hit him, Ram goat came back again and hit him really hard on his head.

Blood started dripping all over Ram sheep's head, his eyes, and his mouth.

Then Ram goat told him: "I have now missed you three times. So, fix your head nicely because I am now going to hit you three times before I give you my horns."

When Ram sheep heard that, He said: "If these are just misses, how would the actual hits feel like?"

His head cracked open; one of his legs is broken, and his left eye shut completely.

So he left the arena and walked unsteadily until he got home.

When his children and grandchildren saw him, they started weeping: "Dad what happened?" "Grandpa, what happened?" "Who did this to you?"

Ram sheep said to them: "Ram goat did this to me. From this day forward, I am putting enmity between his seed and my seed. You should have nothing to do with them ever."

Then he collapsed and died.

That's why our people say envy is a bad thing. Don't envy or hate people for what they have that you don't have.

Stories go, stories come. Now, it is your turn to tell one.

WETIN MEK BRA SPAYDA IN WES LILI SO
[WHY BROTHER SPIDER HAS A SMALL WAIST]

ɔlman no se Bra Spayda na bɛlɛwapi. I nɔ wan de si nyayam na tebul we i nɔ lɛk. Put fufu ɛn bitas bifo am, i go wak. Put jɔlɔf rɛs bifo am, I go mɔndɔ.

So wande afta i dɔn it gud-gud, Bra Spayda ledɔm nain amaka ɔnda di mangro tik de ɛnjɔy di kol briz. Nain di vileg edman in mɛsenja kan tɛl am se the edman de kɔl am fɔ go wan bi-big awujɔ nɛks wik fɔ Mami Abi in wan yia. Mami Abi na pɔsin we ɔlman bin lɛk na di vileg. So, Bra Spayda gladi bad-bad wan bikɔs in no se in bɛlɛ go ful wit ɔl dɛm gbogboaye it we kin de na awujɔ.

I nɔ tu te afta dat, nain Pa Kunika, we tap na di neba vilej, kan nak na in do. Bra Spayda de wɔndrin wetin apin we i kan nak nain do dis awa. Nain Pa Kunika tɛl am se i de mek kuk fɔ in wɛf we day las yia ɛn i go lɛk fɔ

Chapter 9

mek Bra Spayda kam. Na so Bra Spayda in yay de rol nain ed we i yɛri bɔt it. So i aks Pa Kunika ustɛm nɛks wik. Nain Pa Kunika se, nɛks wik Satide. Bra Spayda se, "ɔrayt a go de de." We Pa Kunika dɔn lɛf, nain i fɛnɔt se na de sem tɛm fɔ Mami Abi in awujɔ. In bɔdi brok lɛk udat jɛs lɔs in gud-gud padi.Wetin i go du naw bikɔs i nɔ wan mis natin: ɔl dɛn swit-swit kren-kren sup, da bitas ɛn bɔlɔgi ɛn fufu, ɔl dɛn soba fray plantin ɛn pɛtetɛ. Aw i go mis ɔl dis?

I nɔ no wetin fɔ du, so i kɔl in wɛf ɛn pikin ɛn tɛl dem bɔt di tu awujɔ we dem kɔl am pan di sem de nɛks wik Satide. Bifo i tɔk dɔn, nain in wɛf ala: "eee! Dis na wahala oo! "Yu dɔn fɔgɛt se kɔzin Mabel bin dɔn tɛl wi bɔt in pulnado da sem de de?"

"Lɔdamasi! Wetin wi go du naw?" Bra Spayda de mɛmba ɔl di it we i go mis. Wantɛm-wantɛm, nain i tinap ɛn tɛl in wɛf ɛn pikin se, paopa, in go go ɔl tri awujɔ. In wɛf laf. "Dadi, yu mole dɔn mas. Aw yu go du dat?"

We di de kam, Bra Spayda go nain in lili bafa ɛn pul tri langa-langa rop dɛm. i tay di fɔs wan round in wes; dɛn i uk di sɛken rop to di fɔs wan ɛn gi in wɛf da wande. I tɛl am se, "Yu go to Kɔzin Mabɛl in pulnado. We dɛn bigin pul it, jɛs drɔ di rop ɛn a go rɔn go de go it."

Bra Spayda uk di las rop to in yon rop ɛn gi da wande to in pikin ɛn tel am se mek in go to Mami Abi in awujɔ. I se, "As dɛm bigin pul it so, drɔ di rop kwik-kwik, a go rɔn go it de. Mi go go to Pa Kunika in awujɔ.

So dɛn ɔl ol rod.

As Bra Spayda rich nia Pa Kunika in vilej, in mɔt bigin wata as i de smɛl ɔl di gud-gud it na di awujɔ. Bɔt bifo i mek ɔp, di rop dɛn bigin drɔ. Wan de drɔ to Mami Abi in say, di ɔda rop to Kɔzin Mabɛl in yon say. I tray fɔ rɔn wan say, bɔt di rop dɛm de drɔ am go ɔda say.

Aw di rop dɛn de drɔ, na so in wes de tayt. Dɛn drɔ so te Bra Spayda nɔ ebul bia egen, nain in fɔdɔm ɛn fent. We di wɛf ɛn di pikin nɔ si Bra Spayda dɛn de wonda wetin apin. Wɛn dɛn taya fɔ drɔ, dɛnsɛf rɔn go it bifo ɔl di it dɔn. Nɔto kɔmɔn ɛnjoy dɛn ɛnjoy.

We dɛn de go om dɛm fala di rop sote dɛn fɛn Bra Spayda ledɔm na gras lɛk udat wan giv ɔp di gos. Na so in bɛlɛ dɔn lili we di rop dɛm kwis am. So, dɛn rɔn go gɛt wata fɔ am fɔ drink ɛn ɛp grap fɔ go om—ɛmpti bɛlɛ!

Frɔm da dede nain Bra Spayda in wes nɔ gro egen, te tide.

Na dat mek dɛn kin se, awangɔt nɔ gud. i go kil yu.

Stori go, stori kam i lɛf pan yu.

Krio Stories and Trickster Narratives 209

ENGLISH TRANSLATION OF *WETIN MEK BRA SPAYDA IN WES LILI SO*

Everyone knows that Brother Spider likes to eat a lot.

He has never seen food on the table that he doesn't like.

Put fufu and bitter leaves soup on the table and he will eat with relish.

Put jollof rice in front of him and he would gobble down quickly.

One day after he has eaten to his satisfaction, Brother Spider lay down in his hammock under the mango tree to enjoy the cool breeze.

Then the messenger of the village headman came to his compound to tell him that the headman is inviting him to a big traditional feast next week for Mam Abi's one-year celebration.

Everyone in the village loved Mama Abi.

So, Brother Spider was very happy because he knew he would have a lot of good food to eat out of the many different dishes that would be available in this kind of feast.

Soon after the messenger's visit, Papa Kunika who lives in a nearby village came knocking at his front door.

Brother Spider is wondering why Papa Kunika is knocking at his door at this time.

So, Papa Kunika told him that he is doing a traditional feast for his wife who passed away last year and would like Brother Spider to come. Brother Spider's eyes were rolling with joy when he heard about food.

So he asked Papa Kunika what time next week for the feast.

Papa Kunika said next week Saturday.

Brother Spider said: "Ok, I'll be there."

When Papa Kunika left, that's when he realized that it was the same day for Mama Abi's feast.

He was heart-broken like he has just lost a good friend. What is he going to do now because he does not want to miss anything: the delicious kren-kren soup, the bitter leaf and bologi soup and fufu, and all those mouth-watering fried plantains and potatoes. How can he miss all of this?

He doesn't know what to do so he called his wife and child and told them about the two celebration feasts that he has been invited to the same day, next Saturday. But he finished talking his wife interrupted him: "Eeeee! This is a big problem! Have you forgotten that cousin Mabel had already invited us to a dedication of the child celebration that same day?"

"Lord have mercy! What are we going to do now?" Brother Spider was thinking of all the food he would miss. Suddenly, he stood up and told his wife and child no matter what, he is going to all three events. His

210   *Chapter 9*

wife started laughing. "Daddy, you must be crazy. How are you going
to do that?"

When the day arrives for the events, Brother Spider went into his little hut
and pulled out three long ropes. He tied the first one around his waist,
then hooked the second rope to the first one and gave his wife the latter.
He said to her, "You go to Cousin Mabel's dedication ceremony. As soon
as they start dishing out the food, just pull on the rope and I'll run over
there to get some food."

Brother Spider hooked the last rope to his rope and gave that one to his
child and told her to go to Mama Abi's celebration feast. He said to her,
"As soon as they start dishing out food pull on the rope quickly and
I'll run over there to get some good food. I would go to Papa Kunika's
celebration feast."

So, they all started on their journey.

As Brother Spider got close to Papa Kunika's village, he started salivat-
ing as he smells the good food at Papa Kunika's feat. feast. But before
he knew it, he received a pull on the ropes. One pulling towards Mama
Abi's side and the other toward Cousin Mabel's event. He tried to run to
one side, but the other rope pulled him to the other side.

As the ropes pulled him on either side, so was his midriff getting tighter
and tighter until Brother Spider could not take it anymore. He finally
collapsed and fainted. When his wife and child didn't see him, they
wondered what happened. They got tired of pushing and gave up to get
some food before it was all gone. They had so much fun.

On their way home they followed the trajectory of the ropes until they
found Brother Spider lying on the grass like one ready to give up the
ghost. His stomach was very small because of all the pull of the ropes.
So, they ran over and got him some water to drink and helped him back
up for the journey home—on an empty stomach! From that day onward,
Brother Spider's waist remained very small.

That's why people say greed and gluttony are never good. They could
kill you.

Stories go, stories come, now it's your turn.

TUNDE ƐN IÑ PADI [TUNDE AND HIS FRIEND]

Wan de ya, wan bɔbɔ bin de we nɛm Tunde. Wan de, i ɛn iñ padi bin waka
go insay, insay dis bus ya so. We dɛm rich insay di bus ya so, naim dɛm
yɛri wan bɔd de ala. We dɛm go niaram, deñ si se iñ fɛda fasin pantap
wan tik-an. Tunde fil sɔri fɔ di bɔd.

I no no wetin fo du, so I ron go kol iñ big broda na os.

Iñ big broda dres kwik kwik wan, deñ i sen Tunde go na pantry fo go bring iñ ontin nef. Wen Tunde ker iñ ontin nef go gi am, i put am insay iñ ontin bag en aks Tunde fo go sho am di tik we di bod fasin pan. We Tunde sho am, i ron go de en tek tem pul di bod iñ feda komot na di tik-an.

Di bod shek shek iñ feda lilibit, naim i flay go tinap na Tunde iñ sholda. I no gri komot de. Tunde iñ big broda tel am se mek i fes di bod kan na os. We deñ bringam kan na os, deñ bil wan bibig kej foram. Na so Tunde gladi. From da tem de, iñ en di bod de go olsay.

ENGLISH TRANSLATION OF *TUNDE EN IM PADI*

Once upon a time, there was a young boy named Tunde.

One day, he and his friends walked into the forest.

When they got there, they heard a bird screaming.

When they got close to it, they found out that his feathers were stuck on top of one of the tree branches. Tunde felt sorry for the bird.

He did not know what to do, so he ran home quickly to get his older brother.

His older brother got ready quickly and asked Tunde to get his hunting knife from the pantry.

When Tunde took the knife to him, he put it in his hunting bag and asked Tunde to lead him to where the bird was stuck.

Tunde took him there and his older brother carefully removed the bird's feathers from the tree branch where it was stuck.

The bird shook its feathers for a short while then flew to perch on Tunde's shoulder and refused to budge. So, Tunde's older brother asked Tunde to bring the bird home.

When they brought the bird home, they built a very big cage for it.

Tunde was very happy.

Since that day, Tunde and the bird went everywhere together.

DI BLEN YAY BEGAMAN [THE BLIND BEGGAR]

IL . . .

Aw . . .

Wan de ya, wan blenyay begaman bin de we de waka from os to os de beg. enitem we i go na pipul dem os i kin se, "monin ma, monin sa. Udat du gud, du am fo insef. Udat du bad du am fo insef."

Wan pan dem pipul ya so we i kin go beg to na gentriman, bot i krabit en bad lek shak. I no lek fo mek begaman dem de kan ambog am bikos in no lɛk fo gi dɛm natin. Dis gɛntriman ya so don taya wit dis begaman. i mek op se in go gi am sontin we go mek i no kam na in os egen. So, wɛn di blɛnyay man kan beg na in os da de de, di gɛntriman rap wan bab-bad snɛk na pepa ɛn put am na di blɛnyay man in bag.

As di blɛnyay begaman de go om so, in mit dɛn bobo dɛn de komot skul. Dɛn bigin ambog am. Som pan dɛm de push am, oda wan pan dɛm de dro-dro in bag. Wan pan dɛm put in an insay di bag ɛn opin di pepa we di snɛk de. Di snɛk bɛt am. I fodom na gron ɛn fent. olman bigin ala.

Pipul dɛm komot na dɛm os kan luk wetin bi. Di gɛntriman insɛf kam. We i luk di bobo we ledom na gron i niali day. Na in yon-yon pikin di snɛk bɛt. Yu blant yeri kray lɛk dat?

Nain mek Krio man se, "Yu tink yu du mi, yu du yusɛf."

Stori go, stori kam i lɛf pan yu.

ENGLISH TRANSLATION OF *DI BLƐNYAY BƐGAMAN*

Once upon a time, there was a blind beggar who walked from house to house begging. Whenever he enters a person's house, he would politely say. "Good morning, ma'am, good morning, sir. If you do a good deed, you will be doing good for yourself, if you do evil, you are likewise doing evil for yourself."

One of the people that he would frequently beg from is a rich man, who is also greedy, mean, and wicked. He hates beggars bothering him because he doesn't like to give them anything. This rich man got tired of being bothered by this blind beggar so he decided to give him something that would prevent him from coming to his house again. When the blind beggar arrived that day, he wrapped a deadly snake in some paper and put it in his bag.

As the blind beggar was going home, he ran into some boys coming from school.

As usual, they started teasing him. Some pushed him in one direction, while others tried to yank his bag off his shoulder. One of them went as far as to as to put his hand inside the bag and unwrap the paper parcel. He was immediately bitten by the deadly snake. He fell down on the ground and fainted.

People came outside to see what was happening.

Even the rich man came outside as well.

When he looked at the boy lying on the ground, he almost died with shock. It was his very own son that the deadly snake had bitten.

Krio Stories and Trickster Narratives 213

That is why Krio people say, "Whenever you do something harmful to someone else, you usually end up hurting yourself."

Stories go, stories come. Now it's your turn to tell one.

TA BEBI [TAR BABY]

Dis stori ya we a de kan tɛl una na bɔt Bra Spayda. Bra Spayda na man we i dɔn angri i kin du ɛnitin fɔ gɛt sɔm nyanyam. i ɛn Bra Kɔni Rabit na bin gud-gud padi. ɛvri mɔnin dɛm kin kɔmɔt fɔ go batul fɔ fɛn sɔntin fɔ it.

Bra Spayda in kin go na bus fɔ go luk fɔ smɔl-smɔl tin dɛm fɔ kuk. Bra Kɔni Rabit in yon jab na fɔ go na tɔn go luk fɔ tings lɛk fɔl we nain dɛm go it. Bra Kɔni Rabit fashin wan ples we ɔltɛm na de i de go tif. I kin tif bɔku fɔl pikin dɛm, even sɔm pan di big fɔl dɛn sɛf i kin tif.

Di pipul dɛm we gɛt di ples, dɛn kan ɛng ed togɛda fɔ tray fɔ kech dis tif-man ya so we de kan tif ɔl dɛm fɔl. So, dɛm mek wan bibig ta bebi we fiba mɔtal man so. Dɛn, dɛn put am nia di gɛt we di fɔl dɛn de. Dɛn se, ɛniwan we kan fɔ kam fɔ tif dɛn fɔl, dɛn go fasin pan di ta bebi ya so. Bra Kɔni Rabit insɛf dɔn wach dɛn pipul yaso we dɛn di put dis ta bebi na di gɛt to the fɔl dɛm. So i fred.

Di nɛks de i fɔm sik so i nɔ go tɔn da de de. Bɔt Bra Spayda in go batul na bus ɛn bring it kan fɔ Bra Kɔni Rabit. i it bɛlful. Di nɛks de afta dat we i fɔ go tɔn go fɛn it, i fɔm sik bak egen. i se i nɔ de go bikɔs i nɔ de fil wɛl. Bra Spayda in go na bus ɛn batul-batul so te i ebul fɔ bring it kan Bra Spayda. Egen, Bra Spayda it bɛlful.

Di de afta dat, Bra Kɔni Rabit nɔ wan go fɛn it egen. Nain Bra Spayda se, "Bo dis dɔn pasmak. ɔltɛm yu sidɔm na os. Na mi wangren de go fɛn it fɔ it. A nɔ go ebul dis wok ya o."

Nain Bra Kɔni Rabit se, "Bra, nɔto fɔ se a nɔwan go-o." I se, "Na bi-big bwɛl nain a gɛt, nain mek so."

Bra Spayda se, "Bo we dis bwɛl ya so? Nain Bra Kɔni Rabit se, "Bo luk am, na ɔna mi fut i kɔmɔt." I dɔn tek big ston tayam na in bɔtɔm fut. I bigin tip-to; i bigin tip-to.

Bra Spayda se, "ɔrayt, tide, a go manej yu, bɔt if yu nɔ wok tumara, a nɔ go manej yu atɔl."

Di nɛks de, nain Bra Kɔni Rabit se: "Bra, a nɔ go ebul fɔ go tide egen. Dis fut ya de at mi baaad!" Naim Bra Spayda vɛks. I se "sho me usay yu kin go tif ɔl dɛm fat-fat fɔl dɛm trade. Kan kɛr mi go de ba." Nain Bra Spayda se, ɔrayt. I kɛr am go de. We dɛm rich nia de, Bra Kɔni Rabit si di ta bebi we fiba mɔtal man. Nain Bra Spayda point to di ples we di ta bebi tinap. i se, "yu si da pɛn we de de so, nɔto kɔmɔn fɔl de de. Bɔt luk

Chapter 9

wan man tinap na di domɔt. A tink se nain de gyad di fɔl dɛm. Bra Rabit se, "Bo duya, udat de fred da wan de; a go jɛs pas ɔnda in fut ɛn go insay di pɛn." Bra Spayda se "ɔrayt, go nɔ."

Naim i go. We Bra Kɔni Rabit go, i mit di man tinap na di get wit in fut dɛm opin, jɛs lɛk aw dɛm mek am. i se, "Bra, gudivin." Di tin nɔ ansa. i se, "Bra, una kushɛ-o, aw una du?" Di tin nɔ ansa. i se, "Bo uskayn biznɛs dis, a de tɛl yu adu yu nɔ de ansa." i put in an fɔ shek di tin in an, bɔt i fasin. i fɛt-fɛt so te fɔ pul in an, i nɔ ebul. i se "bo, lɛf me nɔ; bo na angri de kech mi so. Bo lɛf mi."

Fɔs, I mɛmba se na jok, i nɔ no se na fasin in an dɔn fasin de so. Fɛt-fɛt so te, natin. Nain i se, "lɛf, a go kik yu-o." Nain i tek in lɛf fut i kik am, vup! As I kik am so, in fut fasin. i se, "ee-bo, mi nɔ lɛk dɛm kayn ple yaso-o. Bo lɛf mi, lɛf mi." i fɛt-fɛt so te bɔt di wan an ɛn di wan fut stil fasin.

"A go tek dis mi ɔda fut kik yu-o." As i kik nɔmɔ, di ɔda fut insɛf fasin. Nain in laf. "Bo, dis bra ya lɛk ple tumɔs; a se, bo, put mi dɔn, a wan go." i tɔk-tɔk so te bɔt dis tin nɔ de tɔk bak ɛn i nɔ lɛf am atɔl. Bra Kɔni Rabit dɔn fasin gud-gud.

Nain i se, "if yu nɔ lɛf mi, a go bɔt yu-o." i bɛn in ed go biɛn, dɛn i bring am kan bifo ɛn bɔt di tin, bok!! As i bɔt am so nɔmɔ, in ed sɛf fasin. i fɛt-fɛt-fɛt so te in nɔ ebul pul in ed. i fɛt-fɛt-fɛt so te, natin. ɔl dis na nɛt i bi-o.

We doklin naw, di pipul dɛm we gɛt dɛm fɔl dɛn kan wek. As dɛn wek so nain dɛn si Bra Kɔni Rabit fasin pan ta bebi. Nain dɛn aks am: "Bra, wetin yu kan fɛn na ya we yu fasin so?"

Bra Kɔni Rabit se, "Na pas a bin de pas."

Nain dɛn se, "Usay yu bin de pas go?"

i se, "A bin de pas go ɔlɔbɔt in."

Nain dɛm se, "Ya we yu dɔn kan so, yu nɔ go pas go nɔwe egen." Nain dɛm kech am ɛn bit am te dɛn kil am.

Na di stori dɔn so!

ENGLISH TRANSLATION OF *TA BEBI*

The story that I am about to tell you is about Mister Spider. Mister Spider is a person who, when he gets hungry, he will do anything to get food. He and Mister Cunning Rabbit have been very good friends. Every morning they get up to go hunting for something to eat.

Mister Spider regularly goes out into the woods to look for something to cook. As for Cunning Rabbit, his approach is to go to town and look for something to eat where chickens feed. Cunning Rabbit likes a particular

Krio Stories and Trickster Narratives 215

place where he always goes to steal food. He often snatches baby chicks and sometime full-grown chickens as well.

The people who live in this area have tried to figure out how to catch this thief who has been ravaging their chickens. So, they built a huge tar baby which looks like a real person. Then, they placed it near the gate where the chickens are kept. They say, anyone who comes to steal the chickens will get stuck to the tar baby. Cunning Rabbit saw with his own eyes the people putting the tar baby on the gate to the chicken pen. So, he became afraid.

The next day he played sick so he didn't go to town. However, Mr. Spider went hunting in the woods and brought food back for Cunning Rabbit. He ate until he was full. The following day when he was supposed to town in search of food, he played sick again. He said he wasn't going to go because he didn't feel well. So, Mr Spider went into the woods and hunted until he could bring food back for Cunning Rabbit. Again, Cunning Rabbit, ate until he was full.

The next day Cunning Rabbit didn't want to go hunting for food again. At this point, Mr. Spider said, "My friend, this is too much. You are always sitting up in the house while I, alone, go searching for food to eat. I can't keep up this level of work."

Then Cunning Rabbit said, "My friend, it is not because I don't want to go." He said, "Brother, I have a huge boil that is causing this."

"Mr. Spider responded, "Where is this boil?

Cunning Rabbit said, "Brother, look at it here on the bottom of my foot." He had taken a big stone and tied it to the bottom of his foot. He started limping across the room. Mr. Spider said, "Alright, today I will take care of you, but if you don't work tomorrow, I'm not going to help you at all."

The next day came and Cunning Rabbit said, "Brother, I can't make it again today. This foot is causing me great pain!" Mr. Spider became enraged. He said, "Show me where you go to steal those big, fat chickens before. Take me there, Man." So, Cunning Rabbit said, "Okay." He took him there. When they got close to the place, Cunning Rabbit saw the tar baby that looked like a real person. Bra Spider pointed to where the tar baby was positioned and said, "You see that pen right there? That's where the chicken treasure is. But you see the man standing by the gate? I think he is guarding the chickens. Man, please, who is afraid of that one? I would just crawl under his foot and get into the pen."

Bra Spider said, "Alright, go ahead now."

So, he went. When Bra Rabbit went, he found the man standing with his feet spread apart, just as the people had intended. Spider said, "Good evening, Brother." The thing didn't answer. Rabbit continued talking, "Hello, Brother. How are you doing?" The thing was silent. So, he said,

216   *Chapter 9*

"Man, what kind of stuff is this? I greet you and you don't respond." He extended his hand to shake hands, but his hand stuck to the thing. He struggled and struggled to get his hand free, but he couldn't. He pleaded, "Man, please let go of me. I am starving. Man, let go of me."

At first, he thought this was a joke. He didn't realize his hand was stuck there. He struggled and struggled, nothing. Then, he declared, "if you don't let me go, I'm gonna kick you." So, he kicked him with his left foot, pow! As soon as he kicked him, his foot got stuck. He shouted, "Hey, Man, I don't like this kind of playing around! Man, let me go. Let me go!" He continued trying to fight his way out, but his foot and hand were still stuck (to the tar baby).

"I'm gonna kick you with my other foot!" As soon as he kicked, the other foot got stuck. At this point, he, himself began to laugh. "Man, this brother likes to play too much. I'm telling you, Man, put me down. I want to go." No matter how much he talked to the tar baby, it wouldn't respond to him and wouldn't let him go.

At this point Bra Rabit said, "If you don't let me go, I'm going to butt you with my head. He moved his head back and hit the thing with his forehead, bang! No sooner than he hit it with his head, his head stuck to the thing. No matter how aggressively he struggled to release himself, no success. He tried again, no success. And so it went all night.

At dawn, the people who owned the chickens began waking up. Once awake, they saw the Cunning Rabbit stuck to the tar baby. So, they asked him, "Brother, what were you looking for here that led to your being stuck like this?" Spider responded, "I was just walking around here." The people asked, "Where were you going?"

The Spider answered, "I was just walking all around this place."

Then, the People announced, "Because of what you were trying to do here, you will never walk around anywhere again." They grabbed him and beat him to death.

That's the end of the story.

Try your hand at translating the remaining *nansi tori* below:

ANGRI BƆBƆ IT ARATA SUP [HUNGRY BOY EATS RAT SOUP]

Il . . .

Aw . . .

Wan de ya, wan man bin de we go wok na kos. I dɔn de na kos fɔ lɔng bɔt natin nɔ de de egen fɔ-r-am so I kam bak om. Ojo Bɔy kam om wit in

Krio Stories and Trickster Narratives

217

gladston bag. Ol pipul dɛm go no wetin na gladston bag. ɔl in jege jeks kayama de insay da bag de. Ojo Bɔy pul wan tin sigarɛt fɔ smok. Natin nɔ de insay di bag egen. So wi ɔl go ɔp to im mama in os.

We in mama si am nain in se, "ee! ee! Jacɔb na yu yay dis?"

"Yɛs mama."

"Aw yuk am?"

"Wɛl, mama, a nɔ de wok naw naw, nain a se mek a kam om."

" ee, bo, yu jɛs kam, yu nɔ rayt, yu nɔ se natin. Yu sɛf no se na ya, ɛnitɛm we yu want sɔmtin, pas yu go tɔng fɔ go fɛn am. ɛn we wi de fawe frɔm tɔng, i tranga fɔ gɛt tings dɛm we yu want. So, aw wi go du naw? A nɔ kuk yet sɛf frɔm mɔnin."

"Mama duya nɔ wɔri yu sɛf.," Ojo Bɔy se, as i de smok in 555 sigarɛt.

"Dis angri ya so i dɔn mɔna. In fac, na yɛstade we yu dadi go na fam, nain in kech tu *afe,* dat na dɛm bibig arata. i kech dɛm ɛn nak dɛm dɔn. Nain a de kuk so wi go it am wit lili fufu. Na dat nɔmɔ wi gɛt."

"Ah! Mama! Mi? It arata? Nɔ-o. Mi ɛn arata nɔ gri."

Nain Mama se, "ɔrayt, bɔt natin nɔ de ya o. ɛnti yu sɛf no aw yu lɛf os?"

Wɛl, fɔ Ojo Bɔy, i dɔn te we gape de waya. Di angri dɔn mɔna am. Big man nɔ go disgreso. Aw fɔ kan go se, "Mama a go it yu arata sup." So nain I bigin sniz: iiiitzrata!! Iiitzrata!!

Nain i mama se, "Ee, ee Jacob a dɔn tɛl yu, nɔ kan sik ya wit angri bɛlɛ-o. Bo, yu nɔ go tray me sup, di arata sup we a kuk? Tray am si. Afta-r-al yu bin dɔn it am bifo yu go Kos."

Nain Ojo Boy go tek di it we in mama kuk. Angri dɔn sok am. I dɔn di fufu ɛn arata sup, ma! Na wan lili arata fut nɔmɔ i lɛf na in plet.

Naim mek bɔku pan dɛm wan dɛm we kin go na kos, kin klap ɛn klap fut ɛn kam bak wit natin.

Ojo bɔy insɛf mɛmba usay i kɔmɔt-Rigɛnt-we, dɛm de dɛm de, na waka yu gɛ fɔ waka go ɔlsay. Mɔtoka nɔ bin de go de sɛf. Na ɔl dat i mɛmba we mek i it di arata sup ɛn fufu.

The English translation is provided in the Appendix.

NOTE

1. Douglas Odom, "A Comparative Analysis of the Trickster Figure in Africa, the Caribbean, and North America," Undergraduate Honors Thesis, University of Mississippi, 2013, https://egrove.olemiss.edu/hon_thesis/270 (accessed February 2, 2024).

Chapter 10

Poetry in Sierra Leone Krio and Jamaican Patois

Poetry has been a written art form in Sierra Leone since the late 1800s when educated Krios engaged in what can be referred to as "newspaper poetry." Newspaper poetry is a special column or page in major newspapers dedicated exclusively to the publishing of poems of notable Krio writers. However, its appeal was limited because of the lack of standardization of the Krio writing system at that time and because the form and style were noticeably elevated and somewhat Victorian.

One of the driving motivations for Krio poets in the late 1800s and early 1900s was to publicly manifest their knowledge of the art of poetry in their own culture. Equally significant, they wanted to use this art form to examine customs and traditions that many of the early Krio communities took for granted, and they did so by imitating the form and style of British and European poetry. Demonstrating the knowledge they have acquired from British education had to be publicly manifested to validate their introduction to the intellectual cultures of the West.

The *Sierra Leone Weekly News*, which started publishing poetry in Krio in the early 1880s, became the vanguard of newspaper poetry in the Sierra Leone.

Over the years, poetry in Krio evolved to creatively explore and use the rhythms, expressions, and syncopations of the Krio language. Two pioneers in that area are Thomas Decker and Gladys Casely-Hayford, who were instrumental in moving Krio poetry in this direction. As early as the late 1930's Decker had begun to challenge public perception that Krio was nothing but "broken English." He encouraged local Krio communities to embrace Krio as their own language, develop its cultural bases, and find a way to standardize its writing system. All of this, as Neville Shrimpton observes, because Decker "considered that Krio was an expression of the (African) soul of the people who spoke it. As such, its existence could not just be ignored or

220   *Chapter 10*

dismissed."[1] Decker expounded on this in his satirical play "Boss Coker Befo St. Peter," which he presents as a critique of the façade that Krio is "broken English." Gladys Casely-Hayford, a prolific writer and poet in the 1940's, took on Decker's challenge by publishing a book of poetry called "Take Um So," in 1948. Poems in her collection largely introduced readers to the local rhythms of Krio, while simultaneously exploring social issues, identity, and self-expression.

In recent years, several Krio poets have delved deeper into Krio language and culture to create art. For example, Daphne Barlatt Pratt's dramatic cry in "Woyo, Woyo, Wi Kɔtintri" ["Oh dear! Oh dear! Our Cotton Tree!"] captures the power of loss in Krio and more specifically, the pathos and anguish of losing a centuries-old community icon, the cotton tree. Jonathan Peters' poem, "A go fɛn wok, a go kɔl dɛt, dɛm tɛl mi se: 'Go kam, go kam'" ["I went job-searching, or asking for money owed me, they tell me: 'Go and come later.'"] paints a picture of the challenges of cultural roadblocks to achieving one's goals in the community. Even more recently, Tom Spencer-Walters' "Bifo doklin, A de na fo rod fɔ go kech mi kɛkɛ, tret to Funkia" ["Before dawn, I am out in the street, looking for public transport, straight to Funkia"] pictures the resonance of everyday activities of the Krio, in this case a trip to the beach in Funkia to buy fish. Thus, writing poetry in Krio has become a literal effort to (a) showcase the richness and diversity of Krio culture; (b) experiment with the Krio language to address issues that are germane to Krio communities; and (c) examine narratives that shed light on Krio history.

The Krio poems we selected for this chapter are meant to exemplify this thematic shift from merely imitating and valorizing British intellectual artforms, to experimenting with Krio language as a vehicle for intellectual and cultural discourse. This approach provided more leverage for writers to cover issues ranging from Krio cultural icons and the pain of loss, through popular Krio dishes, to building social relationships and practicing social norms.

KRIO POEMS

Poems in this section are carefully chosen because they reference aspects of Krio culture from history to various aspects of everyday life, including a popular past time, gossiping, as well as grafting, food, trading and buying, and inclement weather.

A historical trauma that Krios talk about frequently is their connection to and the lingering effects of the slave trade. For example, whenever they talk about the establishment of Freetown, the capital of Sierra Leone, and its surrounding villages, they always reference the history of how various formerly enslaved groups ended up in these areas.

In the poem, "Futmaleka" ["In a Mighty Hurry"], Spencer-Walters took us back to the advent of the nefarious trade and its deleterious effects on Africans:

"FUTMALEKA" [IN A MIGHTY HURRY]

Original Krio Version

Wi sidɔm na wi abule dɛm
Wit kol at ɛn kol rɛs
Nɔ ambog nɔbɔdi
Dɛn poto kam
Wit gbagbati ɛn shakabula
Dɛn bumbu wi pipul go insay bot
we fiba manawa
ɛn kɛr dɛm go Amɛrika
ɛn di Westinji
Dɛn sɛl wi na makit
lɛk bonga fis na shuku blay
Agba dɛm, kombra dɛm, bɔbɔ ɛn titi dɛm

Bifo jako kɔt yay
Sɔn pan dɛm fɛn dɛnsɛf
Na Gɔla kɔntri na Sawth Karolayna;
ɔda wan dɛn end up na Brazil
bɔku-boku land na Wɛstinji

Dɛn sɛn wi go wok fɔ yando
De kɔt shuga ken ɛn pik kɔtin
mɛn dɛm pikin
ɛn kuk dɛm nyanyam
Frɔm doklin, tete nɛt kam wi de wok.
If yu tray fɔ rɔnawe,
na shakabula go chɛr yu skin ɛn bɔs yu ed.

Bifo jako kɔt yay
Wi pipul dɛm nɔ bi dɛnsɛf egen
Gɔla, Spanish, Inglish, Krio, Creole
Nyu tɔng dɛm
Africa, saful-saful wan, ayd na dɛm mayn
De wet fɔ doklin fɔ flay go om egen

222 *Chapter 10*

English Translation of "Futmaleka"

[We are sitting in our modest huts
In peace, and eating our left-over rice
Troubling no one
Then the white people came
Aggressively and with long guns
They roughly forced our people into boats
That look like warships
and took them to America
and the Caribbean Islands
They sold them in open markets
Just as chip fish in a basket

Men, women, nursing mothers, boys and girls
In the twinkling of an eye
Some of them found themselves
In Gullah country in South Carolina
Others end up in Brazil.
A lot of them landed in the West Indies.

They forced us to work for free
Cutting sugar cane and picking cotton
Taking care of their children
And preparing their meals
From dusk to dawn we are working.
If you try to run away
Bullets will rip your skin and burst your head
In the twinkling of an eye
Our people were never the same again
Gullah, Spanish, English, Krio, Creole
New languages
Africa, lurking patiently in their minds
Waiting for the light of day to shine again.]

Food, as we pointed out earlier, is an important part of the cultural experience of Krios. In all traditional ceremonies, food functions not only to fulfill nutritional needs but also as a symbol of bringing people together as well as a conduit between the spirit and the physical worlds. In everyday life, there are certain foods people like and would regularly crave. All kinds of sauces like *bitas, kasada lif, and kren-kren* are primary on that list, but so are *binch* and *rɛs akara*, and *rayz bred*. However, one food item that is famous for the way it is prepared in one village is *kasada bred ɛn frayfis*. The town of Waterloo,

Poetry in Sierra Leone Krio and Jamaican Patois 223

not very far from Freetown, has the reputation of having the best *kasada bred en frayfis* ever. People would choose to travel to Waterloo to get it even when it may be available elsewhere close to their home. Jonathan Peters captured this food's essence and appeal in his poem appropriately titled "Kasada Bred ɛn Fray Fis."

"KASADA BRED ɛN FRAY FIS" [CASSAVA BREAD AND FRIED FISH]

Original Krio Version

Tide a fil so omsik
Wɛn a mɛmba di wam san na Salon.
ɛn tink se na winta de kam so.
Wan mɔ yia pan dis wakabɔt
Na pipul kɔntri fa we frɔm wi yon

Tide a mɛmba wi fayn-fayn Salon
A nɔ tink bɔt natin pas
Kasada bred ɛn fray fis.
ɛn yu nɔ it fray fis gud yet
If yu nɔ tes Watalo dɛm yon

If yu kɔmɔt ɔplayn de kam Fritɔn
Yu jɛs gɛt fɔ stɔp na Watalo rod
We ɔl dɛm uman treda dɛm kin de
Wit ɔl kayn blay ɛn shayn pan
We ful wit kasada bred ɛn fray fis

A sidɔn na ya so tide
A nɔ de tink bɔt natin pas
Salon ɛn rebɛl ɛn kɔnfyushɔn
We mek i tranga fɔ go Watalo
Fɔ gɛt fayn-fayn kasada bred ɛn fray fis
Tek yu fray fis rɔb am wit grevi
Put am insay yu kasada bred
If yu de go ɔplayn ɔ yu de kam tɔng
Na gud kɔmpin yu dɔn gɛt so.
Nɔ fɔ tɔk bɔt manpawa fɔ swɛla am go dɔng

Naw weting fɔ du na dis kɔntri
Wen otutu de waya, sno de fɔdɔm
ɛn wi lɛf pan wi omsiknɛs

224   *Chapter 10*

Nɔto fɔ manej wetin wi gɛt
So dat wi nɔ go ɛnd pan kekrebu?

Mi gɛt mi kasada, yu gɛt yu fray fis
Tru, kadasa bred ɛn natai nɔ de
Wi nɔ nid fray fray, bɛwl bwɛl
Bɔt wi kin stil put kasada na fray fis
Kɔba fɔ di kol ɛn mek gladi gladi

English Translation of "Kasada Brɛd ɛn Fray Fis"

[Today I feel so homesick
When I think of the hot Sierra Leone sun
And think that winter is fast approaching.
Another year in this constant roaming
In a different country far away from ours.

Today I remember our beautiful Sierra Leone
I don't think about anything but
Cassava bread and fried fish
And you know, you haven't eaten good fried fish
Until you taste Waterloo's fried fish.

If you travel from up country to Freetown
You have to stop at Waterloo Road
Where all the women traders are usually are
With a variety of baskets and shiny containers
Filled with cassava bread and fried fish

I am sitting here today
I am not thinking about anything other than
Sierra Leone, the rebels, and confusion
which makes it hard to go to Waterloo
To get delicious cassava bread and fried fish.
Take your fried fish and smear it with gravy
Put it in your cassava bread
If you're going up country or coming to town
You're in good company.
Don't talk about manpower when you send it down

Now what can we do in this country
When it is bitingly cold and snowing
And we are left feeling homesick
Shouldn't we settle for what we have
So that we will not end up dying?

Poetry in Sierra Leone Krio and Jamaican Patois 225

I have my cassava, you have your fried fish
True we don't have cassava bread and nut oil
We don't always need fried or boiled stews
But we can still put cassava in fried fish
Bundle up for the cold and be happy.][2]

Fish is an important part of many Krio dishes including the one we just described above. To get different varieties of fish and to get them fresh, people would try to get to the beach early in the morning when the fishermen are coming in. Funkia beach in the Western area of Freetown is well known for its supply of *mina* [minnows] which are very popular in many Krio dishes such as *kasada bred ɛn frayfis, bred ɛn fis* [bread and fish], and *fis styu* [fish stew]. Spencer-Walters' "Funkia Mina" poem captures the journey to Funkia beach and the subsequent purchase and preparation of the fish for cooking:

"FUNKIA MINA" [FUNKIA MINNOWS]

Original Krio Version

Bifo do klin
A de na forod fɔ go kech mi kɛkɛ
Tret to Funkia
Fɔ go bay mi
Swit swit mina
Mina Ya . . . !!!

Aw di otutu de waya
Na so di kɛkɛ de tɛtɛ
ɔp ɛn dɔng il
Pas bod os ɛn ton os,
Grani ɛn granpikin
Tete wi rich na di waf na Funkia

Di ples bizi lɛk grɔngɔbi
Fishaman de opin nɛt na san-san
Makit uman de yɛwo na kɔna
Fɔ dɛm mɔlit, tɛni, ɛn mangropej
Bega bega sɛf de pas ɔlɔbɔt
wit dɛm broko bag

Bɔt mi, na mina nɔmɔ a want
Mina we de shayn lɛk shatin
En slipul lɛk drɔ sup na mɔt

226   *Chapter 10*

A bay wan bibig bag
Bifo a jomp na kɛkɛ egen fɔ go om.
A klin mina tete mi an sawa
Dɛn a fray dɛm wit frɛsh natay
Mi Watalo kasada bred dɔn rɛdi
De wet fɔ Funkia mina

Wɛn tit ɛn tɔng jam
Na wa nain bigin so na mɔt
Bitwin Kasada bred ɛn fray fis

Di switnɛs go mi bon sote
A fɔgɛt fɔ drink wata.
Funkia Mina nain swit pas ɔl!

English Translation of "Funkia Mina"

[Before dawn
I am in the street looking for transport
Heading for Funkia
In order to buy my
delicious minnows
Minnows here. . . . !!!

Because it is so cold outside
The taxi was just crawling
up and down the hill
Driving past board and brick houses,
Grandparents with their grandchildren
until we reached the fisherman's wharf in Funkia

The place was as busy as a bumble bee
The fishermen were spreading their nets in the sun
Market women were negotiating prices in the corner
For their mullets "teni" and "mangropej"
Even beggars are everywhere
with their torn and worn-out bags.

But for me, I only want minnows
which shines like white linen cloth
and slippery like "draw sup" in the mouth
I bought a big bag of them
before I boarded a taxi once more heading for home.
I cleaned minnows until my hands got sore.
Then I fried them with fresh nut oil

Poetry in Sierra Leone Krio and Jamaican Patois

My Waterloo cassava bread was ready
for Funkia minnows

When teeth and tongue clash
It is war inside the mouth
between cassava bread and fried fish

The deliciousness was intoxicating
I even forget to drink water
Funkia minnows are the sweetest of all fish!][3]

A favorite past time in Krio culture is gossiping. It entertains, strengthens social ties, and sanctions those who break the norms of Krio society. Gossiping is so popular that it has made its way into the folklore of Krio culture. Songs have been composed about it by local *gumbe* artists like Dr. Oloh and Peter na Lepet, and stories about its effects have been told by prominent storytellers. The poem "Kongosa" by Spencer-Walters demonstrates the use of this past time among the Krio:

"KONGOSA" [PERSISTENT GOSSIP]

Original Krio Version

Kɔna dɛm blayn dɛm
Insay dɛm lili ol dɛm
Biɛn dɛm do dɛm
Yay de rol
lɛk eg insay bwɛl wata
Dɛn no se
Mami Abi de kuk bitas ɛn bɔlɔgi
Yes dɔn kak de wet fɔ di alejo
Dɛm no se
na jɔnks Sera wɛr go chɔch dis mɔnin
Nos de smɛl-smɛl,
i no se
da jɔlɔf rɛs we Jabez de wak so,
na switat kuk am fɔ-r-am.
Mɔt de lebe-lebe
I no se,
Adebayo ɛn Talabi de fɛt fɔ prɔpati
Fut dɛm de waka-waka ɔp ɛn dɔng trit
De luk insay pipul pala
Laylondo!

Chapter 10

Wetin mek pipul dɛm tan so?
Natin pas kongosa
So duya, tot una kongosa bɛnch go fawe

English Translation of "Kongosa"

[At the corners of blinds
Inside little holes
Behind doors
Eyes are rolling
like egg in boiling water
They know that,
Madam Abi cooked bitter leaves and bologi soup
Ears are perked to hear the latest news
They know that
Sera wore second-hand clothes to church this morning
Nose is sniffing
It knows that,
the jollof rice Jabez is enjoying so much
was prepared by his girlfriend.
Mouth is engaging in excessive chatter
It knows that
Adebayo and Talabi are fight over property
Feet are strolling up and down the street
Looking inside people's living room
Persistent liar!
Why are people like this?
Nothing but gossip
So please, take your gossip bench and go away.][4]

Some poets writing in Krio, like Jonathan Peters, are manifestly concerned with issues dealing with extortion or grafting in a country like Sierra Leone, especially in business transactions. Grafting occurs when goods and services are deliberately delayed until the client understands that *put fɔ mi* [offer me something to get something in return] is part of the process for closing successful business deals. By using euphemistic language to extort a bribe, the seller or service person can avoid being openly accused of seeking bribes. Peters' poem, "Go Cam, Go Cam" cleverly demonstrates this fact:

"GO KAM, GO KAM" [GO AND COME BACK]

Original Krio Version

Poetry in Sierra Leone Krio and Jamaican Patois

Una mɛmba tɛm na di tong
We tings bin de go fayn fayn
We if yu wan sɔmtin tide
ɛn yu ɔri pas mekes
Yu kin gɛt am yɛstade
Wɛl, dɛm tɛm dɛm de dɔn pas bikɔs
Tide, na go kam, go kam

A go na kot os fɔ mi kes
Dɛm tɛl mi se: "Go kam, go kam."
A go fɛn wok, a go kɔl dɛt
Dɛm tɛl mi se: "Go kam, go kam."
A go si kɔnsibul, biznɛs-govmɛnt man
Bɛtɛ nɔ kɔmɔt de bikɔs
Tide na go kam, go kam

Bɔt if a se a gɛ fɔ put
Kan si we man de chak
Fɔ mek tings go fuke fuke
A rayt o, a rɔng o, if a jɛs put
Mi we go klia lɛk breeze
Bikɔs go kam, go kam go tɔn
Kam go, kam go, kam

Du ya, dis revolushɔn
Nɔto im fɔ tɔn
Go kam to kam go, witawt
Put fɔ mi a du fɔ yu?
If a put Shaki tɛm, Momoh tɛm
Wetin apin dyɔrin soja bɔy tɛm
If put stil de put, chap de chap
dɛn chenj nɔ lɛf wi stil pan wahala?
Mi pipul dɛm we dɛm se? Dɛn nɔ se
Kapu sɛns nɔ kapu wɔd?
Wetin na revolushɔn?
Nɔto go ɛn kam, kam ɛn go?
Wɛl nain mek fɔ tek tɛm
Wit dis revolushɔn
Bambay go kam, go kam go tɔn
Kan go, kan go, GO!

English Translation of "Go Kam Go Kam"

[Do you remember a time in this city, this country
When things were going well
When if you want something right now

230   *Chapter 10*

And you're in a mad rush
You could get it right away?
Well, those times are gone because
Now, it's go and come back later

I went to the courthouse for my case
They tell me "Go and come later."
I went job-hunting, or asking for money owed me,
They tell: "Go and come later."
I went to see the police, business-government people
Nothing good came out of it because
These days it's go and come later

But if I am willing to give a bribe
You should see how people would be rushing
To make things go smoothly
Whether I am right or wrong, I just have to offer a bribe
I would get what I need as easily as a gentle breeze
because go and come later would become
Come now, come now, come

Now, this new change
Shouldn't it reverse
Go and come later to come now, without
Having to bribe someone to get things done?
If I pay bribes during Siaka's time, Momoh's time
What happened during the military regime reign?
If bribery is still evident and corruption continues
Then hasn't the new change left us with more problems?
My people, what's the news out there? Don't they say
Hold on to the essence of something not just the words?
What is a revolution?
Is it not go and come later, come now?
That's why we should be careful
With this revolution
With time, go and come later will become
Come and go, come and go. Go!][5]

Sierra Leone has one of the highest rainfalls in West Africa and many times when one of these torrential rains hit, poorly designed streets and gutters are flooded becoming flowing streams that carry all kinds of debris that have been carelessly strewn around. Sometimes people get so gravely concerned about these torrential downpours that they worry about the safety of their homes, pets, and livestock. One little respite though from the deluge is that

Poetry in Sierra Leone Krio and Jamaican Patois   231

it will clean up the air and their neighborhoods. Listen to the rhythms of Spencer-Walters' poem "Agbara," as it takes you through the effects of torrential rains.

"AGBARA" [RAIN TORRENT]

Original Krio Version

Di ren dɔn kɔt.
Wata de slayd dɔn ruf
Lɛk ɔkrɔ sup pan agidi
bifo i slipul dɔn wi trot.
Gɔta dɛm ful wit jegbe-jagba
Ples nɔ de fɔ waka na trit sɛf.
Broko bɔtul, ɛmti milk kɔp, rɔtin mangro
Agbara dɔn tek chaj
I de rol dɔng di trit
Lɛk na in prɔpati.
Natin nɔ de we i de lɛf biɛn
Pɔtɔ-pɔtɔ de gɛda fas-fas
bifo pipul dɛn domɔt.
do dɛn de lɔk kwik-kwik
Pus ɛn dɔg de rɔn go biɛn yad
fɔl dɛm go ayd insay dɛm fɔl kup
ɔl fɔ mek agbara nɔ kɛr dɛm go
Da pawa we agbara gɛt
nɔbɔdi nɔ ebul am
na wahala we kin kil animal dɛm
Bɔt na blɛsin we de klin ɔp
wi trit ɛn gɔta dɛm.

English Translation of "Agbara"

[The rain has stopped.
Water slides down roof tops
like okra sauce on "agidi"
before it slides down our throat.
Gutters are full of all kinds of rubbish
There is nowhere to walk on the street path.
Broken bottles, empty milk cans, decaying mangoes
The torrential rain is now in charge
It is rolling down the street
As if it owns it.

Chapter 10

It leaves nothing behind
Mud is collecting rapidly
in front of people's doorsteps.
Doors are closing fast
Cats and dogs are running for cover in the back yard
chickens run into their coops
All, to avoid being swept away by the torrential rain
The power of the torrential rain
No one can challenge

It's a danger that can kill animals
However, it is a blessing which cleans up
our streets and gutters.][6]

Daphne Barlatt Pratt's poems continue to celebrate iconic elements in Krio culture. Her poem, "Una nɔ Westɛm" captures the essence of motherhood in Krio society. Bringing new life into being is not just for the immediate parents' gratification and joy, but also that of the extended family as well as the community at large. Pratt's delightful metaphorical rendering of the process of conception and birth mimics several cultural and mythic beliefs in Krio society. Listen to this very sonorous poem.

"UNA NƆ WESTƐM" [YOU SHOULD NOT WASTE TIME]

Original Krio Poem

nɔ westɛm
fɔ mek dɛn bebi dɛm
na so a yɛri Papa Gɔd se
we dɛn bin de mek mi da de de
una nɔ westɛm
fɔ mek dɛn bebi dɛm
dɛn mama ɛn papa de wet
bebi nɔ redi yet?
bo una dɔn de let
Ayɔdele dɔn taya fɔ wet
fɔ in bebi sista ɔ brɔda
una nɔ westɛm
fɔ mek dɛn bebi dɛm
na rɛd dɔti fɔ tek
miks am dɛn yu mek
di bɔdi, an, ɛn fut
ad sɔm mɛresin rut

Poetry in Sierra Leone Krio and Jamaican Patois

miks am wit sɔm frut
mekes mek yu put
dɛn ɔl fɔ dray na san
prɛd dɛn wan bay wan
una nɔ westɛm
fɔ mek dɛn bebi dɛm
dɛn mama ɛn papa de wet
bebi nɔ rɛdi yet?
mek dɛn fayn
mek ɔl kayn
dak brawn, blak, ɛn yala
chɔklet ɛn milk kɔla
af kas, kol ta, malata
mek dɛn wan by wan
dɛn una prɛd dɛn fɔ dray na san
bebi swit lɛk tin fɔ it
bɔt bebi nɔ mek dɔn yet
bo una de westɛm
fɔ mek dɛn bebi dɛm
mama ɛn papa de wet
bebi nɔ rɛdi yet?

nɔ tek enjɛl we les
fɔ mek bebi in fes
sɔm wokman lɛk
fɔ mek kɔt nɛk
ɔda wan lɛk fɔ
mek bo jɔ
ɔlman get in stayl
fɔ mek bebi smayl
BƆT
bebi in jɛs de pit
bikɔs i nɔ gɛ tit
bebi in jɛs de pu
bikɔs i nɔ gɛ wok fɔ du
bebi in jɛs de kray
bikɔs dɛn put am na san fɔ dray
bɔt una nɔ westɛm
fɔ mek dɛn bebi dɛm
mama ɛn papa de wet
bebi nɔ rɛdi yet?
rɔb dɛn wit dɔni
ɔl oba dɛn bɔdi
te dɛn saf lɛk plastasin
una no wetin a min!

ɔl udat tɔch dɛn skin
go laf ɛn bigin siŋ.
we dɛn rich Salon
ɔlman go gɛt in yon
tek nidul ɛn blak trɛd bo
aylashis de fɔ so
mekes so aybraw ɔp yanda
pan di yay kanda
put tu smɔl brayt yay ɔnda
e! jɛs luk Gɔd wɔnda
naw bɔdi ɛn fes dɔn dɔn
bebi dɔn rɛdi fɔ bɔn
bɔt bifo una sɛn dɛn go
chɛk se ɔlman gɛt tɛn finga, tɛn to
una fɔ tray te te-e-e
una mek dɛn we
tu wankayn bebi nɔ de
na so Papa Gɔd se
bɔt if una mistek mek tu di sem
na Taywo ɛn Kainde dɛn fɔ nem
BƆT
wetin impɔtant
wetin ɔl bebi want
na fɔ kɛr dɛn go
to Papa Gɔd mek i blo
Layf insay dɛn—so
dɛn go it, tɔk, si, yɛri, ɛn gro
na dat impɔtant pas ɔl
fɔ pikin we kam na dis wɔl
bebi dɔn dɔn
bebi dɔn rɛdi fɔ bɔn
nɔ westɛm
sɛn dɛn go wantɛm
dɛn dɔn rich Salon
ɔlman dɔn gɛt in yon
Hmmmm—mmm
bebi swit lɛk tin fɔ it
Bebi saf; yu go laf
we yu ɔl am na yu an
eee! luk in lili fut ɛn an—Aaaaaa!

English Translation of "Una nɔ Westɛm"

[Don't waste time
To make babies

Poetry in Sierra Leone Krio and Jamaican Patois   235

That's what I heard God said
when I was being born that day
Don't waste time
to make the babies
mothers and fathers are waiting
The baby is not ready yet?
I think you're getting late
Ayodele is tired of waiting
for her baby sister and baby brother
Don't waste time
to make the babies
You must take red earth
mix it to make
the body, the hand, and the foot
add some medicinal roots
mix them with some fruits
hurry up and put
all to dry in the sun
spread them one at a time
Don't waste time
to make the babies
Mothers and fathers are waiting
Is the baby ready yet?
make them beautiful
make all kinds of them
dark brown, black, and yellow,
chocolate and milk color
half caste, coal tar, mulatto
make them one at a time
then spread them out to dry in the sun
Babies are so sweet like a delectable platter
but the babies are not ready yet?
Please don't waste time
to make the babies
mother and father are waiting
Is the baby ready yet?

Don' select a lazy angel
to make the baby's face
some baby workers like
to make beautiful neck
others like to
make dimples

everyone has their own style

Chapter 10

to make the baby smile
BUT
the baby is just drooling
because she has no teeth
the baby is just defecating
because she has nothing else to do
the baby is just crying
because they put her out in the sun to dry
but don't waste time
to make the babies
mother and father are waiting
Is the baby ready yet?
Rub them with shea butter
all over their bodies
until they are soft like plasticine
You know what I mean!
Anyone who touches their skin
will laugh and start singing.
When they arrive in Sierra Leone
everyone will receive their own child
Use needle and black thread, please
because eye lashes have to be sewn

hurry up and attach the eyebrows up there
on the skin of the eyes
put two small, bright eyes under
Eee! just look at God's miracle
a new body and a face are complete
the baby is ready to come out
but before you send them off
check to be sure that everyone had ten fingers, ten toes
You should try, very hard
to make them so that
two identical babies are not among them
That's God's wish
but if you mistakenly make two of the same
should name them Taiwo and Kehinde
But
what is important
What every baby wants
is to be taken to Father God
so that He would breathe
Life into them- so
that they will be able to, eat see, hear and grow
that's more important than anything else

for a child who comes into this world

The baby is finished
the baby is ready to be born
don't waste time
send them off right away
they have arrived in Sierra Leone
everyone has received their baby
Hmmmm-mmm!
Baby is as sweet as a delectable dish
baby is soft; you will laugh
when you hold her in your arms
Eee! look at those tiny feet and hands.][7]

Pratt's poem, "Mama Swit-o" is a veneration of the mother among the Krios. Mother is a supreme iconic figure who provides love, nurturing, food and protection to the family.

"MAMI SWIT-O" [MOTHER IS LOVE]

Original Krio Poem

MAMI SWIT O
mek a tɛl yu bo
if yu nɔ no
se mami swit o
wɛn a smɔl a ledɔm sik wan
mama go ol mi an
na mama go koks mi fɔ it
tray. tek dis lilibit
wɛn a rɔn kam wit kray
mama go wep mi yay
nɔ mɛn, nɔ mɛn, ɔshya
sidɔm na mi lap ya
a nɔ bin lɛk stɔdi
a kin wan go le bɔdi
mama kin kɔl mi
kam ol buk Fɛmi
we a dɔn big so i kin se
Frayde nɔto yu bathde?
na nyu klos ɛng so
biɛn in soin rum do
bifo yu go om mɔs kam

238   *Chapter 10*

i go dɔn pak sɔm cham-cham
i go dɔn go na kichin
go fray lili fish ɛn plantin
wɛn i dɔn mɛn mi dɔn
misɛf big a bigin bɔn
i ɛp mɛn dɛn pikin
na dat mami min
mek a tɛl yu bo
if yu nɔ no
mami—swit o

English Translation of "Mami Swit-O"

[Mother is love
Let me tell you
Just in case you don't know
how loving mother is
When I was young and very sick in bed
My mother would hold my hand
Mother would encourage me to eat
Try. Take this small portion of food
When I run over to her crying
She would wipe my eyes
"Never mind, never mind, my sympathy.
Come sit on my lap, please."
I didn't like to study
I just wanted to lie down
Mother would call me
Come and read your book, Femi
Now that I have grown she would ask
Isn't Friday your birthday?
A new dress is hanging
behind her sewing room door
"Stop by before you go home."
She would have packed some snacks.
She would go to the kitchen
to fry some fish and plantains
After she has finished taking care of me
I grew up and started having children
She would help take care of my children

That's what it means to be a mother
Let me tell you
Just in case you don't know
Mother is love.][8]

Poetry in Sierra Leone Krio and Jamaican Patois   239

Perhaps her most celebrated poem in the collection is her ode to the iconic cotton tree in Freetown, the capital city of Sierra Leone. This tree was over 250 years old when it collapsed suddenly in 2022. It was a central point for the enslaved people who were brought back to start a community in Freetown, as well as for the whole country. The poem captures the pathos of loss in all its sonorous details.

"WI KƆTINTRI" [OUR COTTON TREE]

Original Krio Version

woyo woyo kɔtintri
na so yu lɛf wi?
Jɛs lɛk dat? – Vyap!
Tyusde nɛt, yu tinap
Wɛnsde nɛt yu fɔdɔm, bap!
Ebo
aw yu du wi so?
yu, wi gret gret gret gret grani
in yon gret grani in mami
nɔba, a nɔ biliv se dat bi
astafulay, yu tink Gɔd go gri?
a de go luk fɔ misɛf
nɔ tɔk da wɔd de igen. lɛf!
Kɔtintri, kɔtintri, kɔtintri
a nɔ biliv se yu dɔn lɛf wi
a nɔ biliv mi yay
yɛstade yu bin tinap ay ay
na yu ledɔm na grɔn so?
ebo!
woyo woyo woyo
bɔt wet o
tap fɔ kray bo
dis wi kɔtintri ya
bay Gɔd in pawa
i go gro bak ma!
wi granpikin pikin pikin
dɛn granpikin
mɔs no wetin
wi kɔtintri bin min

English Translation of "Wi KƆtintri"

240 Chapter 10

[Oooh! Oooh! Cotton tree
How can you leave us like this?
Just like that? Vyap!
Tuesday night you're up and standing
Wednesday night you fell down, bap!
Oh dear
Why did you do this to us?
You, our great, great, great grandmother
who is your own great grandmother's mother
Never, I don't believe this happened
May the gods forbid this. Do you think God will let this happen?
I am going to go see for myself
Don't say that word again. Stop!
Cotton tree, cotton tree, cotton tree
I don't believe you have left us
I don't believe my eyes
Yesterday you were standing tall
Is it you lying on the ground like this?
Oh dear!

Oooh, oooh, oooh
But wait
Stop crying, please

Our cotton tree
By the grace of God
It will definitely grow again
Our grandchildren's children's children
their grandchildren
must know
what this cotton tree means to us.][9]

POETRY IN JAMAICAN PATOIS

Other than just contributions from Krio writers, we have included in this chapter, selected poems from two award-winning Jamaican poets, Andrene Bonner and Lorna Goodison, both of whom are writing in Jamaican Patois. Jamaican Patois and Krio share some common features that can be attributed to their exposure to and use of linguistic structures and orthographic elements from English, Creole, and the Kwa language family of West Africa that includes Yoruba, Igbo, and Akan. Krio draws much from Yoruba, Igbo, Fante and Ewe, but also from local Sierra Leone languages like Temne and Mende. In the case of Jamaican Patois, a great deal of its vocabulary is from

English, but its phonological and syntactic structures come from the Akan languages of Ghana [Fante and Twi] and to a lesser extent, Yoruba [Nigeria]. Part of the reason for this is that slave plantation owners preferred Africans from this region of West Africa for their skills and strength; so, a vast number of them were shipped to the Caribbean Islands. In Jamaica, many of these enslaved Africans fled to the hills to escape the oppression of slavery. There, they established communities that allowed them to maintain and practice their African culture, as well as nurture remnants of the Akan languages. They did a great deal to preserve what became known as "Coromantee" or "Maroon" culture, which is, indeed, Akan culture in Jamaica.

To demonstrate the similarities and differences between two diasporic languages, Sierra Leone Krio and Jamaican Patois, the readers will find the unusual, if not the only, translations of original Jamaican Patois poems into Sierra Leone Krio ever published.

Starting with Andrene Bonner, her poems explore various strands of Jamaican culture such as racial identity, social injustice, and Jamaican history. In "Troo Di Yeye a Di African" Bonner paints a sad picture of the transatlantic slave trade, specifically referencing its connection with the Akan people

of Ghana and the Yoruba people of Nigeria. Like Spencer-Walters' poem, *Futmaleka,* Bonner's "Troo Di Yeye a Di African" ["From the Perspective of the African"] presents a vivid picture of the oppression and systematic stripping of identities of the Africans in the slave plantations:

"TROO DI YEYE A DI AFRICAN" [FROM THE PERSPECTIVE OF THE AFRICAN]

Jamaican Patois

Mih, Nana fram Kumasi Lan an mi bredda dem, Kojo, Accompong, Quao, Johnny, and Cuffy did si di lan inna di mawni, an lawks di purple mountn a hol up it hed to di cloudy sky.
Di shakkles roun wi foot dem remine wi seh wi no free fi moov mongs di tree dem—throo di mountn an valli—swin inna di uppn seas.
Wi wuk di shuga plantashan lakka mule, dem taacha wi, dem beat wi, dem rape wi—dem hunt wi dung lakka hanimal an lef wi fi ded a sun hot fi john crow nyam wi.

Chapter 10

Wi chat Twi—wi chat Yoruba—we chat Igbo—wi chat Mfantse—wi chat Kikongo—fi wi madda tungs dat shape wi values—shape wi ways. The Maasa dem force wi fi give up wi langwij—we culcharal identity fi Español—Saxon dialeks.

Dem ban wi from worship fi wi deities: *Nyame an Nyamewa a divine creativity, Asase Ya goddess a fertility, Shango a di tunda and ski, Obatala di baba of humanity, Eshu god a di crossroads, Oshun a di rivers, Agwu a medicine*, an replace dem wid one Fadur of heofon and hrofe to spare our sinful soules fi join up wid de Tainos fi kill di Inglish man dem, bun dem plantashan, and bil wi own sociatee.

Wi call dis piece a rock—hell

English Translation of "Troo Di Yeye a Di African"

[I, Nana Abena of Kumasi Land, along with my brothers Kojo, Accompong, Quao, Johnny, and Cuffy saw this land in the morning, and o' the purple mountains raised their heads to the cloud drenched skies.

The shackles around our feet were a bleak reminder that we were not free to move among the trees—through the mountains and valleys—swim the open seas.

We worked the sugar plantations like beasts of burden, tortured, beaten, raped—hunted like wild animals and left to die in the sun—the carrion's paradise.

We spoke *Twi*—we spoke *Yoruba*—we spoke *Igbo*—we spoke *Mfantse*—we spoke *Kikongo*—our mother tongues that shaped our values—shaped our ways. The slavers forced us to surrender our language—our cultural identity for *Español*—for *Saxon dialects*.

They forbade us to worship our gods: *Nyame* and *Nyamewa of divine creativity, Asase Ya, goddess of fertility, Shango of the thunder and sky, Obatala the baba of humanity, Eshu god of the crossroads, Oshun of the rivers, Agwu of medicine,* and replaced them with one *Fadur* of *heofon and hrofe* to spare our sinful *soules* for joining with the Tainos to kill Englishmen, burn the plantations, and build our own society.

We called this land—hell.]

Krio Translation of "Troo Di Yeye a Di African"

Poetry in Sierra Leone Krio and Jamaican Patois 243

[Mi Nana Abena we kɔmɔt na Kumasi kɔntri wit mi brɔda dɛm, Kojo, Accompong, Quao, Johnny, ɛn Cuffy did si dis lan dis mɔnin ɛn di pɔpul mɔntin dɛm es dɛn ed to di bɔku bɔku klawd dɛm ɔp di skay.
Di chen dɛm we dɛm tay na wi fut dɛm mek wi nɔ fɔgɛt se wi nɔ fri fɔ waka rawn di tik dɛm to di mɔntin ɛn vali dɛm- ɔ swim na di big big oshɔn.
Wi wok lɛk dɔg na di shuga ken fam dɛm dɛn tɔchɔ wi, bit ɛn rep wi lɛk dɛn wayl bif dɛn na bus ɛn dɛn lɛf wi fɔ day na san—gud gud yayam fɔ dɛm yuba.
Wi de tɔk *Twi*—wi de tɔk *Yoruba*—wi de tɔk *Igbo*—wi de tɔk *Mfantse*—wi de tɔk *Kikongo*—wi mami langwej we nain mek wi bi wetin wi bi tide. Dɛm poto we kech pipul fɔ go sɛl, fos wi fɔ giv ɔp wi yon langwej ɛn kɔlchɔ fɔ Spanish—fɔ dɛm Saxon tɔn dɛm.
Dɛn nɔ gri mek wi pre to wi yon gɔd dɛm: *Nyame* and *Nyamewa of divine creativity, Asase Ya, goddess of fertility, Shango of the*

thunder and sky, Obatala the baba of humanity, Eshu god of the cross-roads, Oshun of the rivers, Agwu of medicine, ɛn cheng dɛm wit wan *Fadur* of *heofon and hrofe* fɔ lɛ dɛn pre fɔ wi sol bikɔs wi fala dɛn Tainos dɛn go kil wetman, bɔn dɛn fam dɛm, ɛn bil wi yon tɔng dɛm.
Nain mek wi kɔl dis lan ya so—ɛl.][10]

In "Black Hair Deh Pan Trial," Bonner tackles negative perceptions of Black hair that deny Black people the right to cultural expression.

"BLACK HAIR DEH PAN TRIAL"

Original Poem in Jamaican Patois

What a sumting!
Black smaddy hair
deh pan trial
fi vialate di tall,
pretty hair code.

Yes, puppa!
Mi hear seh
Nala daughter get kick out a school,

244   *Chapter 10*

an Maas Rob grandson can't graduate,
sake a im Stokely Carmichael afro
and him Nazarite side burns.

A long time dis foolishniss
a gwaan; now dem tek black pickney
mek pawn—fi dem new-imperial-ism,
cyarry out by di same black
smaddy dem who sake a Bakra blood,
ketch likkle light culla an curly
hair from canefield battarin an rape.

A weh wrong wid dem?
Black smaddy hair gone a jujment seat;
nappy hair, short hair, picky-picky
hair, bumpy hair, Rasta hair.
Every form a wi African hair
meet up inna courthouse.

What a sumting!
Di juhj face black like coal pot,
a hide him coir mattras hair
wid looptail, horsehair bob wig;
outa rispek fi di raahyal crung.
What a ceiful, wutliss smaddy.

Black people hair
deh pan trial, a wonda
wen dis bad-mindid-ness
a goh en.

English Translation of "Black Hair Deh Pan Trial"

[Goodness gracious!
Black people's hair
on trial for violating
the tall, pretty hair code.

Yes, father!
I heard that Nala's daughter
got kicked out of school,
and Maas Rob's grandson
cannot graduate,
because of his Stokely Carmichael
Afro and Nazarite side burns.

Poetry in Sierra Leone Krio and Jamaican Patois 245

It's a long time this foolishness
been happening. Now black children
are pawns for a new imperialism,
fraught with prohibition from the same Blacks
who but for the little drop of white blood,
a trace of lightness, and curly hair,
vexed in cane fields, battering rapes.

What's wrong with them?
Black people's hair face judgment;
nappy hair, short hair, picky-picky
hair, bumpy hair, Rasta hair.
Every form of our African hair,
standing trial in the courts.

Goodness gracious!
The judge's face, black as a coal pot,
he hides his coir mattress hair
With looptail, horsehair bob wig;
sign of respect to the royal crown.
What a deceitful, worthless one.

Black people's hair is on trial.
I wonder when this self-hate,
will end.]

Krio Translation of "Black Hair Deh Pan Trial"

[Lɔd adede!
Blak pipul ia
Nain de kot naw
Fɔ we dɛm go mistek vayɔlet da langa fayn ia kod

Yɛs papa.
A yɛri se
Dɛm ɛkspɛl Nala in pikin na skul
ɛn Pa Rob in granpikin
Nɔ go graduet
Bikɔs ɔf in Stokely Carmichael Afro
ɛn in Nazarite bia-bia
I dɔn te we dis nɔshi-nɔshi dɔn de go ɔn

Naw dɛm de tek dɛm Blak pikin dɛm
Lɛk skepgot fɔ dɛm nyu impirializim
We na di sem Blak pipul dɛm de ep dɛm

Chapter 10

ɔseka di lili wait blɔd,
lilibit panya ɛn kuli ia
frɔm ken fil wahala ɛn rep

Wetin du dɛm?
Blak pipul ia de na jujmɛnt chia
Dada ia, shɔt ia, piki-piki ia,
Bɔmpi ia, ɛn dredlɔks.
ɔl wi difrɛn kayn African ia dɛm
De na kotos fɔ jɔjmɛnt kes.

Lɔd adede!
Di jɔj in fes we blak lɛk kol pɔt
I ayd in chaka-chaka ia
Wit luptel, ɔsia, fɔls ia
Fɔ mojuba to di Royal krawn
Dawande, na kalo kalo, wɔtles man
Blak pipul ia de na jɔjmɛnt chia
A wɔnda ustɛm dis wi-nɔ-lɛk-wisɛf tin go dɔn.][11]

As far as Bonner is concerned, treaties and independence do not mean much because Jamaican people are still suffering under both. Thus, they must take responsibility for their own life and freedom, in "Emancipate Yourself":

"EMANCIPATE YOURSELF"

Original Poem in Jamaican Patois

Wi independent now,
yet wi mouth corner cake-up-cake-up wid white crust;
hunger is di langwij
a wi eye dem, di gurgle
inna wi gut like tines
a rakkle a rumba box;
free edicashan,
but we still noh free
from mental slavery.
Dem seh a ooman run tings;
but last time mi check
a di man dem run wi dung inna di grung
wid dem toxic man-skrewlinity,
deaf ayze political rivalry,
brazen wukplace inequality.

Poetry in Sierra Leone Krio and Jamaican Patois 247

wi independent now,
yet di crown still mek wi bow;
and wen Merica sneeze,
we economy start wheeze;
although Reggae music hypnotize di worl,
and wi dominate in sports,
rank high in science;
dem brand wi culcha wid foreign patent,
sell it back to wi—seh wee got talent.

What hack!
Wi independent now,
yet wi mouth corner cake-up-cake-up wid white crust,
wi dignity splattered gense walls of fragmented identities, a rev-
olushan a change is a mus.

English Translation of "Emancipate Yourself"

[We are independent now,
yet the corners of our mouths
are sticky with white crust;
hunger is the language
of our eyes, the gurgle
inside our guts that rattle
like tines of a rumba box;
education is free
but we are not free
from mental slavery.
They say we are a matriarchy,
but last time I checked,
men have run us into the ground
with their toxic masculinity,
deaf ears political rivalry,
and brazen workplace inequity.

We are independent now,
yet the crown still makes us bow;
when America sneezes,
our economy wheezes;
although Reggae music hypnotizes the world,
and we dominate in sport,
rank high in science;
they brand our culture with foreign patent,
sells it back to us raving that we have talent.
What a hack!

248   *Chapter 10*

We are independent now,
yet the corners of our mouths
are sticky with white crust,
our dignity splattered
against walls of fragmented identities,
a revolution of change—a must.]

Krio Translation of "Emancipate Yourself"

Wi dɔn gɛt indipɛndɛns naw
Bɔt kɔna wi mɔt kɔba wit dray wayt krɔs
Angri na di tin we wi yay de si
Di bɔlɔ-bɔlɔ we de insay wi gɔt
De mek yege-yege lɛk gumbe drum
Dɛn se buk lanin na fri
bɔt wi stil nɔ fri fɔ tink fɔ wisɛf

Dɛn se na uman dɛm na di agba
bɔt di las tɛm we a chɛk,
na di man dɛm dɔn rɔn dɔn dis wɔl
wit dɛm gbagbati,
dɛm fɛt fɔ pawa,
ɛn aw bad dɛn de trit pipul na dɛm wokples

wi dɔn fri naw
Bɔt di poto govament stil mek wi de dɔbale bifo dɛn kwin.
Wɛn Amerika sniz, we icɔnɔmi begin fɔ strɔgul

ivin do reggae dɔn tek oba di wɔl,
ɛn nɔbɔdi kin rɔn-res pas wi,
ɛn wi sabi saɛns bad-bad;
dɛn pent wi kɔlchɔ wit dɛn yon brand
ɛn sɛl am bak gi wi
ɛn dɛn prez wi se wi gɛ talent.
Big big lay!
Wi dɔn fri naw
Bɔt kɔna wi mɔt kɔba wit dray wayt krɔs
Dɛn skata wi sɛlf rɛspɛkt
ɔl oba wi brok dɔng kɛrɛkta
Kuskas na di only ansa.[12]

Jamaican Poet—Lorna Goodison

Lorna Goodison's poems in Jamaican Patois are more philosophical but just as inspirational as Bonner's selections. In "The Road of the Dread" she encourages exploration of life; journeying through life without preconceived expectations. Just as Bonner articulated in her poem "Emancipate Yourself," Goodison points out that the road may not be paved with signs telling you where to go or what to expect. In short, explore life with innate curiosity and an open mind.

"THE ROAD OF THE DREAD"

Original Poem in Jamaican Patois

That dey road no pave
like any other black-face road.
It no have no definite colour
and it fence two side
with live barbwire.

And no look fi no milepost
fi measure you walking
and no tek no stone as
dead or familiar
for sometime you pass a ting
you know as . . . call it stone again;
and is a snake ready fi squeeze yu
kill yu
or is a dead man tek him
possessions tease yu.
Then the place dem yu feel
is resting place because time
before that yu welcome like rain
go dey again?
Bad dawg, bad face tun fi drive yu underground.
wey yu no have no light fi walk
and yu find sey that many yu meet who sey
them understand
is only from dem mout dem talk.
One good ting though, that same treatment
mek yu walk untold distance,
for to continue yu have fi walk far
away from the wicked.

Pan dis same road ya sista
sometime yu drink yu salt sweat fi water
for yu sure sey at least dat no pisen,
and bread? yu picture it and chew it accordingly
and some time yu surprise fi know dat full
yu belly.
Some day no have no definite colour,
no beginning and no ending, it just name day,
or night, as how you feel fi call it.
Den why I tread it brother?
well mek I tell yu bout the day dem
when the Father send some little bird
that swallow flute fi trill me
and when him instruct the sun fi smile pan me first.

And the sky calm like sea when it sleep
and a breeze like a laugh follow mi
or the man find a stream that pure like baby mind
and the water ease down yu throat
and quiet yu inside.
And better still when yu meet another traveller
who have flour and yu have water and a one and
make bread together.
And dem time dey the road run straight and sure
like a young horse that can't tire,
and yu catch a glimpse of the end
through the water in yu eye
I wont tell yu what I spy
but is fi dat alone I tread this road.

Krio Translation of "The Road of the Dread"

[Dat dɛn rod nɔ pev
Lek ɛni ɔda ta rod dɛm
I nɔ gɛ nɔ patikla kɔla
ɛn i gɛ fɛnch na di tu say dɛm
we dɛm bil wit shap babwaya dɛn
ɛn nɔ luk fɔ nɔ saynbod
we go tɛl yu ɔmɔs mayl yu dɔn waka
ɛn nɔ luk nɔ ston se
i dɔn kekrebu ɔ lek yu sabi am gud gud
fɔ sntɛm de yu kin pas sɔntin
we you yu tink se . . . kɔl am ston egen
dɛn yu si se na snɛk we dɔn rɛdi fɔ kwis yu
kil yu

Poetry in Sierra Leone Krio and Jamaican Patois 251

na dayman we de tek im
Prɔpati fɔ skiad yu.
Dɛn di ples dɛm we yu fil se
na kol-at ples bikɔs trade ya
we yu lɛk am lɛk ren
Yu wan go de egen?

Bad dɔg, bad fes wan push yu go bɔtɔm grɔn
we layt nɔ de fɔ mek yu waka
ɛn yu fɛnɔt se bɔku pipul dɛm we yu mit we se
dɛn ɔndastan
Bɔt dɛn jɛs de tɔk so so lebe-lebe nɔmɔ
Wan gud tin nɔmɔ, di sem we we dɛm trit yu
Naim mek yu waka faa
Fɔ mek yu bɛtɛ, yu gɛ fɔ waka faa
from di bad pipul dɛm.

Na dis sem rod ya so mi sista
sɔntɛn de yu go drink yu swɛt fɔ wata
bikɔs yu shɔ se nɔto poyzin
ɛn bred? Yu luk-luk am ɛn cham am so
ɛn sɔntɛmde yu kin sɔprayz fɔ no aw dat ful
yu bɛlɛ
Sɔm de dɛm de we jɛs tan lɛk ɛni ɔda de,
no doklin no nɛt jɛs di sem-ol de
ɔ nɛt, na so yu fil bɔt am
Dɛn wetin mek yu de waka de, brɔda?
Wɛl mek a tɛl yu bɔt di de dɛm
Wɛn di agba sɛn wan lili bɔd
we sabi sing fɔ mek mi gladi
ɛn fɔ tɛl di sɔn fɔ smayl pan mi fɔs
ɛn di skay qwayɛt lɛk di si wɛn i de slip
ɛn briz we de blo lɛk we pɔsin de laf, de fala mi
ɔ lɛk man we fɛn watasay we klin lɛk pikin at
ɛn di wata slipul dɔng yu trot
ɛn mek yu bɛlɛ sidɔm saful
ɛn pantap dat we yu mit da pɔsin na rod de
we gɛt flawa ɛn yu gɛt sɔm wata
ɛn yu ɛn in bek bred togɛda.
ɛn dɛn tɛm dɛm de di rod bin tret ɛn izi
lɛk yɔng ɔs we nɔ de taya
ɛn yu si di ɛnd kwick kwik
tru di wata na yu yay
A nɔ go tɛl yu wetin a ebul fɔ si
bɔt na di rizin dat we mek a waka na dis rod.][13]

252   *Chapter 10*

Goodison continued with the theme of a journey through life in "Heart Ease." Here, the possibilities are endless.

"HEART EASE 1"

Original Poem in Jamaican Patois

We with the strait eyes
And no talent for cartography
Always asking
"How far is it to Heart ease?"
And they say,
"Just around the corner."

But that being the spider's direction
means each day finds us further away
Dem stick we up
Dem jook we up
and when dem no find
what dem come to find
them blood we and say
'walk wid more next time.'

So take up divining again
and go inna interpretation
and believe the flat truth
left to dry on our tongues
Truth say
Heart distance
cannot hold in a measure
it say, travel light
you are the treasure
It say, you can read map
even if you born a Jubilee
and grow up with your granny
and eat crackers for yu tea.

It say
you can get licence
to navigate
from sail board horse
in the sea's gully.

Poetry in Sierra Leone Krio and Jamaican Patois

Believe, Believe
and believe this
the eye know how far
Heartease is.

Krio Translation of "Heart Ease 1"

[Wi we gɛt tret yay dɛm
ɛn nɔ sabi fɔ drɔ map
ɔltɛm a de aks
ɔw fa Heartease de?
ɛn dɛn ansa se
'as yu bɛn di kɔna yu go si am'

Bɔt we da wan de na di rod fɔ go to spayda in os
min se ɛvri de we wi waka di rod luk lɔng
Dɛm ol wi ɔp
Dɛm pinch pinch mi
ɛn we dɛm nɔ fɛn
wetin dɛm kan luk fɔ
dɛm jak wi ɔp ɛn se
nɛks tem, waka wit mɔ

So, bigin fɔ pre egen
ɛn go insay di wɔd gud-gud
ɛn biliv se di tru-tru wɔd
lef na wi tɔng fɔ dray
di tru-tru tin na
di rod fɔ rich Heartease
i nɔ izi-o
rod lɛk dis, nɔ waka wit bɔku lod
na yu na di prayz
i se yu sabi rid map
ivin if yu na Jubiliee we yu bɔn
ɛn na yu grani mɛn yu
ɛn it biskit wit yu ti.

i se
yu go ebul
yu go ebul fɔ fɛn yu we
frɔm sel bod ɔs,
na di si in ol.

Biliv, biliv
ɛn biliv dis

254   Chapter 10

yay no aw fa
Heartease de.]¹⁴

"Inna Calabash," like poems in Bonner's collection and Spencer-Walters'
"Futmalaka," reclaims the history of slavery as it affects Jamaica and Sierra
Leone. The calabash [*kalbas* in Sierra Leone] is the symbolic stomach that
holds yet another Black child to prepare him for slave work in the fields:

"INNA CALABASH" [IN THE CALABASH]

Original Poem in Jamaican Patois

Inna calabash
tell them that the baby
that count in them census already
Inna calabash

One slave child
that count already
while it inside my belly
tell them that the baby
Inna calabash

She show me
Quasheba show me one day
When I faint in the field of cane

When I cry and say
Why I can't be like missus
siddown and plait sand
and throw stone after breeze

Quasheba show me
How the calabash contained
For a slave gal like me
a little soft life and ease.

Pick a big calabash
bore both ends she say,
shake out di the gray pulp belly
run a string through both ends
and tie it across you belly

Poetry in Sierra Leone Krio and Jamaican Patois 255

Drop the little shift frock
make outta massa
coarse osnaburg cloth
over your calabash belly

Nothing Massa like
like more slave pickney
to grow into big slave
to serve slavery.

You will get rest
when you have belly
When you rest enough
just take it off

Say you fall
say you lose baby
Quasheba show me
all I need to know.
Inna calabash

Krio Translation of "Inna Calabash"

[Insay kalbas
Insay kalbas
tεl dεm se di pikin
we dεm ɔlrεdi dɔn kɔnt na dεm sεnsɔs de
Insay kalbas

Wan slev pikin
we dεm bin dɔn kɔnt
we i de insay mi bεlε
tεl dεm se di pikin de
Insay kalbas

I sho mi
Wan de Quasheba sho mi
we a fent na di shuga ken fil
we a kray εn se
Wetin mek a kyan be lεk di jɔmbul in wεf
We sidɔm εn de ple wit san-san
εn trowe ston pan εmpti briz?

Quasheba nain sho mi

256   *Chapter 10*

aw di kalbas we ol
slev pikin lɛk mi
gɛt kwayɛt ɛn izi layf.

Pik wan big kalbas
i se dig ol na di tu say dɛm,
shek-shek da gre swɛl bɛlɛ
pas wan trɛd insay di ol na di tu ɛnd dɛm
ɛn tay am round yu bɛlɛ

Put di lili fri frɔk dɔng
we dɛm mek wit di masa
in rɔf chip klos
oba yu bɛlɛ we luk lɛk kalbas

Natin nɔ de we we masa lɛk
lɛk bɔku-bɔku slev pikin dɛm
we go gro ɔp fɔ bi big slev dɛm
we go gud fɔ di slev trading biznɛs

Yu go blo
wɛn yu gɛt bɛlɛ
Wɛn yu dɔn blo gud-gud
jɛs pul am

Tɛl pipul dɛm se na fɔdɔm yu fɔdɔm
tɛl pipul dɛm se yu kalbas nɔ brok
Quasheba nain sho mi
all wetin a fɔ no.
Insay kalbas.][15]

In summary, the poems that were selected for this chapter show the convergence of language, culture, and history between two African and diasporic nations, whose resistance to the complete annihilation of the elements that give life to their stories, their societies, and their communities, is admirable.

NOTES

1. Neville Shrimpton, "Thomas Decker and the Death of Boss Coker." In, *Africa: Journal of the International African Institute*, 1987. Vol. 57, No.4. (p.533)

2. Jonathan Peters, "Kasada Brɛd ɛn Fray Fis." unpublished (2000).

3. Tom Spencer-Walters, "Funkia Mina," unpublished (2021).

4. Tom Spencer-Walters, "Kongosa," unpublished (2022).

Poetry in Sierra Leone Krio and Jamaican Patois　　　257

5. Peters, "Go Kam, Go Kam," unpublished (1993).

6. Tom Spencer-Walters, "Agbara," unpublished (2019).

7. Daphne Barlatt Pratt, "Una nɔ Westɛm," digitally recorded and circulated.

8. Daphne Barlatt Pratt, "Mami Swit-O," in *Salon Na Wi Yon* (self-published, 2008).

9. Daphne Barlatt Pratt, "Wi Kɔtintri," digitally recorded and circulated (2023).

10. Andrene Bonner, "Troo Di Yeye a Di African;" from "This Land," unpublished collection (2022).

11. Andrene Bonner, "Black Hair Deh Pan Trial," from "This Land," unpublished collection (2022).

12. Andrene Bonner. "Emancipate Yourself," from "This Land," unpublished collection (2022).

13. Lorna Goodison, "The Road of the Dread," in *Collected Poems* (Manchester: Carcanet Press, 2017), 6–8.

14. Lorna Goodison, "Heart Ease 1," in *Collected Poems* (Manchester: Carcanet Press, 2017), 110–11.

15. Lorna Goodison, "Inna Calabash," in *Collected Poems* (Manchester: Carcanet Press, 2017), 176–77.

Afterword

One of the greatest challenges facing the current and future generations of people around the world is identifying a set of principles and objectives which, if followed, will lead humanity to a more harmonious existence in which everyone has the opportunity to develop to their fullest extent, where resources are shared equitably, and when everyone can enjoy a sense of security, both personally and as part of the societies in which they live. A critical principle is access to an accurate history and a responsibility to learn that history, not for the purposes of seeking retribution against those who may have wronged them or their ancestors in the past, but as a pathway to a more positive future. Too many people of African descent do not know their history and, therefore do not understand their present and can only wonder about their future.

From our experience as students of the African World Experience, we believe that one of the major sources of the current challenges and those ahead of us is the fact that too frequently our histories have been distorted in the service of greed and of power. Our histories are littered with examples of distortions to keep us from knowing not only what is really going on, but also even keeping us from knowing who we are. Peoples of African descent have clearly been victims of miseducation and exploitation. A call to reclaim those stories and the cultures to which they are connected comes with a real sense of urgency. How else can African people stand on the world stage as whole people?

It is our hope that in some small way we have contributed to a broader and more accurate understanding of the history, language, culture, and traditions of the Krio people of Sierra Leone and, by extension, the history, language, culture, and traditions of African diasporic people around the world. The authors of this book intentionally chose to outline the history of the Krio people within a timeframe much longer than the nineteenth century because the history of the interactions between the Europeans and the Africans in the Atlantic set the stage for what would happen in Sierra Leone in the nineteenth

260   *Afterword*

century and beyond. Although it was well beyond the scope of this book, the authors could justifiably have painted a picture of the interactions between Africans and other peoples from around the world from the beginning of recorded history. Readers interested in exploring this longer trajectory of history are encouraged to read *They Came Before Columbus: The African Presence in Ancient Ameria*, by Ivan Van Sertima; *Stolen Legacy: Greek Philosophy Is Stolen Egyptian Philosophy*, by George G. M. James; and *African Origin of Civilization: The Myth or Reality*, by Cheikh Anta Diop.

Our efforts to objectively and systematically describe Krio language, culture, and traditions provided us with a foundation for analyzing the Krio society by tracing it back to the ethno-linguistic groups who were active players in the founding of that community. It was critical that we debunk the false notion that Krio is an "English based" creole language, by demonstrating that English words were not borrowed wholesale from English, but were instead inserted into a phonological, grammatical, and semantic grid that resembled the linguistic frameworks of the Kwa languages of West Africa. Similarly, the daily habits, traditions, and cultural apparatus of the Krio people were found to be re-creations of Kwa habits, traditions, and cultural apparatus. Our investigation into the similarities between Krio and other African diasporan communities, leaves no question that the agency of African peoples witnessed in Sierra Leone was replicated over and over again across the Atlantic. The stories of survival, scientific inventions, contributions to progressive governance, and illustrious creativity are legion.

Our final chapter pushes the boundaries of language by offering examples of literary creativity operative in the Krio community. The poems presented here provide opportunities for new learners of Krio to use their language skills, as they translate the poems, and to enjoy the language at play. The poets published here share common cultures, common struggles, and common hopes for the future. Witnessing the parallels that exist between the poetry of kindred African diasporan communities might also stimulate the readers to pick up the pen and record their own experiences in poetic or narrative form. Read and enjoy the literary songs of Africa.

These voices, in narrative form, are beginning to be heard in the international cinematic world. Nigerian filmmakers, find the depth of their creativity in the voices of the people, whether wealthy or common, using Nigerian Pidgin English, a close cousin of Krio. Listening to the playwright's story reveals how closely in touch they are to the pulse of their community, as the actors express their joy, their pain, their passion, and their aspirations through the language of diverse and vibrant communities. However, it is not only in the arts where Krio has gained prominence. In fact, Krio has, for a long time, and continues to be, the medium of commerce and public health across West Africa, from Gambia to Cameroun. It is the undisputed lingua franca of Sierra

Leone and has become widely used for language certification purposes in U.S. colleges and in the military. When the history of today is written tomorrow, Krio and its cousins will figure prominently.

Appendix

Answers to Mystifying Riddles in chapter 8:

a. Bread
b. Ghost, a witch, or an owl
c. Needle
d. Coffin
e. Clock
f. Bottle
g. Age
h. A clock
i. Onions
j. Pɔt sidɔm na faya de wet fɔ fufu tik. [the pot is sitting on the fire waiting for the fufu utensil.]
k. Learn from prior experiences
l. There's much more to it than meets the eye.
m. Pus tinap na tebul de wet fɔ arata. [The cat is standing on the table waiting for the rat.]

Answers to Culturally Related Riddles in chapter 8

a. To ward off evil spirits
b. To ward off bad dreams
c. Unexpected possible travel
d. Money is on the way
e. You need to send money
f. Langa-langa (Explanation: This is a local pseudonym for snake. Its possible origin is probably reduplication of the English word, 'long.') They fear that the snake is evil and if you call it by its name, it would come out and attack you.
g. Minnows

264 *Appendix*

h. Types of Mangoes
i. Colic or loose stomach
j. *Day bɔd kuk sup.* [Dead bird cooks in a stew.]
k. Do something hurriedly, very quickly
l. Because it is coarse and needs refinement as opposed to "dry ball" foofoo which is already fermented and refined.

EnglishTranslation *of Angri Bɔbɔ It Arata Sup* [A Hungry Boy Eats Rat Soup] in chapter 9.

Il . . .

Aw . . .

One upon a time, there was a man who works on the West African coast. He has been working there for a long time but there was no more wok for him to do so he came back home. He came home with his gladstone bag. The older folks would know what a gladstone bag is. All the things that he loved were in this bag. Ojo Boy took out a stick of cigarette out of his cigarette tin to smoke. Nothing else was left in the bag. So everyone went up to his mother's house.
When his mother saw him, she said, "ee! Jacob, is that you?"
"Yes, mother."
"What did you bring home?"
"Well mother, I don't have any job right now, so I decided to come home."
"Ee!!You just arrived, you didn't even write, not a word. You that here, if you want something, you have to go downtown to look for it, and since we are a long way from downtown, it's difficult to get the things that you want. So, what are we going to do? I have not fixed anything since this morning."
"Mama please don't worry," Ojo Boy said in between puffs from his 555 cigarette.
"This hunger is unbearable. In fact, it is only yesterday when your dad went hunting in the farm that he caught two groundhogs, those are the big ones. That's what I plan to cook today for us to eat with a bit of foofoo. That's all we have."
"Ah! Mother! Me? Eat groundhog? Not all. Groundhogs and I are enemies."
So his mother said, "Ok, but nothing else is available to eat in the house. You know how you left us? Struggling?"

Appendix 265

Well, for Ojo Boy, he has been hungry for a long time. The hunger is intense. A mature man must maintain his dignity. How can he now say, "Mom, I will eat the groundhog soup."

So, he started sneezing: iiitzarata!! iiitzarata!!

Then, his mother said, "Eeee, Jacob I have always cautioned you, don't get sick here on an empty stomach, please. Wouldn't you try my soup, the groundhog soup I just prepared?" Try it. After all you had eaten it before you went down the Coast.

So, Ojo Boy got some of the soup his mom had cooked. He was extremely hungry. He finished his plate of groundhog soup and foofoo! The only thing left in his plate was a tiny groundhog foot.

That's why a lot of the people who go down the Coast to work, come back empty-handed.

Ojo Boy also knows this, coming from Regent where you have to walk everywhere to get what you want. There were no cars to take you anywhere. Those were the things on his mind which made him eat the groundhog soup and foofoo.

Glossary

KRIO WORDS/EXPRESSIONS AND THEIR MEANINGS

abɛ dɔnkɔ: A fool; dumb
abɔbɔ: A type of bean that has to be soaked in hot water before cooking
abule: A small hut/dwelling place that's slightly bigger than a "konko"
adɔp: Difficult financial straits
afe: Bush rat
aja: Krio word for Attic/AMuslim woman who has made the trip to Mecca
akataole: A thief
a kɔle: I am impressed
alafia: Good health/peace of mind/freedom from stress
alejo: News/Newsmaker
ambɔg: To tease
ambɔgin: Troublesome
angri de kech mi: I am hungry
ashoɛbi: Uniform dress usually worn by women on special occasions
atare: Alligator pepper
awoko: Very talkative person
ayampi: A professional thief
ayɛn: Iron
badyay: Looking at someone with contempt and scorn
bambot: Live like a prostitute; prostituting
banda: Raised wooden platform use to grow certain vegetables or smoke fish
beberebe: Abundant, plenty
begaman: Beggar
bɛlɛ: stomach
bɛlɛmatande: A gluttonous person
bɛlɛwapi: A gluttonous person
bɛlful: Completely satisfied/well-fed; light-hearted remarks

Glossary

bifo jako kɔt yay: In the twinkling of an eye
bia-bia: Beard
bia: Beer; be patient
bia: To wait patiently and unobtrusively for one's girlfriend
bilolo: Sleepy head
blɛnyay: Blind
blant: Belonging to; or, accustomed to, make a habit of
boto bata: Nonsense, silly talk
braskitul: Take no notice of; ignore
bumbu: Lift and carry
bwɛl: To boil something esp. while cooking/ a boil or lump on the skin
chekere: Small, tiny, a skinny-looking person
cham: To chew
chamcham: Light food
chamɔt: Mumble words; sing without knowing the words
chɛr: Tear apart
chikin cheng: Few coins of little value
chɔstik: Chewing stick
chukchuk: Thorny or prickly plant
dakadeke: Underhanded, crooked, deceitful
diɛ-diɛ: Very cautiously, gradually, go softly
dɛbul: An evil spirit, Satan; masked dancer symbolizing evil or mystical beings
dedebɔdi: Corpse
dodo: Large, protruding navel
doklin: Dawn/morning time
dondo: Absolutely nothing, nothing at all
domɔt: Entrance
dɔbalɛ: To prostrate oneself in front of another as if showing respect
egugu: Masquerade in the *Egungu* secret society
ed: Head
ekuru: Skin disease
es: To lift up
ɛnitɛm: Whenever
ɛnkincha: Large piece of cloth, usually printed cotton tied around the head in a variety of styles
ɛng at: State of suspense or worry
ɛng ed: A conference or formal meeting/discussion
fange: sorcery
fatfut: millipede
falamakata: Imitate blindly, echos person's word, especially derisively
fange pɔt: The pot of the sorcerer

fɛnɔt: Find out
fityay: Insulting, arrogant
fɔl: Chicken
fray sup: Stew
futmaleka: In a mighty hurry, in fear
gbangbaode: In the open
gbo: To become hardened, stale, or old
gbogboaye: Vast amounts; reach great heights
gbosgbos: Trouble, disaster, confusion
gɔngɔli fis: Frog fish
gape: hunger
ibi-ibi: Expression of joy mostly at weddings
igbakɔ :Wooden spoon for cooking and dishing out rice
igbalɛ: A place from which *egungun* masquerade appears
igbɛsi: Type of vegetable or drink made out of it
injalɔ: Brown, driver ants
jakato: Bitter lemon
jɛbu: Counterfeit money
jɛntriman: A rich man
jɛkutɛ: Trouble or sickness one cannot manage or handle
juwini: Witch doctor's potion
kaba slɔt: Long, loosely-fitting print, traditional dress, customarily worn by middle age and older Krio women
kakto: Sore toe
kanda: Skin
kalbas: Calabash
kapɛt slipas: Slipper of wool knitted in canvas
kasada: Cassava
kekrebu: Death, serious trouble
kenkeni: A small amount, something very small
koko: Lump, bump on head, protuberance
kombra: Nursing mother
konkang: Decrepit-looking, ugly, ramshackle
konko: A very tiny hut with not much inside
kongosa: Gossip, deceit, hypocrisy
kɔnsibul: Police
koro-koro: Face to face
kotoku: Pouch or money bag worn by middle-aged or older Krio women
kɔl-dɛt: Request that money owed be repaid
kɔmiɛl: Chameleon
krabit: Mean, stingy, tight-fisted
krenkren: Leaves of the brambly plant used to make soup

langa langa: Snake
lagba: Big, huge
lakpalakpa: ringworm
laylondo: A confirmed liar
lebelebe: Noisy, excessive chatter
ledɔm: Lie down
lɛf fes: Stare in wonder or amazement
majiji: Over-eager, fussy, forward
mandori: Girl acting like a boy
mangropej: Mango Perch, a type of fish
mara: Flirtation, playful sexual attraction
mared: Wedding, or to be married
mɔna: Overwhelming, difficult
mɔndɔ: Grab food greedily and with relish
mɔnki dunyia: A place where everyone is doing what they can to survive. Don't count on anyone for help
mumuyɛrɛ: Tidbits, small things
munin: Mourning
mutmut: Grass flea
nɔba: Not ever, never
nɔ mɛn: Never mind
nain: Then
neba: Neighbor
nyanyam (yayam): Food, snacks
nyɔlɛ: Ceremonial food put in two dug holes to honor the departed
ojukokoro: Envy, covetousness
okele fufu: A bolus of fufu
ojare: Word expressing agreement in a conversation
ogiri: Ground and fermented benniseed
okobo: Sexually impotent male
ɔdɔyɔ: A great fool, a simpleton
ɔdɛ: Masquerde of the hunting society
ɔlɔbɔt: All over, everywhere
ɔkpɔlɔ: Frog
ɔlman: Everybody
padi: Friend
pantap: On top of
paopa: At all costs
papisho: To show off
pasmak: Too much/unbearable
pik-pɔkit: To curse profusely
pini: Groan

Glossary   271

pul dɛbul: Masquerade on special occasions
pulnado: Take out into the open; open ceremony to dedicate a newborn baby to the world
rɔju: Beautiful
rɔrɔm: worms
rop-rop: Small, juicy but stringy mango
ros koko: Unusually irritable person; roasted cocoa
ros kɔn: Set a trap for a person; also, roasted corn
sababu: Good fortune
santibokiat: A notorious thief
satide: Saturday
shalat: Charlotte, a mountain village near Freetown, Sierra Leone
shalat: A shameless person
tabule: A large drum used mainly by Muslims to share messages
tɛtɛ: Walk slowly and unsteadily
tengewule: Very small, tiny
tifitifi: Someone who steals often
tifman: A thief
tinap: To stand up
tɔnkɔbele: A game in which you toss coins
tot: To carry
trowe: Throw away
trɔki: Tortoise
trɔsis: Pants/trousers
udat: Who, whoever
uman: Woman
una/unu: You, your
uswan?: Which one?
wak: Eat with glee
waka: To walk
wahala: Trouble
wan: One
wanfut jombi: A one-legged spirit which struts loudly when it moves
we: Which, where is, to weigh
wi: We
winimalɔsi: A gambling game
yanda: Over there
yɔni: Aggressive ants
yon-yon: Very own
yuba: Vulture
yusɛf: Yourself

SOME KRIO NAMES AND THEIR MEANINGS

aba: "Born on Thursday"
abayɔmi: "I would have died"
ayɔla: "Born to be rich"
abiɔdun: "One born during a festival
abiɔla: "One born into fame"
abiɔsɛ: "Born on Sunday"
adebayɔ: "He came at a joyful time"
adebisi: "The crown gives birth to more"
adebɔla: "The newcomer met honor"
adeniji: "The crown has protection"
adenikɛ: "The crown is provided for"
adeniyi: "The crown has dignity"
adebimpe: "The crown gave me my birth and did a finished job of it."
adeɔla: "Crown has a great deal of honor"
aderele: "The crown is going home"
adeshɔla: "The crown makes a fanfare"
adetokumbɔ: "Honor came from abroad"
adewɔle: "Royalty enters this house."
adeyɛmi: "The crown befits me"
adukɛ: "Much loved"
adwoa: "Born on Monday" (Fante, Ghana)
afolabi: "A child born with high status"
afua (or) ɛfua: "Born on Friday"
agbaje: "One who carries prosperity on to the throne"
aina: "Delivery had complications—umbilical cord twisted around the neck of the baby"
aisha: "Life"
ajani: "He fights for possession"
ajibɔla: "One who wakes up to loving hands"
ajɔkɛ: "Someone we have great affection for"
akindele: "The valiant man got home"
akintola: "Valor is enough for honor"
alaba: "Second child born after twins"
alakɛ: "One to be petted and loved unconditionally"
ama: "Born on Saturday"
amina: "Honest, faithful"
atiba: "Understanding"
ayɔ: "Joy"
ayɔdeji: "Joy has doubled"

Glossary

ayɔdele: "Joy comes home"
babatunde: "Purifying"
bafɔ: "Born on a market day"
balogun: "Leader in war"
bamidele: "Come home with me"
bamijoko: "Sit with me"
bandele: "Born away from home"
bayɔ: "Joy is found"
bunmi: "My gift"
chiku: "Chatterer"—talks too much
dayɔ: "Joy arrives"
durosinmi: "Don't die prematurely; stay to bury me."
(i)dowu: "First child born after a set of twins"
ɛmilɔla: "Spirit of honor"
ɛbun: "Gift of God"
ɛkundayɔ: "Weeping becomes joy"
ɛsi: "Born on Sunday
fayɛmi: "Divination befits me"
fɛmi: "Someone Loves me"
fijabi: "born with difficulty"
filomina: "Flowers"
fɔlashade: "Honor confers a crown"
ibidunni: "Childbirth is great"
ibiyɛmi: "Birth confers dignity on me."
inɛz: "Chaste"
kashɔpɛ: "Let us rejoice"
kayɔde: "Bring joy in"
kɛyinde: "Second born of twins"
kofi: "Born on Friday"
kojo: "Born on Monday"
kwaku: "Born on Wednesday"
kwame: "Born on Saturday"
kwesi: "Strength"
mɔnifa: "I have my luck"
mɔrɛnikɛ: "I have found a person to spoil"
modupɛ: "I am grateful"
nnamdi: "Father's name lives on"
obafɛmi: "The king likes me"
ogunade: "The god of royalty"
ogunlade: "Ogun is our crown"
ojumiri: "My eyes saw trouble"
olumide: "My Lord arrives"

oluwɔle: "The Lord enters the house"
olubunmi: "God gave me"
olufɛmi: "God loves me"
olumide: "My lord arrives"
olushɔla: "God has blessed me"
oluyɛmi: "God rescues me"
onipɛde: "Here comes the consoler"
ɔla: "Wealth, riches'
ɔlabisi: "Fame increases"
ɔlatunji: "Honor reawakens"
ɔlayinka: "Honor surrounds me"
ɔlatokumbɔ: "Honor returns from abroad"
ɔmɔtayɔ: "Children are sufficient cause for joy"
ɔmɔdele: "The child arrives home"
ɔmɔlara: "Children are next of kin"
ɔmɔtunde: "A child comes again"
ɛkundayɔ: "Weeping becomes joy"
ɔladipɔ: "Honors become many"
ɔladuni: "High status is good to have"
ɔrɛ: "Gift of God"
ɔrɛdɔla: "Friendship becomes an honor"
rotimi: "Stand by me"
salakɔ: "Male Child born with head and body covered with ruptured membranes."
talabi: "Female child born with head and body covered with ruptured membranes"
taiwo: "First born of twins"
tunde: "Father returns"
yɛtunde: "Mother comes again"
zara: "Flower-Rose"
zaynabu: "Beautiful"

Bibliography

An Act for the Abolition of the Slave Trade, 47th George III, Session 1, CAP. 36 [XXXVI]. March 25, 1807. Electronic Scholarly Publishing (EPS), Foundation of Freedom. http://www.esp.org/foundations/freedom/holdings/slave-trade-act-1807 .pdf (accessed February 2, 2024).

Adamolekun, Kemi. "Survivors' Motives for Extravagant Funerals Among the Yorubas of Western Nigeria." *Death Studies* 25, no. 7 (2001): 609–19. https://doi .org/10.1080/07481180126579.

Adams, L. Emile. *Understanding Jamaican Patois: An Introduction to Afro-Jamaican Grammar*. Kingston, Jamaica: LMH Publishing, 1994.

Arsenec, Nicole. "Serial Verbs in Jamaican and Martinican." *HAL Open Science*. January 8, 2020. https://hal.science/hal-02910343 (accessed February 2, 2024).

Berry, Jack. *A Dictionary of Sierra Leone Krio*. U.S. Department of Health, Education, and Welfare. Contract Number OE-5-15-028. Evanston, IL: Northwestern University Press, 1966.

Bilby, Kenneth. "Africa's Creole Drum: The Gumbe as Vector and Signifier of Trans-Atlantic Creolization." In *Creolization as Cultural Creativity*, edited by Robert Baron and Ana C. Cara, 137–77. Jackson: University of Mississippi Press, 2011.

Buisseret, David, Daniel H. Usner Jr., Mary L. Galvin, Richard Cullen Rath, and J. L. Dillard. *Creolization in the Americas*. Edited by David Buisseret and Steven G. Reinhardt. College Station: University of Texas at Arlington, by Texas A&M University Press, 2000.

Casely-Hayford, Gladys. *Take Um So*, Freetown: New Eara Press, 1948.

Cole, Gibril R. *The Krio of West Africa: Islam, Culture, Creolization, and Colonialism in the Nineteenth Century*. Athens: Ohio University Press, 2013.

———. "Re-Thinking the Demographic Make-Up of Krio Society." In *New Perspectives on the Sierra Leone Krio*, edited by Mac Dixon-Fyle and Gibril Cole, 33–55. New York: Peter Lang, 2006.

Collins, John. "The Early History of West African Highlife Music." *Popular Music* 8, no. 3 (1989): 221–30. https://doi.org/10.1017/S0261143000003524.

Curtin, Philip D. *The Atlantic Slave Trade: A Census*. Madison: University of Wisconsin Press, 1969.

276 Bibliography

Dallas, R. [Robert] C. *History of the Maroons: From Their Origins to the Establishment of Their Chief Tribe at Sierra Leone*. London: Routledge, 1803; Longman and O. Rees, Paternoster-row, 1803. https://repository.library.northeastern.edu/files/neu:m044rf60h (accessed February 2, 2024).

Davies, K. G. *The Royal African Company*. London: Longmans, Green, 1957. Reprint. New York: Atheneum, 1970.

Decker, Thomas. "Boss Coker Befo St. Peter." *The Sierra Leone Daily Guardian*, October, 1939, 24–25.

Dixon-Fyle, Mac, and Gibril Cole, eds. *New Perspectives on the Sierra Leone Krio*. New York: Peter Lang, 2006.

Dolphyne, Florence Abena. *A Comprehensive Course in Twi (Asante)*. Accra: Ghana Universities Press, 1996.

Donnan, Elizabeth. "The Slave Trade into South Carolina Before the Revolution." *American Historical Review* 33, no. 4 (1928): 804–28. https://doi.org/10.2307/1838372.

Fyfe, Christopher. *A Short History of Sierra Leone*. London: Longmans, Green, 1962; 1964.

Fyle, C. Magbaily. "Nationalism should Trump Ethnicity: The Krio Saga in Sierra Leone." *Research in Sierra Leone Studies* (*RISLS*, eJournal) 1, no. 2 (December 2013).

Fyle, Clifford N., and Eldred D. Jones, eds. *A Krio-English Dictionary*. Oxford: Oxford University Press, in collaboration with the Sierra Leone University Press, 1980.

Government of The Bahamas. "Origins of Goombay Music." https://www.bahamas.gov.bs. See https://www.bahamas.gov.bs/wps/portal/public/Culture/Performing%20Arts/ (accessed February 2, 2024).

Indiana University. Center for Language Technology. "Temne Language Portal, Indiana University" (audio recorded tutorials). 2024. https://celt.indiana.edu/portal/Temne/index.html (accessed February 2, 2024).

Jackson, Rachel. "The Trans-Atlantic Journey of *Gumbé*: Where and Why Has It Survived?" *Journal of International Library of African Music* 9, no. 2 (2012): 128–53. https://core.ac.uk/download/pdf/230340048.pdf (accessed February 2, 2024).

King, Nathaniel. "Freetown's Yoruba-Modelled Secret Societies as Transnational and Transethnic Mechanisms for Social Integration." In *The Upper Guinea Coast in Global Perspective*, edited by Jacqueline Knörr and Christoph Kohl, 58–76. New York: Berghahn Books, 1987; 2016.

Lewis-Coker, Eyamidé E.. *Creoles of Sierra Leone: Proverbs, Parables, and Wise Sayings*. 2nd ed. Bloomington, IN: AuthorHouse, 2018.

———. *Motherland Sierra Leone: Anansi Stories*. Bloomington, IN: AuthorHouse, 2013.

Odom, Douglas. "A Comparative Analysis of the Trickster Figure in Africa, the Caribbean, and North America." Undergraduate Honors Thesis. University of Mississippi, 2013. https://egrove.olemiss.edu/hon_thesis/270 (accessed February 2, 2024).

Ogbonna, Elisha O. *Comprehensive Igbo Language*. Las Vegas: Prinoelio Press, 2020.

Oyelaran, Olasope O. "On the Scope of the Serial Verb Construction in Yoruba." *Studies in African Linguistics* 13, no. 2 (1982): 109–46. https://www.academia.edu

Bibliography

/75193726/On_the_scope_of_the_serial_verb_construction_in_Yoruba (accessed February 2, 2024).

Porter, Arthur T. "Religious Affiliation in Freetown, Sierra Leone." *Africa: Journal of the International Journal Institute* 23, no. 1 (1953): 3–14. https://doi.org/10.2307/1156028.

Pratt, Daphne Barlatt. *Krio Proverbs and Idioms*. Freetown: Sierra Leone Writers Series, 2016.

———. *Krio Salad: Folktales, Poems, Parables, and Wise Sayings*. Freetown: Sierra Leonean Writers Series, 2017.

Rankin, F. Harrison. *The White Man's Grave: A Visit to Sierra Leone in 1834*. London: Richard Bentley, 1836.

Rouch, Jean, and Enrico Fulchignoni. "Cine Ethnography: Jean Routh with Enrico Fulchignoni." In *Ciné-Ethnography*, edited and translated by Steven Feld, 147–87. Minneapolis: University of Minnesota Press, 2003.

Scott-Boyle, Atinuke, Dennisia Lightfoot-Boston, Francois Baudouin, Juliet Sho-Cole, Malvia Coomber, Rhian Milton-Cole, Sharon Sho-Cole, and Yamide Rogers. *Next Gen Krios': Krio-English Dikshɔnɛri (Dictionary)*. Sierra Leone: NGK Oganisation, 2022.

Sengova, Joko. "Aborigines and Returnees: In Search of Linguistic and Historical Meaning in Delineations of Sierra Leone's Ethnicity and Heritage." In *New Perspectives on the Sierra Leone Krio*, edited by Mac Dixon-Fyle and Gibril Cole, 167–200. New York: Peter Lang, 2006.

Shrimpton, Neville. "Thomas Decker and the Death of Boss Coker." *Africa: Journal of the International African Institute* 57, no. 4 (1987).

Sonnenberg, Frank. "Reasons Why Traditions Are So Important." *Weebly*. June 30, 2015. https://selatmeigs.weebly.com/uploads/9/3/2/7/9327727/7_reasons_why_traditions_are_so_important.pdf (accessed February 2, 2024).

Spencer-Walters, Tom. "Creolization and Kriodom: (Re) Visioning the 'Sierra Leone Experiment.'" In *New Perspectives on the Sierra Leone Krio*, edited by Mac Dixon-Fyle and Gibril Cole, 223–54. New York: Peter Lang, 2006.

Thompson, Hanne-Ruth, and Momoh Taziff Koroma, *Krio Dictionary and Phrasebook, Krio-English/English-Krio: A Language of Sierra Leone*. New York: Hippocrene Books, 2014.

Trenchard, Tommy. "Part of Sierra Leone's History Is Being Dismantled Board by Board." *New York Times*. January 20, 2016. https://www.nytimes.com/2016/01/20/world/africa/freetown-sierra-leone-board-houses.html (accessed February 2, 2024).

Turay, A. K. *Peace Corps [Sierra Leone]: Temne Language Manual*. https://fsi-languages.yojik.eu/languages/PeaceCorps/Temne/Peace%20Corps%20Temne%20Language%20Manual.pdf (accessed February 2, 2024).

Turner, Lorenzo Dow. *Africanisms in the Gullah Dialect*. Chicago: University of Chicago Press, 1949; 3rd Printing, Columbia: University of South Carolina Press, 2002.

278 *Bibliography*

Wass, Betty M., and S. Modupe Broderick. "The Kaba Sloht." *African Arts* 12, no. 3 (1979): 62–65, 96. https://doi.org/10.2307/3335581.

Widjaja, Michael. "Igbo Culture/Igbo Language." *IboGuide.org*. 2000-2020. https://www.IgboGuide.org (accessed February 7, 2024).

Williams, Selase W. "The African Character of African American Language: Insights from the Creole Connection." In *Africanisms in American Culture*, 2nd ed., edited by Joseph E. Holloway, 397–426. Bloomington: Indiana University Press. 2005.

Williams, Wayne R. "Linguistic Change in the Syntax and Semantics of Sierra Leone Krio." PhD diss. Bloomington, Indiana University, 1976.

Wyse, Akintola J. G. *The Krio of Sierra Leone: An Interpretive History*. London: C. Hurst, 1989.

ADDITIONAL READING LIST

Akam, Simon. "Freetown's Wood Homes a Link to Sierra Leone's Past." *Reuters*. May 3, 2012. https://www.reuters.com/article/idUSJOE84206Q/ (accessed February 2, 2024).

Anyanwu, K. C. "African Religion as Experienced Reality." *Thought and Practice. The Journal of Philosophical Association of Kenya* 2, no. 2 (1975): 149–57. https://www.africabib.org/rec.php?RID=192649191.

Berry, Jack, coll. and trans. *West African Folktales*. Edited by Richard Spears. Evanston, IL: Northwestern University Press, 1991.

Chucks-orji, Ogonna. *Names from Africa: Their Origins, Meaning, and Pronunciation*. Chicago: Johnson Publishing, 1972.

De Maio, Jennifer L., Suzanne Scheld, and Tom Spencer-Walter, eds. *Critical Dimensions of African Studies: Re-Membering Africa*. New York: Lexington Books, 2023.

Finney, Awadajin Malcolm. "The Sierra Leone Krio: Origin, Properties, and Local & Global Implications." Paper presented at California State University, Northridge, 2007.

Horton, Christian D. *Indigenous Music of Sierra Leone: An Analysis of Resources and Educational Implications* [microforme]. Berkeley: University of California Press, 1979.

Jones, Emile. *An Introduction to Sierra Leone Krio and Its Writing Systems*. London: Glomedia, 2013.

Knörr, Jacqueline. "Out of Hiding? Strategies of Empowering the Past and Reconstruction of Krio Identity." In *The Powerful Presence of the Past: Integration and Conflict along the Upper Guinea Coast*, edited by Jacqueline Knörr and Wilson Trajano Filho, 205–28. Leiden: Brill, 2010.

Marke, Roland Bankole. "Dr. Oloh: A Cornerstone of Sierra Leonean Music." *Patriot Vanguard* (Sierra Leone News Portal). October 20, 2007. http://www.thepatrioticvanguard.com/dr-oloh-a-cornerstone-of-sierra-leonean-music (accessed February 2, 2024).

Mbiti, John S. *Concepts of God in Africa*. New York: Praeger, 1970.

Bibliography

Oduyoye, Modupe. *Yoruba Names: Their Structure and Their Meanings*. Ibadan, Nigeria: Daystar Press, 1972.

Parrinder, E. G. [Geoffrey]. *African Traditional Religions*. 3rd ed. New York: Harper & Row, 1970.

Peterson, John. *Province of Freedom: A History of Sierra Leone 1787-1870*. London: Faber & Faber, 1969.

Shearer, Wendy. *African & Caribbean Folktales, Myths, and Legends*. London: Scholastic, 2021.

Smith, Norval, and Tonjes Veenstra, eds. *Creolization and Contact*. Amsterdam: John Benjamins, 2001.

Spencer-Walters, Tom, ed. *Memory and the Narrative Imagination in the African and Diaspora Experience*. Troy, MI: Bedford, 2011.

———, ed. *Orality, Literacy and the Fictive Imagination: African and Diasporan Literatures*. Troy, MI: Bedford, 1998.

Thomason, Sarah Grey, and Terrence Kaufman. *Language Contact, Creolization, and Genetic Linguistics*. Berkeley: University of California Press, 1988.

White, E. Frances. "Creole Women Traders in the Nineteenth Century." *International Journal of African Historical Studies* 14, no. 4 (1981): 626–42. https://doi.org/10.2307/218229.

Index

a (copula verb in Jamaican Creole), equational sentences with, 128

AAL. *See* African American Language

abana (straw hat), 146

Aberdeen, 24

abstractions, as nouns, 50

academics, 10

ACTFL. *See* American Council for the Teaching of Foreign Languages

Act for the Abolition of the Slave Trade, British (1807), 21

actions: completed, 64, 65; as nouns, 50; in sentences, 74; verbal, 93–94

action sentences, negation in, 74

action verbs, 52, 66

Adamolekun, Kemi, 142

Adams, L. Emile, 126

adjectival verbs, 79, 80–81; in Jamaican Patois/Jamaican Creole, 132

adjectives, 80; demonstrative, 66–67; nouns as, 53

adverbs, 53; temporal, 81–82

African American Language (AAL), 132

African Authenticity, 3, 4–5

"The African Character of African American Language" (Williams), 132

African culture, 9, 157, 162, 241; British community relation to, 4;

Krio culture relation to, 5; Western civilization relation to, 2

African Diaspora, 3, 6; food of, 149; parebulz in, 184

African diasporan languages, 126

Africanisms in the Gullah Dialect (Turner), 131, 132

Africanness, of Yoruba ethnic group, 31

African political entities, 15

African World Experience, 259

afternoon greetings, 62

"Agbara" ("Rain Torrent"), 230–32

Akan language, 18; in Jamaica, 240–41; Jamaican Patois/Jamaican Creole relation to, 130; serial verb constructions in, 117; tone in, 114, 115

Akan people, 23; in Jamaica, 19, 126; *nansi toriz* relation to, 201

Akan tradition, 9

Aku Mohammedans, 141

American Council for the Teaching of Foreign Languages (ACTFL), 11

American Revolution, 22

Anansi, 9, 201

Angola, Trans-Atlantic slave trade and, 16–17, 18

ANGRI BƆBƆ IT ARATA SUP (Hungry Boy Eats Rat Soup), 216–17

282

Index

Annie Walsh Memorial School
(AWMS), 26, 139
anti-slavery sentiments, in England, 21
appeals, 99
Architectural Field Office, 180
Ardra & Whydah, 18
Arsenec, Nicole, 129
Ashante language: co-articulated sounds
in, 44. *See* Akan language
ashoɛbi groups, 147
ashɔkɛ, 145
asientos, 17
auxiliary verbs, 77–78, 119
AWMS. *See* Annie Walsh Memorial
School
AW TUNDE ƐN BƆD NA PADI DƐM
(How Tunde and the Bird Became
Friends), 89–90
awujoh (ceremonial feast), 137
awujɔ, 8–9, 175, 176

Bahamas, 163
bamchu, 137
Barbados, 18
Barbados Code, 18
Benguema, 24
Benin & Calabar, 18
Berry, Jack, 2
benichi. See Jollof Rice
the Bible, 28
Bight of Biafra, 16–17
Bilby, Kenneth, 137
bitalif sup, 152
bitas (bitter leaves), 152, 153, *154*
"Black Hair Deh Pan Trial," 243–46
Black Poor, 7, 19–20, 24; British
philanthropists relation to, 28;
English language relation to, 29;
ethnic background of, 22; religion
of, 139
The Blind Beggar (DI BLƐN YAY
BEGAMAN), 211–13
bod os (wooden houses), 178, 179,
179, *180*

Bonner, Andrene, 9, 240; "Black
Hair Deh Pan Trial" of, 243–46;
"Emancipate Yourself" of, 246–48;
"Troo Di Yeye a Di African" of,
241–43
"Boss Coker Before St. Peter"
(Decker), 220
BRA FƆL ƐN BRA KAKROCH (The
Chicken and the Cockroach), 202–4
Brazil, 17
British colonial influence, 2
British Colony, in Sierra Leone, 19
British community, African culture
relation to, 4
British philanthropists, 20, 21, 28
British slave trade, 18–19
Broderick, S. Modupe, 145
Buisseret, David, 163
Bunce Island, 22

Calabar slaves, 19
Calendar, Ebenezer, 164
Campbell Town, 24
Caribbean Islands, 240–41
carpet slippers (*kapɛt slipas*), 147,
147, 148
Casely-Hayford, Gladys, 219, 220
cassava bread (*kasada bred*), *157*
"Cassava Bread and Fried Fish"
("KASADA BRED ƐN FRAY FIS"),
223–25
cassava leaf soup (*kasada lif sup*), 155
cassava root (*kasada*), 153, 154, *155*
Las Charcas, 16
The Chicken and the Cockroach (BRA
FƆL ƐN BRA KAKROCH), 202–4
child language development, 28, 31
Christianity, 25–26, 27, 139; in
Freetown, 140–41; Liberated
Africans relation to, 31
Christian Krios, 2, 8
Church Missionary Society (CMS), 21,
25, 139; Grammar School for Boys
of, 26, 139

Index 283

civilizing project, Sierra Leone Experiment as, 25

CMS. *See* Church Missionary Society

co-articulated sounds, 44

Cole, Gibril R., 2, 22, 23–24, 123; on Christianity, 26, 139; on loanwords, 111–12; on secret societies, 176; on *Tribal Administration (Freetown) Ordinance* (1905), 141

Cole, Israel Olufemi, 164

collect prayer, 139

Collins, John, 163

colonial administration, 7

colonialists, 4

commands, 98–99

common expressions, 99

communication system, 5; of Krio culture, 138

completed action, 64, 65

completed aspect, 64

complexity, of linguistic systems, 28

concrete houses (*ton os*), 179, *181*

conflicts, 190–92

Congo, 16, 17; Trans-Atlantic slave trade and, 18

Congo Town, 23, 24

conjunctions, sentences with, 100

consonant clusters, 45–46, 114

consonants, 42–44; in C-V-C-V pattern, 113–14; minimal pairs and, 48; nasal assimilation and, 49–50; tone and, 46

contrast, 95–96

conversations: in market, 73–74; question-and-answer, 59

copula verb: *a*, in Jamaican Creole, 128. *See also na* In Krio

Coromantee language. *See* Akan language

cover slut, 145

Creoles of Sierra Leone (Lewis-Coker), 3

creolization, 27–28, 31

creolized languages, 126

crosscultural marriage, 31

Crown Colony, 25

Crowther, Samuel Ajayi, 139

Curtin, Philip D., 15–17; on British slave trade, 19; on Yoruba ethnic group, 24, 25

customs: of Liberated Africans, 138. *See also* traditions

C-V-C-V pattern, 113–14

Dallas, R. C., 22–23; on Maroons, 29

Davies, K. G., 17

de, 46–47; intonation patterns and, 49; locative sentences with, 67–68, 127; multiple realizations of, 69, *69*; as present continuous marker, 56

Decker, Thomas, 219; "Boss Coker Before St. Peter" of, 220

declarative sentences: simple pattern for, 48–49; VP in, 56; Yes/No questions compared to, 77

definite article, 52; *di* as, 64

Demba, Pa, 23

demonstrative adjectives, 66–67

demonstrative pronouns, 55, 66

dɛbul, 176

di, The Definite Article, 64

dialogue, for getting around, 90

DI BLƐN YAY BEGAMAN (The Blind Beggar), 211–13

Dictionary of Sierra Leone Krio (Berry), 2

dignity balls, 162–63

diphthongs, 42

directional function, serial verb constructions with, 85–86

directional verb, 56

direct object, of verb, 70

discourse, full sentence themes in, 95

Dixon-Fyle, Mac, 2, 141

Dolphyne, Florence Abena, 131

Donnan, Elizabeth, 19

Downdrift, 48

dramatization, in *nansi toriz*, 201–2

duplication, 8, 105; in ideophones, 107–8; of verbs, 106

284 *Index*

Egba Town, 24
"Emancipate Yourself," 246–48
emphasis, 95–96
emphatic marker, 92, 94–95; prepositional phrase as, 93
emphatic pronouns, 91, *91*, 93–94; in equational sentences, 92
England: anti-slavery sentiments in, 21; Trans-Atlantic slave trade and, 18–19, 35
English derived vocabulary, 41, 109–10, 111; in Jamaican Patois/Jamaican Creole, 240
English language, 4; consonant clusters in, 46; Krio language compared to, 42–43, 44; Krio language relation to, 5, 7, 28, 32–34, 35, 132, 259; Settlers and, 29–30; subject/verb agreement rules of, 68
Envy (OJUKOKORO), 204–7
equational sentences, 7; with *a* in Jamaican Creole, 128; emphatic pronouns in, 92; with *na*, 66–67; negation in, 75–76
equational verb, *na* as, 88
ethnic background, 22–23
ethnic diversity, in Freetown, 27, 31
ethnic groups, Trans-Atlantic slave trade relation to, 16
ethnolinguistic groups, 16, 259
European powers, 15
evening greetings, 62
exploitation, 259
extortion, 228
ɛnkincha, 146, 169

familiar greetings, 61
Farewells, Formulaic, 62–63
filmmakers, Nigerian, 260
focus, 95–96
folk wisdom, 6
food (*nyanyam*), 149–62, 222
Formulaic Farewells, 62–63
40-day/one year event, 175
France, 19

frayfis (fried fish), 154, 223–25
Freemason Lodge, 27
Freetown, Sierra Leone, 1, 20; *bod os* in, 178, 179; Christianity in, 140–41; ethnic diversity in, 27, 31; Liberated Africans in, *24*, 31; Maroons in, 21, 24; Western education in, 25–26; Wilberforce Hall in, 162; Yoruba language in, 108
frequent action, 64
fricative, uvular/velar, 44
fried fish (*frayfis*), 154, 223–25
"From the Perspective of the African" ("Troo Di Yeye a Di African"), 241–43
fufu, 152, 153, *156*
Fulchignoni, Enrico, 163
full sentence themes, in discourse, 95
"FUNKIA MINA" ("Funkia Minnows"), 225–27
fura, 141
"Futmaleka" ("In a Mighty Hurry"), 221–22, 253
future progressive, 119–20; in Jamaican Patois/Jamaican Creole, 127
future tense, 65; *ga* in Igbo, 119
Fyfe, Christopher, 20, 22–24, 29
Fyle, Clifford N., 2, 8, 32, 90; on English derived vocabulary, 109; locative prepositions on, 121
Fyle, C. Magbaily, 22

ga, future tense, 119
generalized nouns, 51
Georgia, 19
getting around, dialogue for, 90
gɛlɛdɛ, 9, 178
Ghana, Akan tradition in, 9
ginger cake (*jinja kek*), 160, *160*
go, 34
Goderich Village, 105
"GO KAM, GO KAM" ("Go and Come Back"), 228–30
Gold Coast, 17, 18, 19, 126

Index   285

Goodison, Lorna, 9, 240; "Heart Ease 1" of, 251–53; "Inna Calabash" ("In the Calabash"), 254–56; "The Road of the Dread" of, 248–51

Gordon, John, 22

gossip, 227

grafting, 228

grammar, 2–3; in indigenous languages, 28

Grammar School for Boys, of CMS, 26, 139

Granville Town, 20

gras at. See abana

greetings, 62, 63; familiar, 61; pronouns in, 60; question-and-answer conversation in, 59

The Guinea of Cape Verde, 16

Gullah, 6, 8; second person plural pronouns in, 131, 132

gumbe drum and dance, 137–38, 163–64

H. *See* High tone

habitual action, 64, 65

hard work, 186–87

harmonious existence, of humanity, 259

Hastings, 24

"Heart Ease 1," 251–53

High-Low tone, 91

High tone (H), 46–47, 60; completed aspect and, 64; in *de*, 69; with emphatic pronouns, 91; intonation patterns and, 49; minimal pairs and, *47*

History of the Maroons (Dallas), 22–23

humanity, harmonious existence of, 259

Hungry Boy Eats Rat Soup (ANGRI BOBO IT ARATA SUP), 216–17

hunting, 177

Huntingdonians, 25

identity, African authenticity in, 4

ideophones, duplication in, 107–8

idiomatic serial verbs, 88

Igbo language: locative prepositions in, 121–22; *na* in, *122*; second person

plural pronouns in, 131; serial verb constructions in, 117; tense/aspect markers in, 119–20; tone in, 114, 115

"In a Mighty Hurry" ("Futmaleka"), 221–22, 253

Indefinite Quantifiers, 76–77

indigenous languages, grammar in, 28

infinitive clauses, sentences with, 100, 101, *101*

initiating function, serial verb constructions with, 88

"Inna Calabash" ("In the Calabash"), 254–56

instrumental function, serial verb constructions with, 86

international careers, 10

intonation patterns, 48–49; tone and, 7; in Yes/No Questions, 77–78

Islam, 26, 141; Liberated Africans relation to, 140; secret societies in, 176. *See also* Oku Krios

Jackson, Rachel, 163, 164

Jamaica: Akan language in, 240–41; Akan people in, 19, 126; sugar plantations in, 18–19

Jamaican Patois/Jamaican Creole, 3, 6, 8, 241; English derived vocabulary in, 240; Kwa languages relation to, 130; parebulz in, 184; serial verb constructions in, 129, 132; tense/aspect markers in, 126–27, 132; thematic nature of, 128

jinja kek (ginger cake), 160, *160*

jollof rice (*jɔlɔf rɛs*), 151, *153*

Jolof Empire, 16

Jones, Eldred D., 2, 8, 32; on English derived vocabulary, 109; locative prepositions on, 121

kaba slɔt dress, 138, 144–45, *146*, 147–48; with *kotoku*, 146

kam, 33–34

kanya, 159, *159*

Index

kapɛt slipas (carpet slippers), 147,
  147, 148
kasada (cassava root), 153, 154, *155*
kasada bred (cassava bread), *157*
"KASADA BRED ƐN FRAY FIS"
  ("Cassava Bread and Fried Fish"),
  223–25
kasada lif sup (cassava leaf soup), 155
Kicongo group, 163
King, Nathaniel, 176
Kingdom of Kongo, 17
Kingdom of Ndongo, 17
Kise-Kise River, 23
Kizzell, John, 22
kola nut, *158*; in The *Nyɔlɛ*, 175–76;
  rituals with, 157, 158–59
"Kongosa" ("Persistent Gossip"),
  227–28
Koroma, Momoh Taziff, 2
Kossoh Town, 24
kotoku, 145, 146
Kɔmɔjade, 8
kɔngu, 161, *161*
krenkren, 150, *152*
Krio culture, 141–44, 219–20; African
  culture relation to, 5; hard work in,
  186; Liberated Africans relation
  to, 138; ridulz related to, 199;
  syncretic, 167
Krio Diaspora, 3
Krio Dictionary and Phrasebook
  (Thompson and Koroma), 2–3
Kriodom, 35
A Krio-English Dictionary (Fyle,
  Clifford and Jones), 2, 8, 32,
  109, 112
Krio folktales, 3, 9. *See also nansi toriz*
Krio language. *See specific topics*
Kriolization, 27–28, 31
The Krio of Sierra Leone (Wyse), 1–2
The Krio of West Africa (Cole, G.),
  2, 141
Krio parables. *See* Parebulz
Krio Salad (Pratt), 3
Krio villages. *See* Parish system

Kwa languages, 6, 41; co-articulated
  sounds in, 44; *gumbe* relation
  to, 163; Krio language relation
  to, 8, 109, 123, 259; serial verb
  constructions in, 116–17, 129–30;
  Trans-Atlantic slave trade and, 18

L. *See* Low tone
labial stops, 44
language certification, 11
Leicester Village, 23
Lepet, Peter na, 227
Lewis-Coker, Eyamidé E., 3
Liberated Africans, 4–5, 7, 21–22;
  ethnic background of, 23; in
  Freetown, *24*, 31; Islam relation to,
  140; *kaba slɔt* dress and, 145; Krio
  culture relation to, 138; The *Nyɔlɛ* of,
  175–76; The *ɔjɛ* of, 176–77; parish
  systems of, 139; Settlers compared
  to, 30; Settlers relation to, 27, 28–29
life, in parebulz, 192–93
linguistic systems: complexity of, 28;
  simplification of, 3, 4
loanwords, 111–12
locative phrase, 56; stative verbs and, 79
locative prepositions: *na* as, 121–22; *ro*
  as, 125; in Yoruba language, 123
locative sentences, 7; with *de*, 67–68,
  127; negation in, 75
Low tone (L), 46–47; in *de*, 69; minimal
  pairs and, *47*; in pronouns, 60

"Mami Swit-O" ("Mother is Love"),
  237–38
maringa music, 164
market, conversations in, 73–74
Maroons, 7; English language relation
  to, 29–30; ethnic background of,
  22–23; in Freetown, 21, 24; *gumbe*
  drum and dance of, 137, 163;
  Jamaican Patois/Jamaican Creole
  relation to, 126; religion of, 139
Maroon War, 21
marriage identification, 145

Index   287

masqueraders, 176; of gɛlɛdɛ, 178; of The ɔjɛ, 177

MBHS. *See* Methodist Boys High School

McCarthy, Charles, 23

Mende language: co-articulated sounds in, 44; loanwords from, 111–12

mental verbs: serial verb constructions with, 83, *84*, 84–85; in Twi language, 130–31

Methodist Boys High School (MBHS), 139

Methodist Girls High School (MGHS), 139

Methodist Mission, 25, 139

MGHS. *See* Methodist Girls High School

minimal pairs, 47, *47*, 48

miseducation, 259

mission school, in Regent Village, 26

Monuments and Relics Commission, 180, 181

morning greetings, 62

Motherland Sierra Leon (Lewis-Coker), 3

Mother's Union meetings, 140

Multiple African Language Sources for Some Krio Words, *113*

multiple realizations, of *de*, 69, *69*

Murray Town, 24

music and dance, 162; *gumbe*, 137–38, 163–64

Muslims. *See also* Islam; Oku Krios

na, In Krio, 91; as emphatic marker, 92–95; equational sentences with, 66–67; as equational verb, 88; in Igbo language, *122*; intonation patterns and, 49; as locative preposition, 121–22; present progressive, 119

naming tradition, 168–69

nansi toriz, 9, 183; ANGRI BƆBƆ IT ARATA SUP, 216–17; BRA FƆL ƐN BRA KAKROCH, 202–4; DI

BLƐN YAY BEGAMAN, 211–13; OJUKOKORO, 204–7; TA BEBI, 213–16; Trans-Atlantic slave trade relation to, 201; TUNDE ƐN IÑ PADI, 210–11; WETIN MEK BRA SPAYDA IN WES LILI SO, 207–10

nasal assimilation, 49–50

negation, 75; in action sentences, 74; in Temne language, 124

Negative Harmony Rule, 76–77

negative marker, in VP, 78

negative past, in Jamaican Patois/Jamaican Creole, 127

negative present progressive, in Jamaican Patois/Jamaican Creole, 127

Nevis, 18

New Perspectives on the Sierra Leone Krio (Dixon-Fyle and Gibril), 2, 141

newspaper poetry, 9, 219

Next Gen Krios' Krio-English Dictionary (Scott-Boyle), 2

Niger Delta Mission, 139

Nigerian filmmakers, 260

Nigerian Pidgin English, 260

nominalized verbs, 52

noun classes, in Temne language, 124

Noun Phrase (NP), *55*, 86, 91; as emphatic marker, 93; in equational sentences, 67, 75; Object, 56; pronouns in, 54, 55; relative clauses and, 102; in sentence structure, 53; Subject, 77

nouns, *51*, 124; actions as, 50; adjectives and, 53; particular, 51; verbs and, 52, *52*

Nova Scotian Methodist Church, 25

Nova Scotians, 7, 20–21; British philanthropists relation to, 28; English language relation to, 29; ethnic background of, 22; in Freetown, 24; religion of, 139

nɔto, as emphatic marker, 92–95

NP. *See* Noun Phrase

nyanyam (food), 149–62, 222

The *Nyɔlɛ*, 175–76

Object Noun Phrase, 56
Odom, Douglas, 201
OJUKOKORO (Envy), 204–7
Oku Krios, 2, 8, 26; The *ɔjɛ* of, 176–77
oku lapa. See ashɔkɛ
Oku Town, 24
older man, younger person greeting,
 61–62
older woman, younger person
 greeting, 61
Oloh (Dr.), 164, 227
oral traditions, 6, 183; social obligations
 and, 202; thematic element in, 90
Oyelaren, Olasope O., 116
The *ɔjɛ*, 9, 176–77
ɔmɔs, 72
The *ɔntin* society, 9, 177

parebulz, 9, 183–85, 194–97; bravery in,
 187–89; conflicts in, 190–92; hard
 work in, 186–87; life in, 192–93;
 righteousness in, 189–90
parish systems, of Liberated
 Africans, 139
parochial schools, 139
particular nouns, 51
past, in Jamaican Patois/Jamaican
 Creole, 127
past tense marker, 64; in Temne
 language, 125
"Persistent Gossip" ("Kongosa"),
 227–28
personal names, 113
Peters, Frank, 22
Peters, Jonathan, 220, 223, 228
Peters, Thomas, 20
phonetic transcription, 42
phonological patterns and constraints,
 112, 113–16
physical warfare, 4
Pidgin English, 30
plural, 51, 52; second person, 60, 131,
 131, 132

plural pronouns, 60
poetry, 3, 6, 220, 240, 260; "Black
 Hair Deh Pan Trial," 243–46;
 "Emancipate Yourself," 246–
 48; "Funkia Mina," 225–27;
 "Futmaleka," 221–22, 253; "Go
 Kam, Go Kam," 228–30; "Heart
 Ease 1," 251–53; "Inna Calabash,"
 254–56; "KASADA BRED ƐN
 FRAY FIS," 223–25; "Kongosa,"
 227–28; "Mami Swit-O," 237–38;
 newspaper, 9, 219; "Troo Di Yeye
 a Di African," 241–43; "Una NƆ
 WestƐm," 232–37; "Wi KƆtintri,"
 239–40
political entities, African, 15
Porter, Arthur T., 137; on CMS, 139
Portugal, Trans-Atlantic slave trade and,
 17, 35
Portuguese Town, 23
Pratt, Daphne Barlatt, 3, 220; "UNA NƆ
 WESTƐM" of, 232–37
prepositional phrase, 102; as emphatic
 marker, 93
Prepositional Phrase, 70
present continuous marker, *de* as, 56
present progressive: in Jamaican Patois/
 Jamaican Creole, 126–27; *na*, 119
present progressive marker, 65; stative
 verbs and, 80
present tense, 67–68, 84; simple,
 79, 125
pre-verbal tense/aspect markers, 7–8,
 34, 118–20, 133; in Jamaican Patois/
 Jamaican Creole, 126–27
Principe, 17
print dress, 138, 144, 147–48, *148*, *149*
pronouns, *55*, *60*; demonstrative, 55,
 66; emphatic, 91, *91*, 92, 93–94; in
 NP, 54, 55; second person plural, 60,
 131, *131*, 132
proverbs, 99, 183. *See also* parebulz
Pul Na Do, 8
Pulnado/Kɔmɔjade, 168

Index 289

purposive and/or sequential action function, serial verb constructions with, 87–88
Put Stɔp, 8, 169, 170–74

question-and-answer conversation, in greetings, 59
questions: substantive, 69, 70–73, 94; Yes/No, 48, 49, 77–78

"Rain Torrent" ("Agbara"), 230
Rankin, F. Harrison, 29–30; Settler Speech reported by, *30*
rayz bred (rice bread), 161, *161*
Regent Village, 23, 24; mission school in, 26
relative clauses, sentences with, 102, *103*, 103–4
religion: Christianity, 25–26, 27, 31, 139–41; Islam, 26, 140–41, 176
responses, to substantive questions, 71–73
returnees, 137
rɛs pap, 141
rice bread (*rayz bred*), 161, *161*
ridulz, 9, 183, 198–99; as social aptitude tests, 197
righteousness, in parebulz, 189–90
rituals: kola nut, 157, 158–59; *nansi toriz* as, 202; of The *ɔjɛ*, 177; *Put Stɔp*, 8, 169, 170–74; for secret societies, 176; 7-day event, 174–75. *See also* customs
ro, 125
"The Road of the Dread," 248–51
Rouch, Jean, 163
Royal African Company, 17, 18
The Royal African Company (Davies), 17
Royal Navy, 21

Saint Domingue, 19
Sao Thome, 17
sawa-sawa (sorrel), 150, *150*, *151*
Scott-Boyle, Atinuke, 2

second person plural pronouns, 60, *131*; in Gullah, 131, 132
secret societies: gɛlɛdɛ, 9, 178; The *ɔjɛ*, 9, 176–77; ɔntin, 9, 177
selfhood, African authenticity in, 4
semantic characteristics, of Krio language, 32
Senegambia region, 16; Trans-Atlantic slave trade and, 18
Sengova, Joko, 21
sentences: action, 74; with conjunctions, 100; declarative, 48–49, 56, 77; equational, 7, 66–67, 75–76, 92, 128; with infinitive clauses, 100, 101, *101*; locative, 7, 67–68, 75, 127; with relative clauses, 102, *103*, 103–4; tense/aspect markers in, 63–64; word-order in, 70
sentence structure, 53, *54*, *57*
serial verb constructions, 7, 33; with directional function, 85–86; in Jamaican Patois/Jamaican Creole, 129, 132; in Kwa languages, 116–17, 129–30; with mental verbs, 83, *84*, 84–85; with purposive and/or sequential action function, 87–88
"Serial Verbs in Jamaican and Martinican" (Arsenec), 129
Settlers, 137; English language and, 29–30; Krio culture relation to, 138; Liberated Africans relation to, 27, 28–29
Settler Speech, *30*
Settler Talk, 29
7-day event, 174–75
Sharp, Granville, 20, 21
Shrimpton, Neville, 219–20
shuku blay, 173–74
Sierra Leone. *See specific topics*
Sierra Leone Company, 21, 25
Sierra Leone Experiment, 1; as civilizing project, 25
Sierra Leone Weekly News (newspaper), 219

Index

simple declarative sentence pattern, 48–49
simple past tense, 65
simple present tense, 79, 125
simplification, of linguistic systems, 3, 4
Slave Codes, 18
Smeathman, Henry, 20
Smith, Isatu, 181
social aptitude tests, ridulz as, 197
social inclusivity, 3, 4
social interaction, 7
socialization, 6
social obligations, oral traditions and, 202
Sonnenberg, Frank, 167
sorrel (*sawa-sawa*), 150, *150, 151*
South Carolina, 19
sɔndeklos, 140
Spain, 21; Trans-Atlantic slave trade and, 17, 35
Spencer-Walters, Tom, 8, 24, 169, 220; "Agbara" of, 230–32; "Futmalaka" of, 221–22, 253; "Kongosa" of, 227–28; on Sierra Leone Experiment, 25
stative verbs, 52, *53*; *de* as, 67; locative phrase and, 79; mental verbs relation to, 83, 84–85; Present Progressive Marker and, 80
St. George's Bay, 20
St. George's Bay Company, 20, 25
straw hat (*abana*), 146
subject, of sentence, 70
subject noun phrase, 77
subject pronouns, 55
subject/verb agreement rules, of English language, 68
substantive questions, 69, 70; emphatic markers and, 94; responses to, 71–73
sugar plantations, 17; in Jamaica, 18–19
suprasegmental area, of tone, 41
Susu language, 184
sweet mouth, 110, *110*
syncretic culture, 167
systemic changes, in VP, 34
sɛ, as mental verb in Twi, 130–31

TA BEBI (Tar Baby), 213–16
take, 32–33
"Take Um So" (Casely-Hayford), 220
talla dance, 138
Tar Baby (TA BEBI), 213–16
tek, 32–34
Temne language, 6; co-articulated sounds in, 44; Krio language relation to, 8, 123–25, 133; loanwords from, 111–12; nasal assimilation in, 50
Temne people, 20
temporal adverbs, 81–82
temporal or aspectual intent, tense/aspect markers for, 68
tense/aspect markers, 96–98; in Igbo language, 119–20; in initiating function, 88; in Jamaican Patois/Jamaican Creole, 126–27, 132; L as, 47; pre-verbal, 7–8, 34, 118–20, 133; in sentences, 63–64; in serial verb constructions, 84; stative verbs and, 79; in Temne language, 124–25; for temporal or aspectual intent, 68; VP and, 56; in Yoruba language, 118; zero, 84, 120–21, 125
Thaimne language. *See* Temne language
thematic element, in oral traditions, 90
thematic language, 7–8
thematic nature, of Jamaican Patois/Jamaican Creole, 128
Thompson, Hanne-Ruth, 2
to, 88–89
tone, 114–16; High, 46–47, *47*, 49, 60, 69, 91; High-Low, 91; intonation patterns and, 7; Low, 46–47, *47*, 60, 69; suprasegmental area of, 41; vowels and, 46; in Yes/No Questions, 49
tone languages, 7
ton os (concrete houses), 179, *181*
traditions, 8–9, 167, 182; naming, 168–69; oral, 6, 90, 183, 202
Trans-Atlantic slave trade, 34; Angola and, 16–17, 18; England and, 18–19, 35; *nansi toriz* relation to, 201

transcription, phonetic, 42
*Tribal Administration (Freetown)
Ordinance* (1905), 140–41
trickster stories. *See nansi toriz*
"Troo Di Yeye a Di African" ("From the
Perspective of the African"), 241–43
TUNDE ƐN IÑ PADI (Tunde and His
Friend), 210–11
Turner, Lorenzo Dow, 131, 132
Twi language: co-articulated sounds in,
44; mental verbs in, 130–31; serial
verb constructions in, 117; tone in,
115–16. *See* Akan language

udat, 72
"UNA NƆ WESTƐM" ("You Should
Not Waste Time"), 232–37
unmodified phonological form, 34
urban populations, in Sierra Leone, 10
Usay, 62, 70, 71, 80, 90
uskayn, 72
ustɛm, 71
uvular/velar fricative, 44

velar stops, 44
verbal action, 93–94
Verb Phrase (VP), *56*, 96; adverbs in,
81; in declarative sentences, 56;
negative marker in, 78; in sentence
structure, 53; systemic changes in, 34
verbs: action, 52, 66; adjectival, 79,
80–81, 132; auxiliary, 77–78, 119;
directional, 56; direct object of, 70;
duplication of, 106; equational, 88;
in Jamaican Patois/Jamaican Creole,
126; nouns and, 52, *52*; stative, 52,
53, 67, 79–80, 83, 84–85; in Temne
language, 124. *See also* serial verb
constructions
vocal chords, 45
vowels, 41–42; in C-V-C-V pattern,
113–14; minimal pairs and, 47, 48;
nasal assimilation and, 50; tone
and, 46
VP. *See* Verb Phrase

Wass, Betty M., 145
Waterloo, 222–23
West African Methodist Church, 25
Western civilization, African culture
relation to, 2
Western education, in Freetown, 25–26
WETIN MEK BRA SPAYDA IN WES
LILI SO (Why Brother Spider Has a
Small Waist), 207–10
The White Man's Grave (Rankin), 29–30
Why Brother Spider Has a Small Waist
(WETIN MEK BRA SPAYDA IN
WES LILI SO), 207–10
Widjaja, Michael, 122
"Wi KƆtintri" ("Our Cotton Tree"),
239–40
Wilberforce Hall, Freetown, 162
Williams, Selase W., 132
Williams, Wayne R., 41
Windward Coast, 17, 126
Wolof people, 16
wooden houses (*bod os*), 178, 179,
179, 180
word-order, 70
worldview, 5
Wyse, Akintola J. G., 1–2; on *bamchu*,
137; on CMS, 139

Yes/No Questions, 48, 49; intonation
patterns in, 77–78
Yoruba ethnic group, 3–4, 9, 111;
Africanness of, 31; in Freetown, 24,
25; as Liberated Africans, 22; secret
societies of, 176
Yoruba language, 6; co-articulated
sounds in, 44; duplication in, 108;
Krio language relation to, 28, 109,
133; locative prepositions in, 123;
serial verb constructions in, 116–17;
tense/aspect markers in, 118; tone in,
114–15
younger person, greetings of, 61–62

zero tense marker, 84, 120–21; in
Temne language, 125

About the Authors

Selase W. Williams, PhD earned a BA degree in Linguistics at the University of Wisconsin in 1968, followed by a MA in African Languages and Literatures in 1970. In 1976, he earned a PhD in Linguistics from Indiana University. Having studies Swahili as an undergraduate, he engaged in the serious study of Hausa, Mende, Bambara, and Wolof as a graduate student, spending a year in Freetown and Leicester Village conducting his dissertation research on Sierra Leone Krio. In 1975, Williams was appointed Assistant Professor in Linguistics, Black Studies, and International Studies at the University of Washington, teaching Krio Language for over a decade, with Tom Spencer-Walters. He has lectured widely and published on Sierra Leone Krio, African American Language, Black Studies, and Education in the Black Community.

Williams published "Serial Verb Constructions in Krio," in *Studies in African Linguistics* (University of California Los Angeles, 1971); a frequently referenced book chapter entitled "Classroom Use of African American Language: Educational Tool or Social Weapon," in *Empowerment Through Multicultural Education*, ed. Christine E. Sleeter (SUNY Press, 1991); "Substantive Africanisms at the End of the African Linguistic Diaspora," in *Africanisms in African American Language Varieties*, ed. Salikoko S. Mufwene (University of Georgia Press, 1993); "The African Character of African American Language" in *Africanisms in African American Culture*, ed. Joseph E. Holloway, 2nd ed. (Indiana University Press, 2005); and a coedited a book, *The Borders in All of Us: New Approaches to three Diasporic Societies* (New World African Press, 2005).

As an academic leader, Williams has served as Program Director, Department Chair, Dean of Arts and Sciences, and Provost & Vice President for Academic Affairs. He was elected two-term President of the National Council for Black Studies (NCBS), during which time he co-coordinated, with William Little, the first NCBS international conference in Accra, Ghana.

About the Authors

Tom Spencer-Walters, PhD studied at Fourah Bay College, the University of Sierra Leone, where he majored in English and Literature. Upon completion of his degree, he was recruited by his mentors at the college, Professors Eldred D. Jones and Clifford N. Fyle, to serve as one of the assistant editors for the *Krio-English Dictionary* (Oxford University Press, 1980). Spencer-Walters later attended the University of Washington in Seattle, Washington, to further his education in English, Comparative Literature and Linguistics. At this institution, he completed an MA in Comparative Literature, another MA in Communications, and finally, a PhD in Communications, specializing in semantic applications of journalistic writings in Africa.

Spencer-Walters taught Krio to mostly undergraduate students at the University of Washington for a number of years. He accepted a teaching appointment at California State University Northridge (CSUN) where he taught for thirty-eight years before his retirement as Emeritus Professor. During those years, he chaired the Department of Africana Studies, was granted a Senior Fulbright Award to teach and conduct research at the University of Fort Hare in South Africa, served as the Resident Director for the California State University International Programs (CSUIP) at the University of Zimbabwe, and was appointed as Ombudsperson for the College of Social and Behavioral Sciences at CSUN.

Among Spencer-Walters' primary published works are, *Memory and the Narrative Imagination in the African and Diaspora Experience* (Bedford, 2011); *Orality and the Fictive Imagination: African and Caribbean Literatures* (Bedford, 1998); and *Shared Visions: A Multicultural Reader for Writers* (McGraw-Hill, 1996). He has also published several book chapters and articles, including a chapter on creolization of the Sierra Leone Krio, in *New Perspectives on the Sierra Leone Krio*, ed. Mac Dixon-Fyle and Gibril Cole (Peter Lang, 2006), and another chapter on family patterns in Sierra Leone, in *Families in a Global Context*, ed. Charles B. Hennon and Stephan M. Wilson (Hayworth Press, 2008). Spencer-Walters is currently a Certified Language Tester/Rater for Krio at the American Council for the Teaching of Foreign Languages (ACTFL).